Breathing the Fire

FIGHTING TO REPORT–AND SURVIVE–THE WAR IN IRAQ

KIMBERLY DOZIER

CBS NEWS FOREIGN CORRESPONDENT

Meredith Books®
Des Moines, Iowa

Meredith Books
1716 Locust Street
Des Moines, Iowa 50309–3023
meredithbooks.com

Photography credits: **Front Cover** Thorsten Hoefle; **Flap** Jim Hollander/EPA;
Page 98 top Laura Winter; **98 bottom** Megan Towey; **99 top** Thorsten Hoefle;
99 bottom Thorsten Hoefle; **100** Ben Plesser; **101 top** Kurt Hoefle; **103** Agnes Reau;
104 Agnes Reau; **105** Ben Plesser; **106** AP/Khalid Mohammed;
107 top Cal Perry © 2008 Cable News Network. A Time Warner Company. All Rights Reserved.;
108 top AP/Michael Probst; **108 bottom** Nancy Miller; **109 bottom left** Dennis Dillon/CBS News;
110 Don Lee/CBS News; **111 top** Nancy Hoss; **111 bottom** courtesy Jennifer Funkhouser;
112 top Bill Clark/Roll Call; all other photos courtesy of Kimberly Dozier

Printed in the United States of America.

First Edition.
Library of Congress Control Number: 2008920803
ISBN: 978-0-696-23837-6

This book was made possible by every soul who stayed by my side, fighting to keep me alive, and by everyone who prayed for me and pulled for me along the way. It is an attempt to thank them—and to honor those we lost that day.

To my family and loved ones: Sorry I put you through all that hell, but were you really that surprised?

From a wounded Navy SEAL....
this was on his hospital door.

Attention! to all who enter here.

If you are coming into this room to feel
sorrow or to feel sorry for my wounds, go
elsewhere. The wounds I received, I got
doing a job I love, doing it for people I love,
supporting freedom for a country I also
love. I am incredibly tough and I will make
a full recovery. What is full? That is the
absolute utmost physically my body has
the ability to recover. Then I will push
that about 20 percent further through
sheer mental tenacity. This room you are
about to enter is full of fun, optimism,
and intense rapid regrowth. If you are not
prepared for that, go elsewhere.

From the management.

TABLE OF CONTENTS

Every time I sit at my computer to write about the ordeal of the past two years, I find a million other things I need to do—anything but write.

But I know I need to write it, to move beyond it. This ordeal won't let me go. Put another way, many caring and well-meaning people won't let me leave it behind.

Perhaps it's because they never got the whole story and they haven't caught up with my recovery. They can't comprehend how the shattered woman they saw on their TV screens two years ago, unconscious on a stretcher, got better. Maybe they can't quite believe it.

I'm hoping that telling my story will help lay it to rest. And through me maybe I will reveal a fraction of what U.S. troops are experiencing, to say nothing of Iraqi families and anyone else who lives in a war zone.

No one can be the saint worthy of all the prayers that were said for me and the letters, notes, and emails sent to my hospital room. But I understand that I was a symbol for much of what's happening to the servicemen and women, to Iraqis, to loved ones, or to strangers who become as familiar as loved ones.

I only wish I could be more gracious to some of the well-wishers I meet. When a well-meaning stranger chirps, "Oh, how are you?" or "Can I help you?" I sometimes snarl back, "Fine!" or "No, thanks!"— utterly frustrated with people who still think I need help. And worse, I then have to bite my tongue when I hear their sympathetic follow-ups. "Of course you can do it yourself, dear," they say indulgently, as if to a 5-year-old who patently can't.

On Memorial Day, May 29, 2006, I was the victim of a car bomb, along with my camera crew and the U.S. Army foot patrol my crew and I were filming. The weapon was a battered Iraqi taxi, carefully packed with some 500 pounds of explosives with a trigger hardwired to a cell phone inside the car. Someone was watching and waiting for the right moment to dial the phone's number, complete the bomb's circuit, and trigger the explosion.

The taxi was parked on a street used by Iraqi patrols. An Iraqi convoy had been hit on the same street the day before. We had come to ask people what they'd witnessed, whom they'd seen, and if anything seemed suspicious or out of place.

So in we walked, an entire U.S. Army foot patrol—10 soldiers, an Iraqi interpreter, and a liaison officer—trailed by an American network TV crew—a cameraman, a soundman, and me, a reporter. We walked straight into what's called the kill zone of the ambush.

The killers probably could not believe their luck.

Closest to the bomb were my friends and colleagues: CBS cameraman Paul Douglas and freelance soundman James Brolan, just 10 to 12 feet away from the wired car. Next to them was the U.S. Army officer we were following, the Fourth Infantry Division's Capt. James Alex Funkhouser, and his Iraqi translator, Sam. All four were killed, three just about instantly. With the same stubborn will he'd fought with throughout his life, Paul tried to stave off his death, until he lost too much blood. A soldier who had run to help stayed with Paul to the end.

I only found this out later. The soldier who treated me at the site kept telling me, "Your guys are fine."

The blast also killed an Iraqi man who was standing at the wrong tea stand on the wrong corner when we walked into the ambush.

The explosion injured six other soldiers, leaving two of them and me with a yearlong battle to heal our shattered bodies.

Back in the United States, the attack made headlines. Normally a car bomb that kills one U.S. soldier and wounds six more is a sad footnote to a newscast, if it makes the cut at all. But add in a network TV crew with a female reporter on a slow news day, as U.S. holidays generally are, and you have wall-to-wall coverage.

Maybe the attention came because no network had yet lost so many employees in a single incident. And perhaps it was because for most of that first day, I had a 50-50 chance of surviving. There was suspense. It was probably also because I'm a woman. Although women journalists and women soldiers have been in and on the battlefield for at least a couple decades, the public hasn't caught up with us yet.

CBS put together a TV special called *Flashpoint* to tell the story of that day, how one bomb blasted through the lives of so many, including Paul's and James' families, Captain Funkhouser's wife, Jennifer, and his two young daughters, Kaitlyn and Allison, and the six soldiers who were wounded. For U.S. troops this event was sadly routine. As one commander later told me, "Just another day in Baghdad."

This is the rest of my story. Helped by family, friends, loved ones, doctors and nurses, and corpsmen of unsurpassed skills, and I now realize my own will to live—I came back from near death. It meant facing the horror of two lost colleagues I considered friends and a yearlong fight to learn to walk and live on my own again. The bomb changed me—reinforcing some parts and burning away others. In many ways this book is my attempt to put that transformation into words.

One thing I know I'm not: a victim. That's what anyone is called when he or she suffers major trauma: assault victim, car crash victim, Baghdad car bomb victim. But "victims" have no independence. Family, friends, and colleagues, all with good will, coddle you. They tend to you when you first need it, but they don't know how or when to let you out of your cotton-cushioned cocoon.

It's almost as hard to prove you're not a victim as it is to recover. You have to teach those around you that when the "victim" overcomes the trauma—learning from it, changing from it, and moving beyond it—she becomes a survivor, physically, mentally, and spiritually.

I survived. This is a survivor's tale.

just before

NIGHT BEFORE MEMORIAL DAY, MAY 29, 2006

I hate these nights. Stare at the ceiling, turn left. Turn right. Can't sleep. Dread tomorrow's assignment, as usual. In the morning adrenaline will pull me through, as it always does. Tonight worry is getting the better of me, as it always does.

The aircon is noisy, and the thick hotel drapes (of cheesy pseudo-velvet) block out the spotlights on the catty-corner mosque nearby and the lights from across the river. The drapes are meant to catch any flying glass, should a rocket hit the side of the building. But that's only ever happened once, so in my mind that's not the problem. The problem is the next day's patrol.

I'm "safe" here. I've transformed the 12- by 15-foot room into a cocoon fortress—a yoga sanctuary in this half-star hotel floor turned network bureau. I live here about two-thirds of the year. Over three years my personal possessions have migrated to join me. The place is like the *Big Brother* house crossed with a rusting, peeling, leaking Soviet-era submarine, where the carpet sticks to your feet. We've sealed the corridor with steel doors and installed cameras to eyeball would-be visitors.

A ragtag crew of CBS and Iraqi hotel guards protects us (when they bother to stay awake). Our foreign security advisors try to sneak downstairs at odd times of the night to ensure the perimeter guards are awake. They have to make it past the slumbering upstairs guards; otherwise the game is up—the Iraqis upstairs furiously dial their cell phones and wake up all their colleagues at the hotel gates below.

Sleep, damn you.

Tossing and turning is a personal tradition I despise. It happens when I do embeds. I will spend tomorrow morning with a U.S. Army patrol. My two-man crew—my colleagues and friends, cameraman Paul and soundman James—will film the U.S. Army patrol, and I'll trail them. The truth is, after three years as a late-comer network reporter, I'm still a newbie to the two of them—someone they put up with between assignments with "the boys," such as news legend Dan Rather, with whom they've worked for years.

For this shift, they're stuck with me: a workaholic news nerd. They've watched me climb my way from radio to affiliate to network TV. No matter what *I* think I am, to them I'm the former wannabe who is still trying too hard.

I'm also the only reporter I know who has a family with a U.S. military background. My father was a Marine in World War II, surviving the campaigns of Guam and Iwo Jima.

That's probably why I went on assignment with the military a lot, which didn't always make me popular. Sometimes crews said no to my ideas.

But to those of us involved right now, tomorrow's assignment makes perfect sense: There is no other place to be on Memorial Day in Iraq than with U.S. troops.

The three of us had done our preshoot security briefing this evening, not that I could provide much detail. The military press officer who had set up the embed couldn't tell our producers much over the phone, except that the patrol would take place in central Baghdad (so we could get back in time for the 7 a.m. eastern time live shot on *The CBS Early Show*, which airs at 3 p.m. local time). You can't say much over the phone because the insurgents are thought to be monitoring the phone lines.

We don't know exactly where we are going or what we'll see, but the story has something to do with U.S. troops training Iraqis. Since tomorrow is a patriotic day, I suspect the story will be along the lines of "As they stand up, we stand down"—the mantra of the U.S. commanders.

My crew and I suspect this will also be what we call a "dog and pony show," something so sanitized for our cameras that it will be hard to get anything more than an Uncle-Sam-knows-best commercial out of the troops.

But we know that whatever we film will air on the morning show and almost certainly on the *CBS Evening News*. You can't NOT make air on a patriotic American holiday when you spend the day with U.S. troops.

And Paul always said, "Don't risk my life unless we're going to make air."

God, what a horrific way I kept that promise.

Tonight as we talked about what I thought we might see tomorrow, Paul and James had no qualms about the assignment. And they were never shy about sharing their "qualms," that's for certain; only a week earlier James had told *CBS Early Show* anchor Harry Smith that he had misgivings about a daylong embed in Sadr City, so the embed had been cancelled. And Paul had turned down several recent shoots with other correspondent-producer teams.

Another bit of proof I cling to that tells me none of us saw what was coming: Paul always called up his wife and told her if he was going on a shoot he thought was dangerous. I found out later that he did call her, but he never mentioned the next day's assignment.

We settled on an 0800 start, and I've settled in for the usual night of pre-embed brooding.

My subconscious mind knows all too well that we are about to go on yet another U.S. Humvee patrol, the kind of patrol we can see from our hotel rooftop each morning rolling out of the Green Zone. We watch the vehicles leave the sandbagged, barbed-wired, watch-towered gates and move toward their mission in town. And then we hear the distant booms and know many of the explosions are aimed at Americans.

This is the first embed of this reporting shift. For the past three years, I've rotated six weeks in Baghdad, two to four weeks out, and then I'm back again. It's hard, dangerous, and often monotonous, the same sad story over and over. Even my own family thinks I'm nuts for spending so much time covering the war. I was first assigned to Iraq because no one else wanted it. I volunteered to cover "the war that was over." (Remember "Mission Accomplished," the banner on the carrier deck behind President Bush after the 2003 "Shock and Awe" U.S. invasion of Iraq?) At the time, a lot of reporters thought the Bush administration was right. So the network stars came home, their names already made and their reputations won with a victorious story well told.

That's when, in June 2003, I was finally promoted to network as a Jerusalem-based correspondent and sent to cover a war my TV bosses couldn't wait to get out of. Every few months I was warned of another plan to close the Baghdad bureau, and I wondered if that meant I'd lose my job. But the war kept going, and reluctantly my bosses, like all the other TV bosses, churned more and more money into the war, turning bureaus into fortresses and hiring small armies of security guards and a fleet of armored vehicles.

Necessity was part of why I've stayed. Iraq just kept getting on the air, ergo, so did I. Job security, grim reaper-style.

Too, I simply couldn't leave. Like a car crash on the highway—part needless tragedy, part heroes' tale, almost all nightmare—I couldn't, and still can't, take my eyes off the war.

So we've had our briefing, agreed on a time to meet in the parking lot in the morning to take our armored vehicles on the mile-or-so jaunt to the Green Zone to meet our interview subjects, and called it a night.

Like an overachieving schoolkid, I've laid out my clothes, my helmet, and my flak jacket for the morning. I cleaned out a lot of stuff from my flak jacket pocket to try to lighten my load. For some reason I had two casualty bandages. Our security advisors have taught us to carry one bandage with us at all times, just like the military. Two seemed redundant, so I decided to leave one behind. I remember thinking to myself, *We'll be with the military. If anything happens, they have plenty of supplies.* I should have left well enough alone.

I'm finished packing, yet my obsessive-compulsive attention to details still hasn't quieted my mind.

You've done this over and over again in three years. The explosions sometimes barely touch the Humvees. It's a short trip. You'll be back by lunch.

I still can't sleep. I call my boyfriend, Pete, in New Zealand, where it's daytime.

"Hi."

"Hey, babe." He pauses, calculating the time at my end—2 or 3 a.m. "Patrol?"

"Yeah, short one." I'm embarrassed. "No reason to worry. The usual."

He lets me talk. I tell him how ridiculous it is to be afraid. He's heard this on many late-night phone calls before, but he's patient, as always. He's worked in Baghdad and has served many long years in the military in war zones. He understands what I'm feeling without my having to say much. He's lived it. Working in these places does not mean you feel no fear. You feel it, calculate the risks, and push through it.

This has become a ritual: I list my worries. He listens, mostly mute. Then I get a few hours of sleep.

"I hope that all the right decisions are made tomorrow regarding security," Pete says. Decisions by us? We're with the military—they decide where we go. And since ABC News anchor Bob Woodruff and his cameraman Doug Vogt were hit by a roadside bomb four months earlier, the military won't let journalists go anywhere remotely dangerous. Indeed the military is checking all of Baghdad even as Pete and I speak to make sure they are sending us to the safest part.

I decide that Pete must mean he hopes we make the right decisions about bringing our safety gear.

"I'm going with Paul and James. Don't worry, they always bring everything—helmets, vests, earplugs, the works."

I'm calmer. I've talked my fears to sleep, or at least to distraction. I tell Pete I miss him (after three years, we still aren't to the "I love you" stage). He says something Kiwi-male-like, like "G'day, sweetie."

I grab a couple hours of sleep.

Dawn and the alarm clock drag me awake. I jump into the shower, dry my hair, apply my makeup, and mutter to myself that it's a waste of time. I don't enjoy the face-painting part of my job. I apply waterproof makeup so I won't have to pay attention to it.

Paul and James have beaten me to the parking lot, but not by much. Every minute we spend here gives anyone watching us from surrounding rooftops time to prepare an attack. I've been told that it's better to get to the car and out of the parking lot within 15 minutes. I make it a point to be on time.

"Helmets?" I mother-hen. "Flak jackets? Earplugs?" I pull out a ziplock bag of disposable earplugs in case anyone has forgotten his. They protect our eardrums from the shock waves of roadside bombs.

"Have them already, love. Thanks," James says, with his heavy London *Monty Python*-esque accent.

"OK, OK—like I could teach you guys anything about security," I say, shoving the marshmallowlike earplugs back into my flak jacket pocket. Underneath them is my casualty bandage.

We load up and head out.

We drive to the Green Zone: fortified land that's home to several small U.S. military bases, where the American and other Western embassies and a few Iraqi officials who have the good fortune, or political pull, to secure themselves a space in the base there. There are a few American fast-food places and a small, picked-over PX that's still a draw for Americans in search of retail therapy in a war zone. The Green Zone is also the pickup and drop-off point for journalists on short or long embeds.

Our security men drop us off. CNN journalists drive by, bound for somewhere else. We wave to each other. Among them is Cal Perry, the CNN Baghdad bureau chief I met briefly at a military meet-and-greet luncheon a couple days earlier. I don't know any of them well. None of us journalists really meet each other anymore since we're all behind walled compounds, only occasionally daring the gauntlet that is Baghdad to go to a press conference.

Paul cracks jokes with one of the Gurkhas at the guard shack where we wait. James has a last cigarette and adds a jibe or two. Our press officer, Maj. Mark Cheadle, picks us up and takes us to meet someone he calls "a really good guy": Capt. James Funkhouser. We're supposed to call him Alex, Cheadle tells us. He's heading a U.S. team that is training Iraqis (*they're standing up so we can stand down, remember,* I think to myself). And we're going to the Karrada.

The Karrada? I feel relief. *It will be boring, yes,* I think to myself, *but it's a relief.* Sure, the Karrada is technically in the Red Zone, Baghdad proper. It's the neighborhood where we'd all first lived after the invasion. We know the streets. Heck, we know the best sandwich and ice cream shops in the Karrada. There are two dicey squares the insurgents seem to like to hit; but other than that it's tame. I wonder to myself how we're going to get this on the air, even on Memorial Day.

We are introduced to our host for the day. At first I think, *Boy Scout. Rose-colored glasses alert. No one can be this upbeat.* He willingly dons the microphone James supplies and starts answering the questions—truly answering them.

He's not a boy scout. He turns out to be an upbeat realist, and we're all relieved. In the command center before we leave, Alex is candid about the serious challenges he and the Army face. I'm looking forward to hearing his thoughts throughout the day.

Before we go Alex shares that the hardest part of his job—as much as the mission and his men give him purpose—is being away from his girls, his wife, Jennifer, and his two daughters, Kaitlyn and Allison.

Alex gathers the men, and we move to the Humvees. I'll ride with Alex, and Paul and James will ride in another Humvee. There's some hubbub, and the word comes down that our joint Iraqi patrol won't be coming with us.

Great, I think. *There goes the "As they stand up, we stand down" story. Instead we'll be filming the instantly recognizable Iraqi-American theme: "They don't show up, so we do the work for them."*

I'm concerned that they're backing out because of us, that they think we'll show their faces and get their families killed by vengeful insurgents who hate anyone who works with the Americans.

I make my way to Alex and tell him my concerns. I ask if there's any way we can correct the situation, perhaps by promising not to film their faces. He tells me this isn't the problem. The Iraqis simply aren't ready, he insists. So they only send their liaison.

We pull out of the gates in four Humvees, snaking first through the diplomatic traffic inside the Green Zone and then crawling when we reach Baghdad's early morning rush hour, which blends seamlessly into afternoon and evening rush hour.

Riding in the Humvees scares the hell out of me. These are magnets for improvised explosive devices (IEDs). I have my earplugs firmly shoved in both ears and shatterproof glasses wrapped around my head beneath my Kevlar helmet. I sometimes tuck my feet up, pulling them out of the Humvee wheel well, and think that if a bomb goes off under my feet, I'll lose my legs.

I have my guard up until we reach our first stop, pull over, and get out.

I let my guard down.

I pull my earplugs out so I can better hear any exchanges between the young Army captain and the Iraqis he hopes to meet and gently interrogate on the street: "Were you here yesterday? Did you see the roadside bomb hit the Iraqi patrol? Did you notice anything out of place before that? Have any strangers moved into the area?"

But this is your typical wide-avenued Iraqi neighborhood, where every house is behind a high wall. Finding folks to chat with is going to take some effort. The soldiers fan out. They're doing their yard-by-yard security checks. Do you see a threat within the first few feet? Something that looks like a wire or a hidden bomb? No? Another 10 feet out? No? How about 15 feet out?

One soldier later said something didn't feel right—he didn't like the way the cars were parked. But he convinced himself that nothing looked out of place. We walk down a dusty, deserted street with once lovely villas, some now bombed and burned out, others just shuttered against the sun.

The captain and I walk up the avenue a couple feet, and Paul and James gather their gear and catch up. "What are we doing?" Paul asks, looking unimpressed with the surroundings, a dusty, boring street, like dozens of others we'd filmed. "Looking for Iraqis to talk to," I answer.

"Right, OK," he says, scanning the soldiers for a good shot. He and James walk away and start filming the soldiers completing their checks, looking around cautiously, rifles ready—the usual.

The captain turns around, and I follow, walking on his right back down the way we'd come. On our left is a high wall, and behind it is a villa shattered by a much earlier blast.

"See that villa," Funkhouser asks, "to our left?"

"Uh-huh." I try not to stare directly at it.

"We think an insurgent cell has moved in there—the ones who were behind yesterday's bombing. We think they're using it as an OP [observation post]. They could be watching us right now," he adds.

The captain spots his translator, Sam, half a block ahead of us, making his way toward an Iraqi tea stand. *Finally, some Iraqis to talk to*, I think to myself. The tea stand is the usual makeshift affair—a few battered bits of plywood with a cheap awning to keep off the sun, surrounded by a bunch of Iraqis taking a break from work . . . if they had work. Most don't.

Funkhouser jackrabbits ahead of me, outpacing me in a few strides. I trail, trying to scribble his last couple thoughts in my notebook, and think to myself: *He's great, but I'm still not sure how I'm going to make this story stand out.*

As he strides forward I see above his left shoulder the mustachioed face of an Iraqi man in a crisp blue dress shirt and dark blue trousers. He's raising a glass of tea to his lips, tipping it on a saucer he holds in his other hand. He's looking over the tea glass in the captain's direction, the expression in his eyes just a bit hostile and questioning—the same look any Iraqi male gives to a U.S. soldier in full battle dress who is striding toward him.

Out of the corner of my eye, on my right, I see Paul and James. They're moving across my field of vision to intercept the captain and his translator who are about to greet the Iraqis. I assume they're trying to reach the tea stand to capture the classic shot: the Iraqi faces of mistrust and semi-fear dissolving into semi-smiles, as the American captain puts his hand to his heart in greeting and says, "*Salaam alaikum*" (peace to you).

Capt. Funkhouser didn't have to stride down that street ahead of me to greet those Iraqis. He could have kept walking at a leisurely pace, holding forth on his opinion of the world to a network TV reporter, and I would have kept pace with him, walking right up to the bomb. But his mission was more important than his ego, and that surely saved my life.

I watch him draw level with the tea stand, thinking I'll hang back and let Paul get the shot before I step into the frame to listen.

In that moment, the world slammed backward into black.

CHAPTER 2

waking to horror

LANDSTUHL REGIONAL MEDICAL CENTER, GERMANY, JUNE 1 OR 2, 2006

Pinpricks all over my legs like little needles.

Fluorescent light.

Blurry face looking up at me from where she/he is pricking my legs.

Machines beeping.

Trying to speak. Can't.

Ahh, I get it.

My throat is blocked, my mouth wedged open, my tongue a swollen, wooden thing.

I've got a tube in my throat.

More pinpricks draw me back to the blurry person.

I think to myself, *Something happened to my legs, and they're treating them.* Something bad happened recently, I remember that, but I can only pull at the edges of the memory. So my mind grapples with the physical sensation and tries to find some familiar context.

I try to tell the blurry person: "Nice acupuncture." No go.

I don't take well to forced silence.

So I lift my hands and make that universal "please give me my check" motion, one hand writing on the other.

Blurry person "gets it," and within moments presses pen and paper into my hands. I can feel my hands, but I can't see them. My hands are fuzzy pink appendages.

"Nice acupuncture," I write. Or think I write.

"Sorry, can you try that again?" a woman's voice asks. It comes from the blurry person.

I then realize I have woken up mute into a world of mentally slow people who can't read.

I try the phrase again, moving the pen very slowly and very carefully. Penmanship for dunces.

Do you get it NOW? I ask silently, craning my head toward her and holding out the paper.

"Umm, no, I don't get that," says the female voice, all the more frustrating to me for its patient tone. She is trying to soothe my growing agitation.

"Can you try again?" she says.

Hell, lady, that was kindergarten block printing, I think to myself. *Clear as day. Can't you read?*

Months later my family showed me my first attempts at words, wildly scribbled like a child's Etch A Sketch. A team of Discovery Channel cryptographers couldn't have deciphered my writing.

Adding to the confusion, the woman wasn't doing acupuncture, so she wasn't expecting me to write that phrase. My nurse, Capt. Nancy Miller, was changing the bandages on my burned legs and pulling off dead skin as she went, shearing it away from the surviving tissue, which screamed at every tug and tear. I couldn't feel that then.

I did later, and for a time I thought I would never forget that searing, endless two to three hours of pain each and every day as she changed my dressings.

As I try to recall the sensations now, my legs are mute. They remember nothing of the event. I suppose my mind has gone into protective mode. I know there was repeated horrible pain. But it's been wiped clean from my memory.

At the moment I first awoke at the hospital, the pain simply felt distant and small. I was floating, courtesy of some of the best drugs the Western medical profession has to offer. I didn't realize what was happening. I'd been so straight-laced all my life that I had no frame of reference for a Class A drug trip. Versed, morphine, an epidural drip, and IV Dilaudid were now my rotating feast of narcotic companions.

Time fogged by. Even now the memories from Landstuhl aren't sequential. They're a kaleidoscope, overlapping in a daze. But Nancy later told me she didn't expect me to remember my stay at Landstuhl—most people don't.

Maybe it's because I woke up frustrated and angry. I didn't understand why no one could understand what I was writing. There were more pinpricks on my legs, and then she finished whatever she was doing to them. I felt as though my legs were disembodied from me, floating at the end of the bed, swathed in white.

I drifted. Nancy meanwhile had gone straight to find my loved ones to tell them: She's woken up. She's with us.

The next event I recollect is a sea of faces around me. I study them through eyes I can barely open. My family—at least as many members as CBS could gather at that moment—surround me. They were scattered all over the world and rarely gather. The last time I remembered them all in the same room was 1995, for my wedding. (The ceremony produced the only family photo my parents possessed of all their children together, ever. Mom kept the picture on display, despite the reminders that it also heralded another divorce in the family.) So family gatherings are a rare event.

Yet half of my family members are at the hospital—and one new addition, my boyfriend, Pete.

Pete comes into focus . . . then my sister, MeiLee, who is next to Pete (part of my brain thinking, *Wow, my sister only comes up to Pete's shoulder*). Then I see my 80-plus-year-old mom and dad. My brother Mike and his Texan wife, Sherry, my "second mom," are just outside. I don't take them in until later. My three other far-flung brothers, Bob, Larry, and Doug, are missing. Mike is their delegate, so to speak.

My mind scrambles to make sense of this gathering. I think to myself, *Pete's here from New Zealand. MeiLee's here from Ho Chi Minh City, Vietnam. Mom and Dad, who haven't stepped on a plane in a decade, are here from Baltimore* . . .

Two thoughts war in my head, *Wow, I always wanted Mom and Dad to meet Pete* . . . and *Oh, no. Something really bad must have happened.*

"You have both your legs," someone tells me.

Yeah, of course I do. I thought they were doing acupuncture on them.

"You're going to be fine," someone else says.

Yeah, yeah. I think to myself.

"I love you," says Pete.

I freeze. This is a new shock. In three years together, since meeting on the way to Iraq, he's never said that.

My mom later says triumphantly, "He said it in front of all of us. He can't take it back!" My parents don't know Pete. They are watching everything he does, judging his worthiness, while he is grappling with seeing me . . . like that.

I later saw photos my nurse, Nancy, took for me at Pete's request. He said to her, "She's a journalist. She'll want to know." I did, but the pictures were hell to look at—hell to know that's what my family saw and tried not to react to, to keep from upsetting me.

My face and body were swollen with 30 pounds of fluid, the body's response to trauma. In layman's terms, my body panicked after losing more than half its blood and simply held on to all the IV fluid that was pumped into it. But there was no room for the excess fluid in my blood vessels or my organs, so it filled my extra spaces, such as my abdominal cavity, my lungs, and, most visible, my neck tissue and limbs. I looked like a pale Jabba the Hut, with Michelin Man-sized arms and legs swathed in white cotton bandages. There was still dried blood under my fingernails and crusted on my puffed-up hands. Tubes were in my nose and mouth, and IV lines ran directly into my blood vessels. A large burn visible on one of my arms was oiled with unguents. My head was half shaved, and there was a stitched incision. The doctors had opened my skull to remove shrapnel, then riveted it back in place with titanium screws with plates attached to either side to hold the floating bone in place. When I look at the photo, I see another *Star Wars* image: Darth Vader's glowing, scarred skull.

My face and the right side of my body were peppered in red and blackish cuts where shrapnel had bored into me. It will be working its way out of me for the next several months and years.

In the hospital, though, at that gathering, I can't see any of this. I only know Pete has just said he loves me. I think, *He said he loves me. Oh, God, if he said that, I must be in real trouble.*

I fade out again. Pete said I could barely keep my eyes open—later, when I could speak, I would even drift off midsentence.

I wake again. Nancy is doing something with the tubes or the wires or the bandages—I'm so critical, she is doing "one-on-one" care, meaning she almost never leaves my side for an entire 12-hour shift. I am going to take advantage of that constant presence and get some answers.

Ever so carefully I pick up the pen and try again, writing with intense, determined concentration.

I think to myself, *She won't know what I mean if I write, Where are Paul and James?*

So I write ever so carefully: "WHERE . . . IS . . . MY . . . CREW?"

All I know for certain is that the LAST moment I remember before this blazing white world, I was with my crew—though Paul and James hated that phrase. "We're not *your* fucking crew," Paul would tell anyone who called him and his soundman that, chip prominent on his shoulder.

But *my* crew was with me. I was *their* correspondent, whether they liked it or not, and now we are forever linked by this event.

Nancy came into focus, her kind brown eyes with arching brows, her reddish hair covered with some sort of puffy hat, her blue scrubs, a gown, and gloves. She may have also been wearing a mask. I was peering so intensely at her eyes, looking for a reaction, that I hardly took in the rest of her face.

She was expecting this question.

"Where is my crew?" she asks, forming the words carefully. "You want to know about your cameraman and soundman."

I think I nodded, or tried to.

"I'll get someone for you," she told me.

That was another vague answer, and frustration welled up in me again. This was all people gave me. I don't remember much of those early hours or days, but I know that wherever I was, I asked about Paul and James. And I kept receiving the same answer: silence.

Nancy sought my family in a nearby waiting room.

"She's asking about her camera crew," Nancy says. "Do you want to tell her?"

My dad calls it, immediately. "If she's asking, she needs to know," he says. "We have to tell her."

As they're deciding who will deliver the news, I'm in my own evanescent world.

Memories of the explosion start to come back. I work hard, snatching at those edges and puzzling together the memories—but they don't always stay where I put them. They keep sliding away from me. There was an explosion, I know that. I want to know what type—I will be told conflicting things over the next few weeks about what it was.

I remember some of what it felt like. Sulfur smells, like fireworks burning just under my face. Jagged images: I had been at work, in Baghdad, filming something with Paul and James, and the world had slammed backward like I'd been knocked into a black dimension.

I didn't know when that was or where Paul and James were. But I needed to find out.

My family decided my Baghdad producer, Kate Rydell, would tell me what had happened. I didn't know at that point that she had been at my side since I reached the Baghdad emergency room.

She walks into my Landstuhl hospital room and slowly comes into focus. At 5-foot-nothing, she seems dwarfed by the medical equipment around me, small in the fluorescent, glowing white room. Kate is a lady, always dressed perfectly in understated, quiet linens and silk sweaters—her defiance against the awful places we work, I guess.

Now she is crushed, her face shrunken by grief, pinched in on itself. She has none of her usual composure. I see the way she steels her face to look at me, takes a deep breath, and starts what she's been endlessly rehearsing in her mind.

She says, "I wanted to be the one to tell you."

She doesn't need to say another word. I don't really want her to.

"Paul and James didn't make it," Kate chokes out.

She cries.

I can't.

The tube is still in my throat. My face is frozen and numb. My mind does an instinctive "this is not happening," and I close my eyes. I am so paralyzed, it's as if I have lost the power to cry.

If I could have spoken, all I would have said was *no*.

Kate later told me that my whole body imploded, trying to ball up and drive backward into the hospital bed. My body said what my voice couldn't: *no, no, no*.

She leaves. My mind starts scrambling. Now I desperately need to remember what happened—what killed them.

We'd been filming something. Then impact. A shuddering crash, then black. *It was a bomb*, I think. *Where were they? Where was I? Where was the bomb?*

Minutes, or hours, later I reach for my pen and paper again—my family has to hold it for me and try to switch the pages when I run out of space—I'm completely unaware.

I write things like "I remember it. BOOM. An explosion."

My writing has gotten sharper.

"I heard screaming," I wrote.

My drug- and pain-scattered memories stumble to catch up. My brain starts sentences it can't finish and picks them up minutes, or hours, later. I am an indifferent conversationalist at best.

In the jumble, some facts are now crystal clear: I am in an intensive care ward in Landstuhl, Germany. Other soldiers from my patrol were in rooms nearby. My family is here; my CBS colleagues are here.

And Paul and James are gone.

Another unwelcome realization creeps into my consciousness within a day or so of waking up, about three days into my stay—the world was waiting outside. My survival, and my condition, is news.

I wasn't ready to think about that. I didn't know how to respond or what to say. My mind was stuck in a Baghdad street, trying to remember.

My sister was the first to hear my halting account. She didn't encourage me to keep talking. The fact that I remembered the blast shocked her. My family hoped I'd remember nothing. She hid her horror; she didn't want to hear about the blast, but she didn't let me know that.

I also didn't know that the first time she'd come into my room, she'd seen me swollen, bandaged, with blood-streaked hands, and she'd burst into tears. My mom, ever the German policeman of our emotions (and her own), pulled MeiLee aside and said, "Don't let her see you like that.

Smile. We have to be strong for her." My mom didn't want anyone to be the mirror that showed me how bad I looked. They were parceling reality out to me slowly in horrible—but, they hoped, manageable—bites.

Still I knew more than they did. They couldn't protect me from my memories. If they could have, I'm sure they would have tried to take them away, but that would have damned me. I've learned that one of the best ways to avoid the recurring nightmares, the anxiety, and the host of other symptoms that are part and parcel of posttraumatic stress disorder is to relive everything you can, moment by moment, and bring it all into the light. Only then can you move on.

I started that process in my hospital bed. In between the doctors, the nurses, the endless surgical procedures, the drug drifts, and my loved ones holding my hand, there were moments of clarity when the pieces started coming back, sticking where I put them.

I told MeiLee that Paul and James were walking ahead of me, a bit to the side, trying to move ahead of Alex. I don't remember how much detail I told her at that moment. I had to work backward in my head from the single moment that stayed with me clearly: the instant of the explosion. It was like when you hit your head hard and momentarily see stars, only a thousand times worse. There was pitch blackness, a smell like a thousand burning matches, and a feeling of being strangely weightless, as if I were diving underwater. Once I'd grabbed the edge of that memory, I kept revisiting it, repeatedly, for weeks. I'd remember the blast and the slam sideways, and my body would be frozen in space with the memory, locked in that moment.

CHAPTER 3

one bomb refracted

Over the next few days, I pulled together the sequence, from blast to pain to rescue to unconsciousness, reliving it as if I was there.

I remember in that blackness saying to myself, *Bomb, some sort of bomb.* The sulfur helped prove that to me.

I knew the what but not the where or the how. At first there was no pain, no sound, no sensation of my arms or legs or face. I didn't even have time for horror. Just awareness: This is happening.

I was flung into the air, but I don't remember landing. By the time I did, both legs were smashed from the sheer force of being knocked back, and the explosion had scorched much of my right leg, some of my left, and parts of my arms. I was peppered with bits of molten metal and car parts, which were embedded in me from head to toe.

Where are Paul and James? my brain stuttered. I was searching for familiar points of reference, and that meant them.

I tried to remember where they'd been standing. I tried to remember where I'd been standing.

Then I tried my voice. Pauw-hhhh. No sound. I didn't know both my eardrums were blown out. If I was speaking at all, I couldn't hear myself or anything else. Then Ja-hhhhh, I tried.

It was like those nightmares when you try to call for help but your screams are mute. You wake up hearing a long, useless "Hhhhhhhhh" coming from your throat. You're powerless.

My brain started ticking, trying to figure out why there was no input, no sensation. A colleague's words floated back to me. I'd read them in an article only the day before the patrol. It was in a stack of a couple hundred pages of newsprint I'd made my way through to catch up on whatever my colleagues have been up to. It was my routine every time I started a new shift in Baghdad.

This time my "homework" saved me from panic. I'd read the account by ABC cameraman Doug Vogt about what it felt like to be hit by an improvised explosive device (IED). He'd been hit by a blast while filming anchorman Bob Woodruff as he recorded an on-camera web chat out of the top of an Iraqi armored vehicle. They'd been attacked exactly four months prior to when our patrol was attacked: January 29, 2006. They both took shrapnel and rocks to the head.

Doug's words came back to me. "When the bomb hit, I couldn't move," he wrote. I remember thinking how awful that must have been to be aware of what was happening around you but remain paralyzed, shell-shocked.

I knew Doug from brief introductions in various hellholes. He was a wizened pro, who had seen it all before and greeted you with gruff "Hi, how are you." I didn't know him well, but in that moment of panic, I immediately trusted his words.

I told myself, *OK, Doug, you were right. I can't move.*

And then, what seemed an eternity later, *OK, Doug, I still can't move.*

Then louder in my head, losing patience now, *Doug, when can I move?*

I drifted into blackness.

The next thing I saw was bright, blazing hell. I was lying face-to-the-sky in the debris. My legs were burning, searing. Pain and heat. I lifted my head and saw a burning car, maybe 20 or 30 feet away. The chassis burned bright orange, the tires, a little darker. I thought the heat of the car's fire was hurting me. Again my brain was trying to make sense of the moment, putting the clues together that it could see or feel, trying to make some logical whole. My car theory wasn't right. The burning I was feeling was from damage already done, the blast-molten shrapnel embedded throughout my body, car-parts-turned-missiles, literally searing into my flesh and melting parts of my clothing into my skin.

Luckily for my sanity, as I lay there on the ground, I could only see the bulk of my flak jacket, not the ruin of my legs.

Even if I could have seen them, I don't know how much I would have taken in. I lifted my right hand and failed to see the cut on my pointer finger, a seven-inch gash that started at the top of the finger, to the back of my hand, bloody and tendon-deep. My mind blocked it out.

I started crying out for help, still weak, but this time I said words I could hear.

"Help! The car's burning me. Help!" *God, how pathetic*, I thought. My inner critic barked that I sound like a cliché.

I heard other voices, choked by pain, calling for help. They sounded otherworldly and unidentifiable. "Help me! Somebody help me!"

Did my voice sound like that too, strangled and high-pitched? I asked myself.

Should I be calling for help? chimed in another voice in my head. In triage, you go to the people who aren't making any sound first. It's the rules of the ABCs: airway, breathing, and circulation. You first ensure all your quiet casualties have an airway and are breathing. You make sure their hearts haven't stopped.

Then you help the ones who are making noise. They obviously have an airway, as I did. Just by calling out, I knew I'd made myself a lower priority for the medics.

Next I thought, *The hell with that. The car's burning me.* That meant I was in immediate danger, and I needed to get away. I gave myself permission to scream.

Louder now, "Hellllp!" I rasped. "It's burning. Helllllp!" It must not have sounded like much. One of the soldiers later said I was crying. I don't remember that. I remember a take-charge voice in my head barking orders at me and then only somewhat more gently at my rescuers.

Within a minute or two, as near as I could tell, a soldier was dragging me away from the blaze. I couldn't see his face. When I lifted my head, I still couldn't see anything but the front of my flak jacket and the fire.

A voice spoke to me. "Hello, ma'am," a soldier said with that universal Midwestern/Southern twang all U.S. troops seem to pick up. I don't know how long it had been since I was dragged from the burning car. A second? A minute? Two minutes?

I didn't even give him time to ask my blood type.

"I'm O positive," I told him.

"O positive," I heard him say back.

Near me were three dead men: James, Capt. Funkhouser, and Capt. Funkhouser's Iraqi translator. Paul was near death. And there were six wounded soldiers, two of whom were injured as badly as I was. I couldn't see or hear any of that. I was in my own tunnel with the sky, the top of my flak jacket, the voice, and, dimly now, the burning sensation in my legs.

"I'm going to tie a tourniquet on your leg," the soldier told me.

"I have an extra bandage in my flak jacket," I said. "Do you need it?"

I started unzipping my jacket's left pocket and pulling everything out to get to the bandage I knew was there.

"I don't need it, ma'am," he said.

"Okay," I replied and started stuffing everything back.

His voice came again. "I *do* need it, ma'am."

Uh-oh. That's not good.

I started unzipping my flak jacket's left front pocket again, digging past the spare earplugs, before pulling my hands away and saying, "You do it. You're in better shape than I am."

All through this, I didn't see that huge gash across my hand any more than I saw my rescuer's face. I was bleeding everywhere, and I was oblivious.

I heard my impromptu medic say to someone over my head, "Time of tourniquet . . ."

Then another, "Time of tourniquet."

My brain registered that meant both my legs. Somewhere during all of this, I remember trying to ask about Paul and James. I thought I heard one soldier say to the other, "She's asking about her guys," followed by silence—no reply. I was sure they heard me.

"They're going to be just fine, ma'am," the soldier said to me. "Let's worry about you right now."

Some explosions interjected with loud pops and bangs just a few yards from us or just a few feet. I couldn't tell. The flames had reached the random mishmash of leftover ammunition in one of the Humvees that had been parked near the car bomb.

I thought it was the car bomb that had been cooking off. That's what sometimes happens if the car doesn't burn up at the moment of the explosion; as it turns out, our Humvee had. A car bomb is composed of a few huge leftover artillery shells or tank mines hooked to a trigger. Then the individuals who constructed the bomb toss in anything else that could add to the mayhem, such as grenades, bullets, and screws or nails or other seemingly innocuous objects that can become deadly when propelled by a bomb.

I'd visited enough car bomb-aftermath scenes in Baghdad in the previous three years to know that when you heard the popping sound of leftover ammo, you were too close and had arrived too soon after the bomb had exploded. You ducked and got out of the way.

I asked my medic, "Is that the car bomb cooking off?"

He replied with a gruff "Yeah."

He didn't bother to explain that it was actually M4 and/or 50-calibre ammo cooking off in the floor of a burning Humvee near us—same difference, I guess.

I remember wondering where my helmet was and badgering the soldier accordingly.

"Do I still have my helmet on?" I needled. "Can you tell me if I have my helmet on because I don't want to get hit by shrapnel from the car bomb cooking off, you know?"

Silence. "Excuse me . . . my helmet?" I kept pushing.

If he heard me at all, he must have been thinking, looking at the rest of me: "Lady, that's the least of your problems."

Mercifully for the soldier, I passed out at that stage, or think I did.

That was all I could remember. For the soldiers treating us it was far worse—they had no shock to kick in and obliterate their memories. For some it would become what they called "a movie in their head that wouldn't stop playing" for weeks and months following the bombing. Once I was released from the hospital, during months of rehab I slowly sought them out, tracking them down through emails, then phone calls, then interviews. I was trying to rebuild the day from their memories and fill in all the blanks.

For the soldiers May 29 in the Green Zone had started much like ours. They weren't exactly looking forward to the mission, and they wanted it to be over. They had been told they would be driving around with a group of reporters—something they did often because their articulate boss, Capt. Funkhouser, was a popular spokesman for Army press officers. So they were used to it, but babysitting the media wasn't their favorite assignment.

They'd done this often enough and had already decided what I would report.

"Just yesterday there was an IED that went off right here, leaving this crater," Sgt. Daniel Mootoosammy aped me in his best reporterese. He knew our first stop was the spot where an IED had hit an Iraqi patrol the day before, killing at least one man.

"And then, you know," Sgt. Mootoosammy went on, "these bad things happen all the time. But look at the progress that's happening." He described what would have been our next stop: U.S. checkpoints that Iraqis were slowly taking over. "They'll have a 100-percent control of this district, you know, in a matter of months."

"But, of course, we never really got that far," Mootoosammy added, one of the understatements of the day. Mootoosammy started the day as a gunner atop one of the Humvees, far down the chain of command. Less than 15 minutes after leaving the Green Zone, he was the ranking soldier on the ground, and in charge.

Equally unimpressed with the media junket was Capt. Funkhouser's driver, Sgt. Justin Farrar, a sweet, round-faced kid. He'd started Memorial Day as most soldiers did, completely unaware of the point in time on the calendar. Troops in Iraq live their own version of *Groundhog Day*.

But Farrar did know how many days it had been since he'd gotten back from his two-week visit home to see his brand-new infant daughter. (It had actually been two and a half months since his trip home, but he spoke about it as if it had been the day before.) Farrar had arrived at his wife's hospital room at 1:18 p.m. on March 18, 2006. Arianna Hope Farrar was born at 1:20 p.m. He owed Capt. Funkhouser that memory—Captain Funk, as the guys sometimes called him, had insisted Farrar make the trip.

"He was like the daddy to the company," Farrar said.

31

Funkhouser was new to the unit. He—a young, green officer—had only been assigned to it just before deploying to Iraq six months earlier. It wasn't a great way to begin. But his men respected that he'd begun his Army career as a regular soldier before going for command. And soldiering was in his blood—his father, a well-known colonel.

Most important, Funkhouser had already proved himself on the ground. He always took the lead truck, which traditionally was the position that usually got hit. (We rode lead that day.) He couldn't be talked out of it, although his men sometimes tried. "If something happens, it will happen to me first," he'd say.

Out of respect for him, his men put up with the constant round of reporters. From Sgt. Farrar's point of view, the only good thing about having a TV correspondent along in the lead vehicle was that he had a new audience to brag to about his baby girl.

When we pulled up at the first stop of the day, Farrar prepared to get out and "pull security" for Capt. Funkhouser, as he always did. Farrar later told me the captain turned to him and said, "You stay with the reporter—keep an eye on Kimberly."

I was oblivious to the fact that the officer had just given me his guardian, and oblivious too that Justin was trailing me as I walked next to Capt. Funkhouser down the street.

Meanwhile, minutes after we pulled up, S. Sgt. Nathan Reed had cleared us to get out, after the men finished their preliminary survey from atop the Humvees.

The captain was in charge of conducting the interviews with the Iraqis. But Reed was in charge of running the patrol. Their mission today was pretty straightforward, Reed said. "To provide security for Capt. Funkhouser and the CBS crew and take them to Iraqi checkpoints that were in the process of being turned over to the Iraqi Army."

At the security briefing beforehand, Reed didn't have any particular threat to report. According to headquarters, we were going to what was statistically the safest part of Baghdad. I later found out the U.S. battalion commander of the area made sure of that when he signed off on the CBS News embed the night before.

Still, from the moment they pulled up on the wide, deserted street, Reed thought the area looked "kind of shady" with its row of dusty, high-walled villas shuttered up tightly.

He ordered the patrol to park all four Humvees in a row, noses pointed down the street, and he looked for a reason to jettison the mission. There were few people about, which to him could mean the locals had been warned of an imminent attack.

But it could also mean the Baghdad summer heat had driven everyone indoors. With no visible threat, he couldn't justify to himself calling the stop off.

Still, as Capt. Funkhouser got out of his Humvee, Reed kept searching, ordering the men to run extra checks around us.

His instincts were telling him something was wrong, but what? Where?

He had the men reposition the Humvees, to make them a wall of armor between us and the opposite lane of traffic. Then he studied a nearby row of parked cars, which all the men knew from experience were sometimes used by insurgents to hide roadside bombs.

He ordered two soldiers to check the cars. But he didn't have to. They'd already spotted the cars and were headed that way.

Funkhouser; his translator, Sam; and Paul and James were already closer to the cars than Reed. They were standing opposite the tea stand, just across the narrow side street that connected with the wide avenue.

Farrar remembers trailing the captain and me down the avenue, trying to keep up. He says when Funkhouser spotted the tea stand, he strode quickly ahead, and that I waited a beat, but then followed, walking so fast that Farrar—weighed down with 80 pounds of flak jacket and weaponry—had to jog to catch up, trying to flank me on my right.

I thought Paul had been filming Funkhouser. As it turns out the troops say he was filming them as they checked the parked cars. Paul and James were attuned to the soldiers and the fact they'd spotted danger.

Reed was zeroing in on a car parked next to the tea stand, and Paul was zeroing in on him. Paul and James were standing with their backs to the other row of parked cars, just 10 feet behind. They were the ones Reed had ordered his troops to check next. The car bomb was second in the row, a battered orange-yellow taxi, one away from Paul, James,

Capt. Funkhouser, and his translator. That was the weapon that was about to go off.

Inside, apparently in the trunk, the bombers had packed a 25- to 30-millimeter illumination artillery shell that was loaded with incendiary phosphorus. Next to it were one or two smaller shells that were loaded with the high-density explosive RDX. Illumination shells are supposed to light up the battlefield at night. Used as a weapon on the ground, the chemicals would burn into us.

The trigger was a Motorola cell phone. The bombers only had to dial the number to complete the trigger's circuit. The battalion commander later surmised that the car bomb had probably been left over from the attack the day before, designed as a secondary explosion that would have blasted through any rescue workers who came to the aid of the Iraqi patrol that was hit.

But the day before, the roadside bomb had failed to disable the Iraqis' vehicle. So they'd thrown the wounded into the back of their blast-damaged truck and raced to the hospital. The secondary car bomb had nothing to hit; the triggerman had to wait for another target to come into view.

Twenty-four hours later we walked in. Up to a dozen members of our patrol were converging on the little intersection where the tea stand stood, just opposite the line of parked cars and the bomb.

The captain and his translator and Paul and James were within 10 or 12 feet when the hit man called the number.

Farrar said he'd just drawn level with me when he saw the flash, felt the boom, and then heard only a dull, buzzing sound. His eardrums had been blown out.

Then darkness. Farrar said a dozen thoughts warred in his head, foremost among them "I can't do this to Amy," his wife.

He was still standing as he resisted unconsciousness. He looked to one side and saw the burning Humvee and then looked to the other side and saw the man he was sworn to protect falling backward.

"I can't tell you how I knew," Farrar said, "but I knew he was gone."

A fragment of shrapnel had penetrated Capt. Funkhouser's brain, killing him instantly. His men said he looked like he was sleeping.

Farrar tried to take a step toward his commander—the man he'd sworn to bring back to his family in Texas, safe and sound.

That's when he realized shrapnel had shredded much of his right side, peppering his upper thigh and shattering his jaw. His M16 fell to the ground, twisted and useless. He followed, collapsing into the dirt but still trying to crawl toward his captain.

Some 30 feet back from the kill zone, Specialist Izzy Flores Jr., the platoon's medic and the man who was to be his unit's savior that day, was knocked back by the blast. He saw his buddy next to him, Specialist Leon Snipes, throw himself to the ground. Specialist Flores followed suit, curling himself into a protective ball.

When the second wave of shrapnel finished falling, Flores said to himself, "Maybe it didn't get us. Maybe no one's hurt."

Snipes tossed a rock at Flores, trying to get his attention. For some reason, though Snipes wasn't sure why, he couldn't speak.

Flores turned to see his buddy's face full of blood. Shrapnel had blasted through the front of Snipes' mouth, removing part of his lips.

Flores said to himself, "OK, we've been hit." The 20-year-old medic was faced with his first multiple casualty scene. He handed Snipes a bandage and headed for those wounded the worst. Snipes, spitting out teeth as he went, headed for the radios to call for help.

Just on the other side of the Humvee that was parked nearest to the car bomb, Sgt. Ezequiel Hernandez and Corp. Michael Potter were caught in the backwash of the flames. Sgt. Hernandez had been walking toward the parked cars—and the car bomb—when Corp. Potter stopped him to ask if it was okay to allow the traffic through on the opposite side of the road. That extra couple of seconds' delay surely saved both of their lives.

Shrapnel had hit Sgt. Hernandez, and flames had scorched Corp. Potter's hands and face, rendering his weapons useless, but the Humvee took the brunt of the blast. Sgt. Hernandez remembers seeing the blast lift the roughly 5-ton armored vehicle and toss it a couple feet, like a child's toy.

The Humvee's gunner, Specialist Alfredo Perez, was literally shell-shocked, the back of his head peppered with shrapnel. He said the world had gone black for a moment. When he came to, everything was blurry. It took him a moment to realize his glasses and goggles had been blown off. He felt warm liquid run down his back, not understanding that it was his own blood.

Hernandez started yelling at him to get off the truck. Perez just stared at him, hearing the order but not understanding why. He started trying to obey, crawling toward the front of the Humvee. That's when he saw that the whole front end of the Humvee was on fire. He scuttled backward, finally rolling off the back side and onto the ground.

Mootoosammy had been in position at his gun. He'd just dropped down from the hatch into the Humvee to answer a call when the blast hit.

He popped up and looked back and saw a fireball, sending burning scraps of twisted metal slicing through the air. He ducked, thinking something bad had just happened. Then a second wave started hitting his truck, molten metal falling from the sky. The metal must have been blown 100 feet into the air before arcing back to earth.

Finally, it was over, and Mootoosammy looked back toward the blast site. "Everyone was lying down," he said, splayed out from the center of the blast like hands on a clock.

Flores shouted to him, "Can you cover me?" Mootoosammy manned the gun, aware insurgents often attack in two waves: a blast and then small arms fire or rocket-propelled grenades.

He manned the gun, shouting to the medic to "go do his thing."

Following their training, Potter and Hernandez made their way to Mootoosammy in the first Humvee, which was farthest from the blast and the safest place to shelter.

Potter, his burned hands already torturing him, said, "Give me something to do." He wanted something to concentrate on—anything but his hands.

Mootoosammy asked him, "Can you handle the gun?"

Potter climbed up into the Humvee's turret, and with his fingers already turning reddish purple and swelling, he manned the 50-caliber gun. Mootoosammy started trying to take stock of what had happened, how many were injured, and how to get help there fast.

Flores was going from victim to victim on the ground. First he came to Reed, who was already bandaging himself.

Reed wanted to know who else had been hit. "You know I can't tell you," Flores said. You're not supposed to upset victims who are already in shock.

"I can take it," said Reed. The sergeant in him needed to know who was alive and who was lost.

"Captain Funkhouser is gone," Flores said.

"You're kidding me," Reed said flatly.

"No."

Reed was able to take the information in, and when Mootoosammy walked up to survey the scene, Reed told "Mootoo" what he already knew: He was in charge.

Flores had already completed a quick survey. He saw that Capt. Funkhouser and his translator, Sam, couldn't be helped. "There were obvious signs of death," he said later in the most diplomatic way he could describe. James, too, had been killed instantly. He was still half clutching his microphone boom.

Paul was fighting for his life.

And so was I. I was lying where I'd fallen. Flores said he'd done a visual check on me and gotten me to speak to him. "Speak to me. Show me you can breathe," he'd said. Just as I suspected, because I was speaking, he'd assumed my injuries were less severe, so I could wait. He also didn't want to move me at first. With one of my legs jutting out at an inhuman angle, he assumed I might have spinal trauma—another reason to leave me where I was.

Flores moved back to work on Farrar, whose right side had been shattered by the blast, his jaw busted, his mouth full of blood, and his right leg laced with shrapnel. Farrar kept asking him about Capt. Funkhouser. Although some part of Farrar knew what had happened, he wanted to know for sure. Flores dodged the question.

Mootoosammy later said that just like Farrar, I kept asking about my own guys and calling out their names. He says he finally told me my crew wasn't doing well, but I guess I didn't hear or my mind shut it out.

Somewhere after those first moments of chaos, the cavalry arrived—literally. C Troop, 1-113 CAVALRY (FWD.), a unit of the Iowa National

Guard, had been driving through an adjacent traffic circle when the blast hit. They were so close that their commander, Staff Sergeant Jeremy Koch, thought the blast hit his rear vehicle. His was the voice I would fasten on to a few minutes later.

The blast "was so close. Then everyone was like, we're OK. But we had to find out what it was," he said, describing the moment, when I met him at his home months later. He ordered the convoy to whip around the next roundabout and race back. As they reached the original circle, Koch looked down the street and saw U.S. troops lying on the ground. His medic, Specialist Lacye Presley (110th MP Company), grabbed her bag and ran into the scene between one of the parked cars that was in flames and the burning Humvee. That meant Flores now had some backup, but there were still too many casualties for two medics to treat.

Right behind Specialist Presley came Guardsman Sgt. Patrick Flattery with his weapons "low and ready," as he later described.

Presley went straight to work, kneeling between Reed and Farrar, who'd been dragged to the shelter of one of the high villa walls away from the burning vehicles.

The soldiers didn't exchange greetings. They were just a group of men and women in uniform, wordlessly running into the chaos, and setting to work, side by side with the first group of soldiers.

Guardsman Flattery said he ran into the scene, dashing between the two burning vehicles, then froze for a moment. He hadn't known what to expect, and seeing fellow soldiers on the ground, wounded and killed, "just gets to you," he said. He told himself to pull it together and be professional.

He went straight to Paul and pulled him away from the burning Humvee. Flattery noted a tourniquet was already on Paul's right leg, only minutes after the blast. Paul's eyes were open, and he was trying to speak. Flattery turned him over to Iowa Guardsman Specialist Cory Heaberlin, who knelt at Paul's side, speaking to him softly. "Heaberlin was an expert with IVs," Flattery said of him. "He practiced on it every day." Heaberlin would use those skills to fight to keep Paul alive and would stay with him until his last breath. Months later he shared with Paul's wife, Linda, what it was like to be with Paul in those final moments. If Paul had any final words, Heaberlin chose to share those with Linda alone.

Flattery turned to me next. He said I was calling out, asking to be moved away from the burning vehicle. He said I hadn't yet received any medical care, as far as he could see, so he dragged me near the other casualties. I asked him, "Was my helmet on?" and he thought I asked for my camera. He spotted Paul's TV camera next to the burning Humvee, where it had landed after the blast, and told me he couldn't get to it.

There was debate later on a couple military blogger websites, criticizing me for badgering the frantic soldiers for "my camera." I don't remember that, but it would have been a bizarre request since it was Paul's camera. I didn't know at that time what had happened to him, and a correspondent knows better than to touch a cameraman's $40,000 prized possession.

Yet that's what some of the troops remember hearing me say, because perhaps that's what they expected me to say.

Flattery's commander, S. Sgt. Koch, would end up spending the most time with me, and he remembered it slightly differently He said throughout the incident that I was asking for my "camera bag," which makes more sense to me. I carried a satchel-like camera bag as a purse. He said I kept explaining that my cell phone was in my bag and that I needed it to call my producer and my boyfriend in New Zealand. He didn't want me calling anyone, so he kept telling me he didn't know where my bag was. (And he truly didn't know. My bag was in Funkhouser's Humvee, where it would remain until soldiers found it later in the day and locked it up for safekeeping.)

It was Koch who ended up tying on the tourniquets that saved my life. He later said he'd ended up treating me "by process of elimination" because I was the last injured person waiting for hands-on aid when he ran into the scene.

His medic and Flattery had run directly to the casualties, but Koch had taken a moment to position his patrol's vehicles in a security perimeter, a couple dozen yards back. He quickly organized an outer cordon of Iraqi soldiers who'd responded to the blast to keep gawkers back and then ran in.

Koch said he first went directly to Funkhouser, lying peacefully, as his guys described it, almost as if he were sleeping. "You see a fellow soldier in uniform, fallen, you go to him," he later explained.

The other soldiers waved him off. "You can't help him," they said.

So he looked around and saw me and went to work. Since I was the last to receive help, it comforted me months later to know that Paul didn't die, nor did any of the soldiers' conditions worsen, because I received help before they did.

Koch knelt down and started talking to me calmly, as he'd been trained. I remember the voice, but I never saw, or perhaps registered, his face.

The first thing he told me was his name and that he was with the Iowa National Guard, although I don't remember that. I only remember that he said ma'am a lot.

Koch filled me in on plenty of other details I hadn't absorbed at the time. He says my eyes were shut for most of the incident, except briefly at the beginning, which explains why I don't remember him or much of the bomb scene. He also told me that from the moment he ran up to me, he didn't think I'd make it. But he knew he had to do what he could.

"I kept asking you your name," he later said. "You were like, my name's Kimberly Dozier. I'm with CBS. Whatever. And for some reason, I kept forgetting it. It's like—maybe I was too busy doing other things." (Yeah, like keeping me from bleeding to death.)

He asked me where I was from, and I told him my parents were from Baltimore—that's what I usually say because I've moved around so much. I'm not exactly *from* anywhere, so I just say where my parents are from.

"I asked you the same questions maybe 100 times," he said. "I asked how old you were, and you said 39. I told you that you didn't look a day over 28." He said I smiled, just a little.

He confirmed that I asked repeatedly about "my boys" and that he'd decided that wasn't the time for me to find out. "It's one thing the Army teaches you," he later explained. "You don't tell casualties about other casualties. You don't want them to lose hope."

As he spoke to me that day, he was working quickly. All soldiers are taught basic combat lifesaving skills, and he'd always taken that seriously. He carried two bulky casualty bandages, instead of the required one, and he used to get ribbed about it—until that Memorial Day.

He had needed both his bandages and the one I offered him to tie tourniquets on my legs and stop the bleeding. My left leg was splayed from midthigh at a 90-degree angle, and I had a massive cut across that leg. (Everyone assumed the left leg was hurt the worst because of the leg's odd angle. But it was the nicked femoral artery in my right leg, and the deep burns from hip to ankle, that were killing me.)

He knew my legs would survive roughly an hour without the oxygen supply from circulating blood. After that, the tissue would die, and the doctors would have to amputate (so goes the conventional medical wisdom, though the current war is pushing those boundaries). He asked the nearest soldier for a Sharpie to write on my forehead the time he tied the tourniquet. He couldn't find one, so he tried the fallback method: writing on me in blood. But it kept smearing, "maybe because of the latex gloves I was wearing, or maybe because it's something they tell you about in class" that simply doesn't work in the field.

Off and on throughout, the rounds in the Humvee were cooking off. When they first started, everyone was thrown into momentary panic.

One of the men shouted "Sniper!" The Iowa National Guardsmen said the Fourth Infantry Division soldiers had shouted the word, and the Fourth Infantry Division soldiers insist the Iowa National Guardsmen shouted it. Regardless, almost everyone hit the dirt.

Near Koch and me, Flores was in the middle of patching someone up. He later said all he could think was "Please don't shoot me now; I've got to finish this." And he kept going.

Meanwhile I was in the middle of asking Koch if I still had my helmet on. He confirmed my recollection that I had been stubbornly insistent about the helmet.

"But that isn't what frustrated me," he later told me. "What did, though, was that you kept trying to sit up, and I told you repeatedly to stay down" so as to keep the blood from rushing to my legs. He knew if I lost any more blood, I was "a goner."

I managed to sit halfway up once before he could stop me. That's when he saw my helmet was full of blood and the back of my head was sticky matted red. He realized something had ripped into my skull. He gently pushed me back down and called for the medic from his patrol, Specialist Lacye Presley. She helped him put on another bandage.

While he worked, he continued his steady patter of questions to try to keep me awake, and I kept talking. He said I wasn't panicked or moaning and groaning in pain. "You just needed someone to talk to."

But the entire time, my shrapnel-strewn body was leaking blood like a sieve. And he started losing me.

"Your voice became very weak, and you started drifting off," he said. "I feared that if you lost consciousness, you'd never wake back up. I was like, 'Hey Kimberly, please stay with me. You're gonna make it. You'll be all right.'"

And I replied from my stupor, "Yeah, yeah, yeah. OK, all right."

He called out to Presley again, who scrambled over and started an IV and then another and another, every time I started to go under.

By the time the casualty evacuation (Casevac) team reached us from the Green Zone, close to an hour had passed. "That was the longest hour of my life," he said.

Meeting Koch months later was surreal. The TV crew captured our awkward reunion at his home in Iowa, me walking in his front door to see a 6-foot-tall guardsman with piercing blue eyes who was totally unfamiliar to me—until I heard his voice. I remembered that. He and his wife, a schoolteacher with a haircut I envied (just like the one I had before my brain surgery), had tracked every detail of my story they could get off the web.

Koch tortured himself for days and then months after the event, first saying, "If she dies, is it because I tied the tourniquets wrong?" Then he wondered, "What could I have done better? What tourniquet could I have tied tighter? What bandage could I have applied? What could I have said to her?"

I only found out that Koch and his men had helped save me and the others that day thanks to the persistence of his commander at the unit's base. Capt. Grant Kaufman had fought a frustrating battle to get his guys included in the official bombing report. They weren't from the Baghdad area of operations. They'd simply been driving through, back up to their base a few hours north, in the Sunni hot zone of Diyala. For months after the incident, their role in the rescue was lost in the chaos at the scene and the twists in the Army's chain of command.

When I released my first public statement, thanking only those in the Fourth ID patrol I'd been with for saving my life, Capt. Kaufman realized I still didn't know the whole story. So he broke Army rules and went to a local CBS station in Iowa to try to reach me. He told them about Koch's role in hopes of getting the inside track on my recovery. The station reached me via email in late August where I was in a rehab hospital. It took me until early fall to reach Kaufman and then Koch and find out who'd most directly saved my life, although every single person on the ground that day played a role.

Later in my hospital room in Landstuhl, maybe three days after the blast, the Fourth Infantry Division's Corp. Potter came to my room to apologize for "taking so long" to get us all rescued from the bomb scene. I told him, "Hey, I'm here, aren't I? It's OK."

I was a bit baffled by his apology as I had no idea it had taken almost an hour to get us out of there, though we were only a couple miles from the Green Zone. And I didn't know then how close I'd come to not surviving.

The reasons for the Casevac team's delay fit neatly under the old-fashioned term "fog of war." Amid the chaos Mootoosammy was trying to get the rescue team the right coordinates. He later blamed himself, as did others, for a series of mistakes that stole precious minutes from our rescuers.

He shouldn't have—what none of them took into account was that in addition to the shock and adrenaline pumping through them from the attack, they were all close enough to the blast to sustain mild to moderate traumatic brain injury (TBI). TBI covers everything from a mild concussion sustained when a blast makes the brain bounce around inside the skull to the damage of penetrating shrapnel. Symptoms include confusion and a distorted sense of time. TBI victims can seem drunk. You could say that every man in that patrol was walking wounded.

In their initial panic and confusion, they were convinced the radios were off-line though Humvee radios are engineered to continue operating after that kind of blast. Snipes was trying to get them tuned back in but was working through the fog of pain from the shrapnel to his mouth.

So Mootoosammy and Hernandez were trying to reach their base via cell phone, an open form of communication that troops aren't supposed to use because the insurgents can monitor it. But at that moment, cell phones were the only thing they knew for sure were working. Mootoosammy called his platoon sergeant back in the Green Zone and said, "We have some men hurt. We're at this location . . ."

But the coordinates he'd given were incorrect. He'd rebooted the Humvee's satellite computer tracking system, which *had* been blown off-line. He didn't realize the coordinates the computer spat out were from the last known location the Humvee had locked on to: their base in the Green Zone, where we'd started the morning's mission.

As the Casevac team scrambled to leave, they checked the coordinates, realized the error, and called Mootoosammy again. He then had to pull out a map and give them grid coordinates the old-fashioned way.

As all this was happening, it didn't even occur to the Fourth Infantry Division soldiers that the Iowa National Guardsmen had working radios and working satellite coordinate systems in their Humvees, parked just yards away. And it took the Iowa guys at least 15 minutes to realize the Fourth ID patrolmen were having communications problems and had therefore failed to send a "nine-line," the official call for help that summons rescuers for casualty evacuation. The nine-line gives rescuers everything they need to know about whom they're picking up, including how to find them and what to expect at the scene when they arrive. So the Guardsmen sent in the message, and, Koch said, within minutes Apache helicopters were flying overhead.

Koch said I heard the birds from my place on the ground and asked, "Is that my helicopter?" I'd seen so many Casevac helicopters fly past my window over the years that I must have assumed we'd be flying out of there—my helo pilot boyfriend, Pete, would appreciate that.

We were parked on a wide avenue, but it was still too narrow for a helicopter landing, which needs an unobstructed open area of about 100 feet square (100×100) to land safely. Too many wires were strung across the avenue where we were hit, and a statue stood smack in the middle of the nearest square, where the Iowa National Guardsmen had established the security perimeter.

So the Casevac had to reach us by ground, navigating Baghdad's twisted, traffic-choked streets. And even once they got the right coordinates, the Casevac team couldn't find us. Mootoosammy later explained that they were almost to our position when the rescuers spotted smoke and rushed to what turned out to be the site of a different car bomb. Less than a mile away, another explosion had gone off, hitting Iraqi civilians—one of five car bombs in all that hit the capital that day. So the Casevac team took the time to dismount and establish a security cordon at that scene before calling Mootoosammy's cell phone again and asking where he was.

"Did you guys already drive back to the Green Zone?" the rescuers asked.

"We're right here," Mootoosammy barked. He repeated the coordinates, his frustration reaching stratospheric levels. The rescuers jumped back into their Humvees. Yet somehow in the confusing Baghdad streets, they drove past us once more, stopped, and called again.

That's when Iowa National Guard S. Sgt. Mitch Hall threw a red smoke grenade. He'd overheard all the confusion, so he ran out to his vehicle at the traffic circle, grabbed one of the grenades, and threw it.

But Mootoosammy is convinced he himself threw it. Maybe they both did. In any case the grenade or grenades sent up billowing red smoke.

"Do you see THAT?" Mootoosammy barked.

Time had run out for Paul, and it was fast running out for me. By the time the Casevac team lifted my stretcher into their Humvee, I was screaming and fighting them. I'd gone hypoxic, meaning my body had so little blood that my brain was running out of oxygen. A trauma surgeon at Baltimore's Shock Trauma Center later explained my behavior: Like a drowning swimmer, I was fighting the oxygen loss, and anyone who came near me, with my last gasp of adrenaline.

Medic Presley later told me it scared the hell out of her.

"I knew then that you were about to die."

CHAPTER 4
combat support hospital–green zone

Somehow the adrenaline carried me through the Humvee dash across Baghdad traffic. Reed, Farrar, and the other injured men were each loaded into additional vehicles.

Completely by accident, cameras were waiting at the Green Zone's Ibn Sina Hospital. The colleague I'd passed earlier that day, CNN's Cal Perry, and his cameraman, Dominic Swann, had been filming Baghdad's main combat support hospital for months. They were at the front of the battered, dusty entrance to the Saddam-era building, which was now a trauma center, filming what for them had become a routine event—incoming casualties—until they figured out who today's casualties were.

Cal and Dominic split up, tracking the six Humvees carrying us in and the barely organized chaos of the trauma staff inside, who were rushing back and forth between patients and stacks of supplies and making room for multiple casualties in their makeshift trauma operating room. They'd built it out of the old hospital's emergency room. Ibn Sina had been one of the most exclusive hospitals in Iraq under Saddam, devoted solely to his relatives, political cronies, and top officers. Its walls were covered with cold white, gray-flecked marble (which the docs say I matched perfectly in bloodless pallor). The irony was that for all the fancy marble, the toilets barely functioned and the oxygen outlets on the wall weren't connected to anything.

So the U.S. military had done its best to transform the building into a proper trauma center, cramming in almost everything you'd find in a stateside hospital. Every bed had monitors for blood pressure and heart rhythm (or lack thereof) and portable oxygen saturation and respiration units, which measured whether the oxygen from the lungs was actually reaching the blood. There were also two state-of-the-art cardiac defibrillators, an old portable X-ray machine—a "workhorse," as one doc called it—and a new CT scanner that was housed in a trailer outside.

Cal and Dominic tracked the soldiers easing the stretchers gently and awkwardly out of the Humvees, then, after they'd cleared the Humvee doors, racing inside.

Cal later wrote about that on the CNN website: "I could tell immediately that something truly horrible had happened; this was much worse than only a few wounded. Bloodied, screaming, and scared soldiers are lifted out of the vehicles. A gunner yells to one of his buddies, 'You're going to make it. You're going to be OK.'"

Soldier after soldier was stretchered past. Then Cal later told me he saw something that didn't look right, but it didn't register at first. A civilian was being carried out of one of the Humvees, a woman.

He stood well out of the way and filmed through the Humvee's window, a shot I saw later: red shirt, red hair, face slack, body slumped. Then my stretcher raced by him, soldiers pounding past through the dirt and slamming open the doors of the ER.

Inside, Cal's camera (or maybe Dominic's) caught a surgeon rushing into the hospital from his morning run, sweating in his gray Army shirt and black shorts, with an M16 slung across his shoulders. Again, just like at the bomb scene, I just happened to be at the end of the line, waiting for medical care. There was no VIP nonsense here, despite what some later claimed.

Off and on I was screaming, so the video showed.

To Cal, who was filming in my ER, I was just some screaming woman they were working on, another sad case for the trauma docs. That was until they tilted me and Cal spotted a bloodied microphone, still pinned to my shirt, from the morning's shoot.

He felt a rush of nausea, he later wrote, and broke out in a sweat. Someone rushed by, asking, "Do you know her? That's Kimberly Dozier from CBS."

Cal stopped filming and switched into bureau-chief mode, calling his desk in Atlanta, simultaneously reporting the news and ordering them to observe a news blackout until CBS could reach our families.

Watching me fighting for life, he kept asking himself, "Where's her crew?"

He later told me that when I first came in, I was "amazingly coherent, even telling the doctor your name and that you weren't allergic to anything."

Coherence didn't last. The surgeon, Capt. David Steinbruner, slid a tube down my throat to take over my breathing, and he started pumping in Versed, a drug that puts the brain into a low-functioning state.

In the video you can hear me making low, guttural screams through the tube. I don't remember any of this. Versed has a side effect mostly welcomed by doctors. It scrubs your memory, even erasing memories of events from before the drug started coursing through your system. Maybe that's why I can't remember fighting my rescuers.

Or perhaps I don't remember because I was slipping away. Sitting outside my operating room, Cal and Dominic heard someone inside shout, "I don't have a pulse." As the team started chest compressions, he and Dominic couldn't bring themselves to film it. They sat stunned, staring silently at the wall.

Twenty seconds later they heard someone shout: "I've got a pulse . . . a strong one."

I'd made it out, that time. As the doctors and nurses stabilized me and moved me upstairs to a bigger operating theatre, my heart was about to shut down again.

Capt. Steinbruner later explained the battle on the operating table, a day seared into his mind in detail. A horribly ordinary day as it happened was made special only when he became aware of the generals and the U.S. ambassador crowding his waiting room. He wrote me a long, detailed email—one of several we would exchange, as he patiently explained everything he could remember from that day.

I was called down from my room by Dr. Sam Mehta, one of the other ER docs, who said that a VBIED (vehicle borne improvised explosive device) had gone off and several people were coming in. I ran down from my room to be met in the hallway by an anxious charge nurse, who said that there was a badly injured patient in the back room.

I ran around the corner to find you laid out on the trauma room table. You were very pale, the same color as the mottled white marble in our ER. Your legs had many holes, which were bleeding, you had a tourniquet around each thigh, and a small wound over your right temple, I believe.

You were just barely conscious, trying to sit up and trying to pull the oxygen mask off of your face. I asked you your name, and you said "Kim" in a soft whisper.

You also answered a question about allergies, but I don't think that you were really there. I really just wanted to see how sick you were and if you could answer me. I told you I was going to put you to sleep and did so without too much difficulty.

Several people swirled around you and began cutting off your clothes and tightening the tourniquets around your legs. At some point, we lost your pulse. I remember asking several people to check, as I couldn't feel it anymore.

Someone started chest compressions, and I had the nurse push epinephrine and blood into you as quickly as she could. We probably pushed on your chest for about 30 to 60 seconds, although I did lose track of the exact time.

You never had a shockable rhythm, so I didn't have to use the cardiac defibrillator on you, but I could have if necessary. For the record, you were in what we call PEA (pulseless electrical activity): a very scary rhythm but fixable if you can figure out what's wrong. In your case, it was pretty straightforward. The trick was fixing it quickly. But don't dwell on that, all is well that ends well.

I rechecked your pulse, and it had come back. The many units of blood that you sucked down were pumped into your veins with a power infuser, which definitely helped save your life. This was one of the most critical pieces of equipment we had. You were hooked up to a small, portable respirator that most definitely wasn't state of the art but worked well enough.

The lab and blood bank did an awesome job analyzing your blood, chemistries, and blood gas as well as getting us blood product very quickly. I believe I took a quick look inside your body, putting a portable ultrasound device on your belly, just to reassure everyone that you had no large intra-abdominal bleeding. This may have saved you a laparotomy scar and the surgeons' unnecessary rummaging around your belly.

I decided with the surgeon Chuck Fox and the orthopedic surgeon (who has asked to remain anonymous) who was stabilizing your legs that it was time to send you upstairs for surgery.

We all said it at the same time, just looked at each other and said: "Let's go now."

Now, just to really blow your mind, this was going on at several tables at once [as doctors worked on some of the critically wounded soldiers].

Just so you understand, I don't think that your heart ever truly stopped; it's just that you had so little blood that it wasn't enough to generate a pulse. So it's fair to say that for a brief moment, you died. But I believe that you have a lot more yet to do in this world because you came back with just a little help from us. . . .

Let me say that the soldier who put the tourniquets on saved your life. Everyone who laid hands on you and the injured soldiers that day and over the next several days did everything right: from medic to air crews to us to the surgeons and anesthesiologists to the crew transporting you to Balad [the Air Force Theater Hospital at Balad Air Base Hospital—the top U.S. military medical facility in Iraq] to the neurosurgeons, nurses, and critical care teams that shepherded you back to Germany. When you woke up at Landstuhl, your broken body had been touched by dozens of people, all of whom wished you God speed and a swift recovery.

For my family the news was grim. They were told I might die. But I was still in the fight.

A horror without hope was visited on the families of Paul and James, Capt. Funkhouser, his translator, Sam, and the family of that Iraqi who'd simply been standing on the street, having a cup of tea.

I imagine if you saw it from above, you could see rings of horror spreading out from the bomb in all directions—waves, which when they hit, would leave those struck forever changed. One wave came in the form of the two stricken officers in their green dress uniforms, who had to walk to the front door of Capt. Funkhouser's house in Ft. Hood, Texas, to tell his wife. Jennifer Funkhouser had been vacuuming when she answered the door. She took one look at them, ashen and ramrod straight, one of the officer's lips trembling, and she knew. "But I just spoke to him yesterday," she said.

And then to herself, "How do I tell my daughters?" Kaitlyn, 4 years old, and Allison, just 2 years old, were upstairs playing.

Jennifer didn't want the image of exploding cars in her daughters' heads, so she told them there'd been a car accident. Kaitlyn looked at her mother and said, "Daddy's dead." And she said, "Yes."

It took a day for all of Capt. Funkhouser's loved ones to be reached, so the Army released his name 24 hours after they released Paul's and James' names. Some in the public, ignorant of how the military reporting system works, lashed out on conservative blogs, saying the media's failure to name Capt. Funkhouser proved reporters only cared about their own and not about the man in uniform who'd fallen with them that day.

I don't know how Sam's family was told; it would have been too dangerous for U.S. troops to go to his house. He kept his name anonymous to protect his family and hid the fact from anyone in his neighborhood that he worked for the U.S. military. Working for the Americans can get you killed. So what must the family have said to neighbors? What cover story did they create to explain their loss and their grief?

The news hit our CBS bureau in Baghdad with a phone call to my friend Agnes Reau. Lt. Col. Barry Johnson made the call. He was the head Coalition press officer whose quiet, raised-eyebrow sarcasm had turned him into someone we liked and relied upon.

Agnes answered the phone and went still. Kate Rydell, sitting at the desk across from her, said her face changed. She hung up and said, "Our crew has been hit. You have to get to the Green Zone right away."

They realized later that they'd both heard the bomb, and one of our translators had run in to report it: another car bomb, this one in the Karrada. It was an event so normal they hadn't risked sending a crew to film it.

Kate, as the senior producer, had been in charge of our story but wasn't allowed to go with us. The Army said there wasn't enough space in the vehicles. Thank God. That made one less of us hit that day. Kate is a hands-on producer. If she'd been with us, she would have been standing right next to Paul and James.

Now she raced downstairs, scrambling drivers and our foreign security team. Kate said that even as she threw herself down the hotel steps, her cell phone was ringing. Reuters news agency called and asked if we were alive or dead. All she could say was that she didn't know, and she asked for a news blackout.

In the back of her mind, guilt was already growing. She later blamed herself for fighting for a space for James on the trip so he could watch Paul's back if we ran into trouble. (The Army prefers one-man bands—cameramen who also do sound—because they want a minimum number of journalists on an embed. Every space they make for journalists means a soldier they have to leave behind.) But the Army press officer, Maj. Cheadle, doesn't remember that. He said the only debate was whether she could come too.

Kate raced out of our high-walled hotel compound to the Green Zone, accompanied by two of our foreign security advisors, who are in charge of helping us stay as safe as we can in a place like Baghdad. As former military operators like my boyfriend, Pete, they prefer to keep their names out of the media, so I only use their first names. Karl and Jim talked their way through the gauntlet of Green Zone security checks in double time and came to a halt at the Cash (the casualty support hospital, or CSH). They ran in and stopped in what was essentially a large entryway, empty save for a bunch of bloodied stretchers. There's no front desk clerk at a combat hospital.

The surgeons had seven casualties to treat, three whose lives were in danger. Justin Farrar and Nathan Reed were screaming in pain. So was I by then, those low guttural cries muffled by my breathing tube.

The CBS team rushed through the hallways until they stumbled into a doctor who asked them to make an identification.

Kate froze, thinking for a moment that perhaps he meant that all of us had been killed.

Our security team walked her around a corner and almost straight into me, where I was "lying on a gurney, surrounded by 10 people," she later described. I was still alive, soaked in blood, but the doctors wanted me "identified."

Kate tried to look in over the crowd of people working on me, but she couldn't see over them. So one of our security men moved around to the other side, peered in, and said, "Yes, that's Kimberly Dozier."

The surreal nature of the questions hit Kate later, as she thought, "How many red-headed female Western journalists can be wounded in Iraq at the same time?"

That was her first chance to see me, drenched in blood, with one leg still askew, the left foot splayed outward at an unnatural angle, twisted from the point where the femur shattered. By then my face was covered in ventilating tubes and my body going porcupine with IVs.

"There was so much blood," Kate said. "I thought we just had to kiss you goodbye."

Kate and my two security friends sat on a bench outside, watching the chaos as the doctors treated the other soldiers. Different surgeons came out to brief them, each one with an ever grimmer prognosis. One of the doctors described the massive shrapnel injuries and burns to my legs.

"He didn't seem to be too sure you'd keep your legs," Kate later said.

He told me that he was "very pessimistic" and that I only had "a 50-50 chance of making it." Kate's notes were staccato, disjointed: "pelvis okay, loss of blood, heart stopped 2X, 50/50."

I'd lost more than half my blood at the bomb scene, and it kept leaking out. The doctors pumped in 30 to 40 units—that's more than one adult's worth. Between Farrar, Reed, and me, we'd literally bled the blood bank dry.

A call went out. Within minutes there were 50 soldiers, contractors, and medical personnel crowding the hallway, waiting to give blood, including some of the men who were injured on our patrol.

"They were carrying their own warm blood down the hall," Kate said. The blood would be screened using new technology not yet approved in the States since it's only 95 percent accurate, not the FDA-mandated 99 percent. But it would do the trick, working so fast that the donor blood was practically going from one warm body to another to try to keep us alive.

Meanwhile Kate said it took an age to confirm that Paul and James were lost, and then hours to get them both from the blast site to the hospital. At the bomb scene troops were still mopping up and collecting evidence. Within hours Army commanders were sending Special Forces teams into action, looking for those who set off the bomb.

Paul, James, and Capt. Funkhouser were being watched over by the captain's own men, the bunkmates and battle buddies of the patrol that had been hit. The grandmother of one of those soldiers later contacted me. She said her grandson and his mates had rushed to the scene, unable to stop the bomb, but risking their lives to stand guard over the dead in the center of Baghdad for three hours.

But the soldiers could not spare the fallen some of the minor indignities war produces. They had run out of body bags at the scene, so Paul and James had been wrapped in one together, waiting to be carried to the Green Zone. They would have had a thing or two to say about sharing such close quarters.

That necessity didn't reach those back at base, where Kate and our security guys were waiting to identify Paul and James for their families. Various commanders and diplomats crowded into the hospital to see what they could do. Kate snapped at one, "You've lost James' body. Where is it?"

Paul's and James' friends, our security men, identified their bodies like they'd just identified me on the operating gurney. They assured us later that neither man felt a thing, although I knew Paul had fought his damnedest to stay alive.

Months later I spoke with Paul's wife, Linda Douglas. I had never met Linda, nor James' wife, Geri Brolan. Geri did not want details, but Linda did, so a mutual friend thought talking would help us both. She had many questions, and I tried to answer them the best I could—what I felt at the scene, from the initial distant pain to the numb shock that replaces it and then how the mind takes charge until blackness fades in. I pretended for a time that the conversation helped her, but I fear it only helped me and drove her pain deeper.

As the news spread from the military's frantic central command centers and then across the Green Zone, a host of diplomats and American commanders headed for the CSH. Paul and I had worked as a team in Iraq through maybe a dozen shifts over three years. Together, we'd interviewed just about anyone who was anyone. James had racked up just as much time on the ground at ABC News Baghdad before coming to work with us. The diplomats and commanders wanted to see if they could help and wanted to see for themselves if it was as bad as they'd heard.

One visitor was our patrol's overall commander, the Fourth Infantry Division's Maj. Gen. James "JD" Thurman, whom I'd only just met two days before for a press luncheon. We took a picture afterward—ranks of scruffy journalists and the Southern, good-old-boy general, all of us with those goofy, pasted-on grins you wear for a picture with a bunch of people you don't know very well.

By then Kate was frantic between waiting for news from the surgeons operating on me and delivering the news of Paul's and James' deaths to London and New York. She was now trying to figure out how to get the two men home and where to fly me, if I survived.

So Maj. Gen. Thurman bowed out quietly and went back to doing what generals do: in this case, keeping track of a rapid-fire investigation already underway. U.S. forensic specialists and military bomb experts were examining evidence from the scene, and Iraqi police were busting in doors across the Karrada and gathering more. Within hours they had enough information to move in on two different Iraqi cells, both made up of hard-line Sunni extremists with connections to Al Qaeda and both with the materials in hand to make the type of bomb that had hit us. We'll never know for sure which one was directly responsible, but it matters little. Both groups were bent on killing someone in the same manner we'd been attacked.

Meanwhile Kate was learning about the present: which in my case meant good news—and bad news. The doctor had successfully clamped my femoral artery by performing a cut down, a procedure where they went in above my hip bone and stemmed the artery's flow, so they could then stitch up the nick in the artery lower down in my leg. Along the way they had to restart my heart twice. Somewhere in there they'd put X-fixes on my legs—external metal rods drilled into my bones above and below the breaks in both femurs—to keep my legs temporarily straight until orthopedic surgeons could hammer rods into place. My right leg, the tissue blasted and burned from hip to ankle, had started swelling. They'd had to perform a fasciotomy to the calf, scoring straight down my leg on both sides from knee to ankle with a scalpel, right down to the muscle, to release the pressure. The fasciotomy worked, but the battle to save my leg was far from over.

After all that, there was one problem they discovered that was beyond the surgical skills of the doctors in the Baghdad casualty hospital. After they'd stabilized my heart, stopped the artery from bleeding, and topped up my blood, the medical team checked the rest of me and found that the nasty cut in my head was a lot more than that. A fragment of shrapnel had entered my skull, and that meant a new crisis.

They had just told Kate that I was stable and would be staying in Baghdad overnight when, minutes after the head wound was found, I was on the emergency evacuation list for Balad, stat. They flew me north to Balad within the hour.

Kate relayed the bad news to the office and went to work finding a way to join me. I would be flying by medical evacuation chopper, but there was no room for Kate. U.S. Ambassador Zalmay Khalilzad, who'd just walked in to check on the situation for himself, instantly offered up his own Blackhawk, replete with its twin-Apache attack helicopter escort. This was much to the consternation of his staff, who had to get him to important meetings.

Ambassador Khalilzad already had two of his top people working with us. His press officer, Liz Coulton, herself a former journalist, was helping Kate deal with releasing details to the press, and his aide, Susan Phalen, flew with Kate to Balad to sort out the red tape, including dealing with the military's insistence that I not be permitted to fly to Germany until they had my Social Security number since they presumed my passport was burned at the scene. (It wasn't, though. It was sitting in my bag in the Humvee with several thousand dollars, the cash CBS had just floated me for that trip but I'd been afraid to leave in my room. The Fourth Infantry Division soldiers guarded it like it was their own, safely returning everything a few days later.) Susan, working together with a Pentagon aide, sliced through the bureaucracy and got me on the plane to Germany the next morning.

Gen. George Casey stepped into the breach for transport, taking Kate and Susan with him on his own chopper to Balad. The commander of multinational forces in Iraq had missed us at the CSH and wanted to see the injured from our patrol for himself.

Gen. Casey had met Paul and me during a brief day's filming a couple months earlier. We'd been invited to follow him for a day, flying to Fallujah as he briefed newly arrived commanders on his game plan for Iraq.

As I took notes inside, Paul and soundman Adam Haylett had waited outside, where they heard an emergency call blare out over the Fallujah base's PA system. A patrol had been hit with mortars, and the base hospital needed A positive blood. Without a word, Adam—A positive himself—had rushed to the hospital tent to give blood. Paul rushed after him, with the camera, and filmed. He never missed a news shot.

So Gen. Casey remembered both Paul and me, and from the moment of the bombing, he and his aides tracked our progress.

They got me into the operating room in Balad by about 9 p.m. Balad lies a short helicopter flight due north/northwest of Baghdad, not much to look at from the air, just a collection of tents on a dusty, flat airfield.

But inside is some of the best medical equipment in the world and a team of top surgeons, including the 207th Head and Neck Team, 332nd EMDG/AFTH. Susan took Kate aside to a waiting area, and the surgeons went to work on my skull.

Neurosurgeon Maj. Hans Bakken was warm but very clinical and matter-of-fact in later emails, when he explained to me the process of taking a cranial saw to my head. Lopping off part of a skull to dig out some excess metal is all in a day's work for him. This wasn't the adrenaline-fueled fight to keep me alive that the trauma surgeons in Baghdad experienced. This was a careful, measured operation to remove something that didn't belong in my head, all the while keeping an eye on my vital signs to make sure I didn't tip over the edge again.

Maj. Bakken later explained that there was "only one fragment in the head, just underneath the skull, and so I removed it." He added that he "then cleaned things up and put the skull back together with titanium plates and screws." My skin was then stapled into place in an arcing semicircle. Monitors were left in place through a hole in my skull to make sure my brain wasn't swelling from postoperative bruising. Swelling spells brain damage.

They kept me under with more Versed to keep my brain at a low operating speed to let it come back slowly. From then on at each hospital, doctors were on the lookout for brain damage: What had that small chunk taken out or done to what was left behind?

I was also later warned at Bethesda Naval Hospital that there might be small fragments left in the brain matter, too small for the surgeons to spot. Maj. Bakken reassured me that he didn't think "there's much material, if any, remaining within." But that measure of doubt is enough to keep me far, far away from MRI scans—magnetic resonance imagers are, as the name implies, basically huge magnets. An MRI scan could drag any leftover fragments of metal through my brain, not to mention what it would do to the fragments floating throughout the rest of my body.

The surgery over, it was time to move me to Landstuhl. Kate was with me every minute, and like any reporter facing a crisis, she dealt with everything by taking copious notes. My medical chopper arrived at Balad at 9 at night, and I'd gone straight to neurosurgery, less than 12 hours after I'd been hit on the Baghdad street. I'm not sure how long the surgery took, but we left around 6 a.m. on one of the large C-17 transport planes, which had been turned into flying hospitals called C-Cats, and was bound for Germany.

"The whole method of moving you was amazing," she wrote. "They packed you on a stretcher and essentially loaded a mini ICU onto it. They wheeled you onto a bus, and they hung the stretcher on hooks, sort of like a hammock. Then, because it's such precious cargo, the bus driver drove very slowly. And I wanted to yell, 'Hurry up. We have to get to Germany!'"

Kate said 10 soldiers were waiting next to the plane to wheel me on board, executing a very precise military maneuver to get me off the bus and onto my rack on a side of the plane, without jarring the equipment or me.

Inside, a doctor, a couple of nurses, and a respiratory specialist were among the team of people in charge of keeping me and the dozen or so other patients on board alive through the journey, through every change in altitude and temperature, and through the juddering motion from the roaring engine of a military cargo plane.

Even in that unconscious state, my usual attitude started reasserting itself, Kate said. Despite the brain surgery and the copious amounts of drugs I was on, I was fighting to wake up. I had questions, and I needed answers.

Kate said, "They were giving you a bunch of pain medication, but you kept coming out of it, so at one point the doctor called me over and said I could talk to you."

Kate said she put a hand on my shoulder and started speaking to me, trying not to yell but still somehow making herself heard over the din of the engines. "You're on a plane to Germany," she told me. "You've been injured in a bombing, but you have your arms and legs. You're going to be fine," she added.

Kate said I blinked my eyes and nodded my head ever so slightly.

"I absolutely knew you heard and understood me," she said. I have no memory of it, but it must have given me peace at the time.

After that I slept all the way to Germany.

CHAPTER 5

word spreads

Back at the bureau Agnes' first phone call was to Andy Clarke, CBS's new deputy bureau chief in London. He'd worked as a producer there for years and was one of Paul's best friends. She told him what she knew at first: There had been an incident, and "Our guys have been hit." She'd never been through anything like this before, but she instantly knew what the news would do to our small London bureau. Within 10 minutes, word would spread and her Baghdad office phone would be ringing nonstop with people in London desperate to know what had happened, what she knew, and how she felt about it.

So Agnes issued a strict order to Andy: Only you call me, no one else from the bureau, no one from New York—just you. That way, she clawed back some small measure of control over the horror.

I counted Agnes among my best friends and one of Paul's good friends. Agnes—pronounced, as this French-born daughter of a diplomat always explained with a wink, "Ahn-YES"—was one of the constant presences in the bureau. She held it together, waking before anyone else and tearing through the newspapers, wires, and local translators' translations for story ideas, then organizing a morale-building barbeque by the pool before many of us had even had breakfast. She'd organized such a barbeque for Paul, James, me, and the outgoing correspondent, CBS News anchor Harry Smith, just three days before Memorial Day. Harry had played grill master for the bureau, giving chef Paul and his sous-chef James the night off. In the pictures I look haggard from the lack of sleep and a roiling stomach as I'd unwisely eaten at the hotel's bacteria-laden buffet for lunch. But we're all grinning, especially Paul, James, Agnes, and me, because we've spent so much time here the past three years that we feel like we're home.

Now Agnes was left in a surreal world where she'd said goodbye to us in the hallway that morning and then no one came back. My desk was empty and the kitchen clean and quiet without Paul and James cooking some large daily feast. Nor would Kate be coming back. She would fly straight to Germany with me, wearing the clothes on her back.

In the silence Agnes was picking up her phone over and over to deliver the worst news of her professional career, knowing with each call she was starting a horrible telephone chain around our company, families, and the world.

That done, her next task was worse. Together with our foreign security advisors, who mercifully for Agnes and Kate identified the bodies, Agnes was responsible for organizing a way to bring Paul and James home.

Meanwhile, our Iraqi staff was devastated—once Agnes was able to tell them. She had to hide the news from them for hours until she knew for sure, and even then until she was certain that Paul's and James' families had been reached. It wasn't just that the Iraqi staffers were losing friends— we'd all known each other for years. The tragedy also spelled new personal terror. They'd all had close calls themselves of one sort or another. But they'd almost convinced themselves that bad things didn't happen to the bureau's foreigners, at least not to us, which gave them a false sense of comfort. Now it had, which meant it could happen to anyone.

Across the company we were not prepared for the tragedy either. Andy, new to his job as deputy bureau chief and waiting for his new boss to move to London, had to face alone possibly the worst task in two decades at CBS News: calling the wife of his friend Paul and telling her Paul was gone.

Then, although he didn't know James well, he had to call James' wife and find the words to tell her. And then, somehow he had to figure out how to help both wives tell their children before the news broke in the international media.

In the military there's a tradition of honoring loss. It's an accepted part of the job, which gives the patriotism of that service its bittersweet edge.

In journalism we may be the Fourth Estate, doing our service by questioning our country's leaders, but we generally don't exhibit our patriotism in blood. Logically we all knew violence could hit us in a dozen different ways in Baghdad: car bombs, roadside bombs, gunfire, rocket fire, kidnappings, stray rounds. But we hadn't actively prepared for it.

Although a military commander is trained on how to deliver this message and knows in the back of his or her mind that a horrible event will likely occur someday, this news blindsided my colleagues and sent them reeling for weeks and months, possibly for years to come.

Since an attack wasn't supposed to happen, the fact that it did meant someone must be to blame—or so the grief-twisted logic went. Someone should have seen it coming. So new deputy bureau chief Andy tortured himself with guilt over the assignment. He'd double-checked the week before Memorial Day to make sure we were planning on shooting something with the troops.

When Andy called Paul's wife, Linda, to tell her of Paul's death, she simply refused to believe it, especially since Paul hadn't told her in the phone call the night before that he was going on assignment. In her mind he couldn't have been on the shoot, and there must have been some mistake.

For the next year Linda interrogated everyone about what exactly happened and when. She wanted an almost forensic level of detail, as though if she could master exactly what happened, she could figure out what or who was to blame and could take her anger out on the source of blame and keep such a tragedy from ever happening again. She practically cross-examined her grief, according to those in whom she confided. I understood her quest. I wanted to help her, but after our first disastrous phone call, I decided that the journey and the quest for information was and is part of the grieving and healing process for both of us, and that I shouldn't try to shortcut that. Besides, after that one initial conversation early on she didn't want to talk to me again. I understood that too and let it be.

Geri, James' wife of 20 years, handled it in almost completely the opposite way. She didn't want to know the details. She was at work when Andy reached her. James' 15-year-old son, Sam, was at home, miles away. Geri also had to contact her 12-year-old daughter, Agatha, who was at school. At the combat hospital Kate worked with U.S. embassy officials to call every news organization and keep the blackout in place until Geri could reach her children.

According to those close to her, Geri coped by blocking out the tragedy—or trying to. She told herself, "These things happen, so just get on with it," just the way her husband always refused to let the world's various hellholes get him down.

At the London bureau, there were grief, anger, and lots of blame. I had been one of the correspondents who had tried hard to make the starting lineup in our management's new team, post-Dan Rather. Some immediately presumed I'd taken the Memorial Day assignment as part of the competition. Even as I was lying in the hospital bed fighting to survive, some in London shouted and recriminated, asking if the new spirit of intercorrespondent rivalry had gotten Paul and James killed. Even my friends were asking themselves the same thing.

Those who stayed my friends concluded that the day's shoot was standard, the type any of us would have deemed safe, rather than a pushy TV correspondent's grasp for glory. But a couple of my former London colleagues will forever blame me. If I'd just stayed in the hotel that day, all would have been well and Paul and James would be alive.

In the shattered Fourth Infantry Division patrol, some of the soldiers were also asking the same questions: "If we hadn't been out with the media that day, would this have happened to us?" Farrar was already blaming himself for not being at Capt. Funkhouser's side, and I was part of the reason. He'd been stuck guarding me. He was asking himself, "If those reporters hadn't gone with us that day, would we have stopped there at all? Or would the task have gone to some other patrol with a less media-friendly, less articulate commander?"

When Farrar woke in his hospital bed, these questions formed and stuck. He later told me that he briefly hated me and even Paul and James. He only started changing his mind after he read a statement I wrote for the CBS news website months later. I had described my recovery in brief and thanked the Fourth Infantry Division troops and

Iowa National Guardsmen for treating me as their own and keeping me alive. After that, Farrar says he started seeing Paul, James, and me as three people who'd simply been caught up in the same terrorist hell that had killed his captain and had nearly killed him.

Meanwhile, across the world, my family and loved ones were also being contacted. The first phone call went to my boyfriend, Pete. Our foreign security advisors had served with him in the military and later in Baghdad. That's how we met, just after the fall of Baghdad. He'd been a foreign security advisor for CBS News. He wouldn't date a client, so I asked him out—three times. He finally said yes after informing his boss (proving chivalry isn't dead). As our relationship grew serious, he decided that dating a journalist and working with her colleagues was a conflict of interest, so he stopped working with the media. (As people liked to say to me, "Great, he meets you, and you wreck his career.") Now I was about to keep him out of gainful employment for a good six months or more as he stayed by my side.

It was 11:30 p.m. in Auckland, New Zealand, and 3:30 p.m. in Baghdad when one of his old military colleagues, Don, called him up. Don was a fellow Kiwi who worked on the CBS Baghdad security team.

Pete had been expecting my call at some point before he went to bed, my traditional "Embed was OK, all clear" call, but the call hadn't come. Then a bit late for me, the phone rang, and he saw it was an overseas number.

But it wasn't my voice answering his hello.

"Hello, Pete. It's Don."

Pete stopped him. "Wait a minute. Let me get my earpiece in." His phone speaker was dodgy. By the time he had the earpiece in his ear, he was prepared for bad news. "What's happened?"

Don kept it brief, telling Pete there had been an incident and that I'd been wounded, but they didn't know how badly. At that point they weren't sure what had happened to Paul and James either.

Pete doesn't get visibly upset, unless you try to tell him he took a wrong turn when he's driving. Like most Kiwis he's the king of understatement, and like most military operators at his level, he exhibits an almost inhuman ability to put a lid on strong emotion. When necessary, like on a jungle or desert stakeout for days at a time, he can go into goal-oriented mode, where he becomes like a machine. He'll stay like this for hours, days, or weeks until the job is done.

That self-control would fail him for just a moment. As insane as he knew it was, Pete sat down and emailed me. Months later, working back through thousands of emails, I found his. He sent it right after he received the phone call.

> Don just rang me. I haven't got a clue what happened yet, but I could imagine. hell, I felt like I wanted to warn you about the patrol. you better answer this damned email!! !! please.

Don called Pete again after Kate and the security team reached me at the hospital. He told Pete, "It's 50-50 she'll make it." CBS booked the fastest flight they could find for him: a first-class flight to Germany that left midmorning the next day, Auckland time.

That was about when Pete's usual force of will kicked in. He simply told himself I'd survive, so his job was to get to me. He spent the 12 hours before the flight packing, closing up his house, and breaking the news to his two kids, Rhian, then 13, and George, then 11. He told them a gentler version of reality: I'd been hurt very badly, but I'd be OK, and he had to get to me now.

Rhian and George always knew that what I did had an element of risk but that it mostly was something cool that landed me on the Auckland evening news a couple times a week, where they could see the pieces and comment on what flak jacket I was wearing. We'd bonded on camping trips with their dad, sharing an unspoken pact as we pretended we really liked Pete's campfire cooking. I was too infrequent a visitor in their lives to be a secondary parent, so I became a friend to them and tried to show them what kind of life they could lead if they tackled it head on. Each time I visited we'd sync together like no time had passed, just like Pete and I did. The kids would tease their dad that it was time for us to get married. After seeing so many couples in their young lives split, including their mother and father, they feared the slightest conflict between us, as if it meant one of the few stable and happy things in their lives was being threatened.

Pete couldn't risk telling them how touch and go it was for me at that moment. He wasn't going to tell them I'd almost died and still might. When it came to my injuries, Pete kept them in that netherworld parents often try to put children, somewhere between the awful reality and the place we'd like to be reality. But they'd heard enough of the headlines to figure it out. They knew it was bad.

Meanwhile CBS News foreign editor Ingrid Ciprian Matthews had located contact numbers for my family.

I'd made a will and an emergency contact sheet a couple years into my Baghdad assignment, right before one of the Marines' assaults on Fallujah. I hadn't told my brother Mike or sister, MeiLee, that they were in it. Indeed, I hadn't told them anything at all. They'd never wanted me to go to Iraq in the first place, and the longer I'd stayed, the stronger they had argued I should leave. They made their pleas in phone calls and emails and during my rare visits. I wasn't going to give them more ammunition by informing them of my will. I'd simply signed it and sent it to my managers in London and New York.

Unfortunately for the holiday staff at 4 a.m New York time, my will had been misplaced. CBS started calling anyone they knew I knew to find numbers for my family. They called photographer friends in Jerusalem who had keys to my house. They rifled through my files and papers, looking for anything that looked like an address book, then anyone with the name Dozier.

Our foreign editor, Ingrid, meanwhile, had raced into work when she received news of the attack. She had the emergency information locked away in her files. She waited until 5 a.m. eastern time before calling one of my four older brothers, Michael, and his wife, Sherry, in Nashville. For me Mike and Sherry, some 20 years my senior, had always seemed like surrogate parents. I'd left word that they were to be contacted first. I thought it was better for Mike to break the news to my elderly mom and dad in Baltimore.

Sherry says that when she answered the predawn phone call and heard "This is CBS News," she burst into tears, handing the phone to

Mike before Ingrid could say another word. Ingrid explained to him that I had been "caught in a roadside bombing in Iraq." My retired-banker brother, Michael, was used to dealing with crises. He went into lock-down mode, speaking calmly, getting all the contact information, and confirming that he and Sherry would fly from Nashville to Baltimore to accompany our parents to Germany.

Sherry said the morning from then on was "just a blur of phone calls from around the world." Friends and fellow worshippers from their church, and then it seemed like every church in Tennesee, started calling or sending word they were praying for us all.

MeiLee, meanwhile, was harder to track down. She'd moved within Vietnam from Hanoi to Ho Chi Minh City. Vietnamese by birth, she'd tried to locate her original family years earlier. She never found them, but she did find a whole new life. She met her Vietnamese-American partner, Hahn, and had three children. She'd stayed in Vietnam, running a Texas BBQ restaurant that Hahn thought would do well (but they eventually closed—the Vietnamese aren't big meat eaters) while Hahn ran the country's first pro golf shop, which is going gangbusters.

I hadn't updated the CBS contact list with her new numbers when she'd moved to Ho Chi Minh City, so the first she heard of the bombing was from a friend who saw the breaking news on the web. Without calling CBS or even checking with my mom and dad to find out where I was being sent, MeiLee simply packed her bags, said goodbye to her children—Evan, Ryan, and infant Gracie—and raced to the airport. She guessed I'd end up at Landstuhl, so she boarded a plane to Germany.

My parents received their first phone call from Mike, and neither of them have wanted to talk about that moment.

After that, Dad's phone was ringing every few minutes. The information was coming from Mike and CBS. I later found my dad's first notes tucked under the phone in his and Mom's condo. In block print scribble, I can see Dad going into "get the job done" mode, with the simple underlined words like notes I'd watched Dad take over the years when an engineer called from his job site with a crisis: Concrete poor faulty. Low PSI (pressure per square inch).

One of the notes read:

State Dept.
Will be glad to help with passports.
Open eyes—
Told her on Milstrans
FACE OK

Dad apparently took this note while I was in transit from Balad to Germany. Someone had told Dad that I opened my eyes on the military transport. I was dismayed, months later, reading the "FACE OK" note—throughout, there was a bizarre emphasis on my face. I guess people thought even if I lost my legs, if my face was OK, I could still do my job on TV. It seemed to be the first question asked after people knew I would live: "How's her face?"

As for the State Department contact, he was helping my parents get new passports (theirs had expired). The small army of CBSers who descended on their condo an hour north of D.C. in Baltimore included a photographer, who took their pictures and rushed them, together with my parents' old expired passports, to the State Department. My parents had emergency travel documents within a few hours.

CBS's goal was to get my mom and dad to my bedside as quickly as possible. They still weren't sure I'd live and, if I did, whether I'd have brain damage or be able to keep both legs. Even if I was OK, I'd need family members to help me heal and to make some major medical decisions for me.

Friends and family were already reaching out to my parents. One of the first phone calls they got was from my ex-husband, Daniel Casson, and his family in London, asking if there was anything they could do to help—typical of Danny, who is always there for anyone in need. After our divorce in 1999, Danny had remarried to a high-powered British lawyer, settled down in London, and was busy juggling working for a couple aid agencies and raising two little girls. Our marriage had foundered in large part over my insistence on continuing working in war zones, and his worry that I would end up just as I had, in that hospital bed in Landstuhl. It wasn't a day for "I told you so," but I wouldn't have blamed him for thinking it.

Meanwhile CBS News President Sean McManus had come into CBS at 5 a.m. Memorial Day morning as soon as he'd heard the news. Already the president of CBS Sports, he'd spent less than a year juggling the two jobs. Like Andy, nothing he'd done in the news business to date prepared him for this tragedy. Shortly afterward he was en route to Las Vegas for his first all-CBS-affiliate conference. That's when Secretary of State Condoleezza Rice contacted him. She was closely following the situation. I had many friends in the State Department, including senior members of Rice's staff. She offered to help McManus in any way she could. Hers was the first phone call from the Bush Administration. The second came from White House Press Spokesman Tony Snow, who also asked what he could do.

Those phone calls helped McManus realize his place was in London: to be there for the memorial service at the airport when Paul and James were brought home to their families. He flew directly from Las Vegas to London to join Paul's and James' loved ones, and our whole bureau at London's Heathrow airport, as the coffins arrived. Then he traveled to Germany to see my family and meet me, one of his Baghdad correspondents, for the very first time on one of the worst days of my life.

As all of this happened, America was watching. Iraq had become, for the most part, a reason to change the channel: the same bad news over and over. But this single bombing seemed to strike a new chord of horror—at least it did with the media. They communicated the tragedy wall to wall to America. A news crew out with U.S. soldiers on Memorial Day was cut down by a car bomb, paying the price that troops had been paying in blood and lives every day since they arrived in Iraq. It drove a three-year-old reality home in a new way.

Headlines reached as far away as tiny New Zealand. "I remember it well," my Auckland physiotherapist later told me. "The story just stood out. A cameraman and soundman were killed just for filming soldiers, and a woman journalist was fighting for her life. I thought, 'A woman out there doing something like that. Good on her. I hope she makes it.'"

My survival seemed to be the thing people were clinging to—as if somehow the horror of losing Paul, James, and Capt. Funkhouser would be more manageable if I lived, if at least one of the bombing victims escaped the bastards who'd tried to kill us all.

As I lay unconscious in a hospital bed in Baghdad, Balad, and then Germany, thousands upon thousands of people were willing me, and praying for me, to survive.

CHAPTER 6

landstuhl

Landstuhl Regional Medical Center is a way station, a place where doctors patch people up and then move them on within 24 to 48 hours. The military usually only suggests bringing families there if the patient is so touch-and-go that they don't know if the patient will make it to the next stage: a stateside military hospital.

Pete reached me first. My main nurse, Nancy, prepared him for what he'd see in my ICU room—the tubes, the bandages, the shaved skull, the swelling, and the multitude of beeping machines.

All the patients on the intensive care wing had separate rooms where they were kept in isolation in case we were infected with Acinetobacter, a multidrug-resistant bacteria that can multiply in an immune-compromised person to fatal effect. As it turns out, I was infected. And it caused me a lot of trouble later. Pete had to wrap himself in a disposable gown and gloves before he could walk into the room. He and the rest of my family had to do this in every hospital from that point on.

Pete had spent plenty of time in an ER training to be a medic, which was all part of his military training. But none of that or anything he'd seen on the battlefield took away the horror of seeing someone he cared about in such a state.

Or to put it in Pete's understated style, "I'm glad Nancy told me what to expect." Months later, when I asked Pete what it was like to see me at that moment, he looked off into the distance, remembering. The way he steeled his face even thinking about it told me more than anything he could have said out loud.

Prepared by Nancy, Pete walked into my room, took my hand, and said my name. Then came the best moment for him since Don had called him with the news from Baghdad: I squeezed his hand back. Nancy says my heart rate steadied and slowed—a pattern repeated whenever Pete came into the room.

Usually, Nancy later explained to me, people have a mixed reaction to their loved ones that manifests physically. All those "issues" seem to come out, floating upward from the subconscious. So when a relative or loved one tries to speak to a near-comatose patient, the patient's vitals often become erratic.

With Pete, however, I was immediately at peace. So the nurses pulled up a chair for him and asked him to sit down and stay by my side. (But they needn't have asked.)

My parents, Mike, and Sherry arrived a few hours later, followed by MeiLee and Pualani, one of my nieces I hadn't seen in a decade. They gathered and waited for me to show signs of life. Some of the world's major media were also outside the hospital waiting to see if I'd survive.

Pete, being in the security industry, outright refused to go on TV. He doesn't like the media much. My parents—and in a few cases Mike—were left to explain my condition. My parents sat down and spoke with CBS News' Sheila MacVicar, an interview was shared with the other networks.

When I read the interview later, it was my first insight into how my parents must have felt seeing me that destroyed. At the time, jailed within the confines of a broken body and a screaming mind, I was not thinking about how hard this must be on my family—I was in survival mode.

For my parents their highflier, overachiever daughter had just come crashing down. They didn't cry on camera, nor even in the privacy of my hospital room. They weren't part of the Dr. Phil confessional couch generation. They came from the Great Depression and World War II, when imminent crisis was always around the corner and people didn't complain about it. They got through it.

And that's exactly what my mom and dad did in Landstuhl.

In the interview my mom told MacVicar, "When I walked into the room and saw her, it really impacted what this was all about and how close we came to maybe losing her. To hold her hand and have her little thumb wiggle showing she knew us. I'm just delighted with the improvement in the time we've been here."

My father jumped in, "She's sharp as a tack, really."

"She knows where she is?" MacVicar asked.

"She knows where she is. She knows the questions to ask. One of the very first questions she asked was how her teammates were. She didn't know at that point," my dad answered.

"And how did Kimberly react?" MacVicar followed up.

"You could tell that it had—it upset her," my mom said. "She kind of closed her eyes. When she can voice her feelings, it will be much easier for her,"

It was strange for all my loved ones to be around me and for me to be mute. I asked MeiLee to write for me what it was like.

The group that gathered at Landstuhl Regional Medical Center for Kim numbered a hefty 10, an unlikely gathering of people from all over who had rarely or never met: There was her boyfriend from New Zealand who'd just met her parents from Baltimore; me, the adopted sister from Vietnam; Mike, the second-oldest of our four brothers; Sherry, her Texan sister-in-law; Pualani, a Hawaii-born niece she hadn't seen in a decade; CBS network higher-ups out of Washington, D.C., and New York; and her producer, Kate.

Kate was wearing the same clothes she'd worn to travel with Kim on the military plane out of Iraq. It looked like she'd been to hell and back. Producer Penny Britell, normally high on the food chain in D.C., personally accompanied my parents to Germany. She carried luggage, ran errands, bought magazines, and some sized 0–2 clothes that petite Kate could finally change into. Linda Mason, CBS VP, kept conversation flowing and as upbeat as she could manage, when she wasn't in the hallway on her cell phone arranging a gazillion things.

Then there were our parents. Though physically slow, our mother did not miss a beat. One of the first things she did as matriarch was to handwrite a letter of consolation from our family to the families of Paul and James, a task made all the more challenging with Parkinson's disease, which miniaturized her normal cursive penmanship. The sentiment, however, remained true.

Also, as our mom was a veteran patient advocate for our father over years of surgeries and medical emergencies, she had had plenty of practice waging little battles for the best care and second and third opinions from too-busy doctors. Our father, now healthy, benefited from her vigilance, and the pair were ready to do the same for their daughter. Protecting Kim from whatever was coming her way was their top priority.

Putting on a show of strength, they made their way slowly but steadily, arm in arm down the shiny, spotless hospital corridor toward the ICU. Not far from them were my oldest brother and his wife, who are like second parents to Kim. Then there was me, tagging along. With three kids and a restaurant with a 65-plus-person staff, I'm used to being in charge. But here the baby daughter in a family of eight, I took my rightful place as official nail biter. The only one lower on this filial food chain was our niece, Pualani, who got to do Burger King deliveries and hold her grandmother's purse.

Kim asked me if I was shocked when I first saw her. Well, I had heard you'd been hit by a bomb, I told her. I didn't know what to expect, but I didn't expect pretty. On the flight over from Vietnam to Germany, my imagination went wild with the horrific possibilities. When we were finally able to see her, she was unconscious, with a breathing tube down her throat, her face, neck, and arms puffed like the Michelin Man and spotted with dried blood and shrapnel. Because hospital linens hid the horrendous injuries to her legs, I was not as upset as I probably should have been. I was also just relieved to see her alive, a fact I wasn't certain of less than 24 hours before. That she was not yet in the clear and facing the prospect of a long and tortured recovery had yet to rain on my parade. She's alive! Alive was good. Good enough for now.

While I was still in the room, I saw the nurse gingerly tugging at what I thought was a tiny tuft of tissue sticking out of a pea-sized hole in Kim's hand. I watched with increasing alarm as she pulled out a thin, foot-long strip of gauze stuffing a large hole where shrapnel had been removed. Out of curiosity, I took a peak in the hole and spied bare white hand bones. The nurse nonchalantly bandaged it over, this pea-turned-golf-ball-sized hole clearly the least of her worries.

Not being able to see most of Kim's body, the most disconcerting sight initially was her head, which was crudely shaved on one side with Frankenstein staples running a half circle across it. On the other side, what was left of her hair, which Nancy, the nurse, had earlier braided into a short pigtail. Because her normally soft, fine hair was still dirty from bomb smoke and heaven knows what else had come down wind, the reddish pigtail stuck straight out from her head, channeling Pippie Longstocking. It was a look I hadn't seen on a seasoned war correspondent.

The fact that Kim's face, in stark contrast to the rest of her body, sustained so little damage was a relief to most everyone. Perhaps it's because she works for a living on network TV, and almost definitely because she's a woman. I suspect the gut reaction also has a lot to do with how people are emotionally wired to judge well-being from a face. Somehow it seemed like a small victory. There in the midst of the battleground of her body was a petite, triumphant nose, surrounded by swollen, blood- and shrapnel-specked but otherwise undamaged eyes and lips.

Later, we were briefed by the neurosurgeon that a piece of shrapnel had been removed from her right temporal lobe and with it a little brain matter. He reassured us that if a person were to get a traumatic brain injury, this was the best way to get it. What a relief! What's a little brain matter, right? Needless to say, we were all just a tad concerned. Sure she might never walk again, but we all knew the essence of Kim was not her legs. Everything that makes Kim who she is was up in that packed attic of hers: the clever comeback queen, a Häagen Dazs fiend, the neat freak and Battlestar Galactica geek, the workaholic-talkaholic, news-obsessed, adrenaline junkie, and cat lover. Now the question was: Were all of those Kims still in there?

The first time I went in to see Kim after she regained consciousness, she still had a tube down her throat and was unable to speak, no doubt a unique form of torture for her. When she saw me her eyes widened and she lifted her head the half-degree her condition allowed. The fingers on her bandaged hand perked up. Her eyes did all the talking. "MeiLee," her eyebrows said in surprise, "What the heck. You're here too?" That's when I cried for the first time since I'd heard she'd been hit. No, she hadn't actually said any words, but I knew instantly that Kim was still Kim. However she may have been altered physically, those bastards had not gotten the best of my sister. Thinking I was upset by her physical condition, our ever-protective mother tried to shoo me out of the room. Kim shook her head ever so slightly. "No, no," her eyes beckoned, "please stay."

Amazingly the next time I saw her, she had the tube out of her throat and was able to speak. By the following day, my birthday, she was speaking clearly. It was a surprisingly quick transformation from just days ago, drugged, dumb, and probably deaf, to alert and asking me, "So . . . how was I enjoying this birthday?" And "now that she'd been hit by a bomb, hello, what more would she have to do to get me to email that Christmas picture of me and the kids she'd asked for?"

I decided to work on digging out the dirt and blood from under her nails, something I knew was driving the neat freak—now that I knew she was still in there—insane. Pualani had the pleasure of feeding her ice chips. While we were there serving as her personal Candy Stripers, she suddenly began to recall details of the blast. Her monitors started bleeping like mad.

We had all talked in the waiting room about what to do if Kim started to remember, whether or not the trauma of remembering would set her recovery back. The general consensus from our protective elders was that we were not to encourage it.

But with the floodgates open, the words and memories flowed forth so fast there seemed to be no stopping them. I knew then as we had expected before, whatever the consequences, we could no more stop her determination to piece together the events of that day than we could stop a tidal wave. It was not just her profession, but also her core instinct to process events as she sees them. There was no stopping her.

My memories flooding back was actually encouraging for my doctors, who'd been watching for signs of possible brain damage. The fact that I'd woken up and recognized my family and then proved I could speak had dispelled the worst of their fears and, as MeiLee wrote, my family's.

When they'd taken the tube out of my throat, I'd had to start slowly testing my voice. My throat was sore and scored, my mouth dry and swollen. Speech only came in whispers at first.

Then came the disgusting part: the coughing and spitting into an ever-present, hissing vacuum tube. Lying in the dirt and smoke, I'd done what every other soldier there had done. I'd breathed in the poison. Our lungs were clogged with a back draft of noxious material, which we now had to retch out over weeks, lest it settle in our bed-bound, immobile lungs and turn to pneumonia, one of the trauma patient's killer enemies.

I also became aware of the countless other souvenirs left behind, lodged in my body. In my right hand and arms, I could see red and black flecks of shrapnel floating under the skin. In my X-rays you could actually see some marble-size chunks of molten car metal floating in my hip, a couple in my leg. There was even a small speck on the bridge of my nose and a couple tracing the outline of my right jaw.

In Landstuhl, I wanted it out—all of it, immediately. The doctors explained that unless it was a large piece or located in a spot where it could do damage, most of it would stay right where it was. They told me it actually did more damage to dig around the soft tissues to remove it.

Nancy brought in some of the chunks the doctors *had* removed from my leg. She had them gathered in large plastic bags and specimen cups. The first—a flat piece of metal, twisted by the heat of the blast, which spilled over the sides of my hand—was recognizable as some sort of car part. It had been embedded in my right leg.

A second piece was a completely intact metal wheel weight from one of the tires, about the size of the top of a finger. I never even noticed that part on a car before. Every time I spot a wheel weight on a car now, I think of the one that was lodged somewhere in my thigh.

What Nancy didn't explain then was just how close I'd come to losing my right leg. I didn't learn that until months later when I revisited Landstuhl with Nancy to film for the CBS News program on the bombing, *Flashpoint*. She said in the first 24 hours, my right leg turned nearly black. As I mentioned earlier, doctors in Baghdad had relieved the pressure in my lower right leg with the fasciotomy, when they'd sliced open the skin from knee to ankle down to the muscle in 2-foot-long cuts on either side of my calf.

But the blood circulation was still far from normal. The black color could mean my leg was bruised and still struggling to flush out the bad blood from so much damage. Or it could mean my circulation system had been irretrievably destroyed, so there was no way to oxygenate the leg's muscle tissues, tissues that might already be dying.

My doctors were faced with a stark choice: They could gamble and hope what they were seeing was temporary bruising. But if the tissues were actually dying, that meant the doctors were giving the bacteria breeding in the dead tissue a chance to course through the rest of my body and kill me.

Many doctors new to the field will take the more conservative course of action. They'll amputate the limb and save the patient. But my surgeons had been deployed in a war zone for about two-thirds of their yearlong tour, some of them for more than that. They'd gambled before and won. Nancy explained that after some debate, they took a chance with me, putting heating pads on my legs, changing them frequently, to help stimulate the circulation.

After about 36 hours, the gamble paid off. By the time I was awake enough to be aware of my legs and what had happened, the risk of amputation had mostly already passed.

It remained a possibility the doctors wouldn't openly share with me, though. The jagged, burning chunks of shrapnel had done major damage to my quadriceps, the four major muscles that power my upper leg. So many muscles were shredded that by the time the dead tissue was painstakingly removed from the living, my broken femur bone was exposed. In later surgery at Bethesda Naval Hospital, the remaining muscle had to be rearranged to cover it. And then doctors could only hope the grafts they put on the massive burn, a foot and a half by 8 inches, would take. If they couldn't cover the femur again, they'd have to consider taking the leg off. (They opted not to tell me about that possibility until after the surgery had been carried out and had worked.)

In order for my muscles to heal and for those later grafts to take, the surgeons at Landstuhl knew they had to clean the area of the damaged flesh, dirt, and bacteria that the blast had blown in. Otherwise the area would contaminate any future grafts and slow or stop healing.

So, according to my mom, every day at Landstuhl, surgeons would powerwash the dirt and dead, burned tissue from my legs. Picture strapping a patient to the operating table and turning a fire hose on her at full blast. It was Nancy's bandage change on overdrive. These "washouts" were so painful they had to be done under full anesthesia and each one counted as surgery. By the time I was discharged from the last hospital weeks later, the surgeons had lost count of how many procedures I'd undergone. The guesstimate was "at least two dozen." Detailed records hadn't been kept at the Baghdad or Balad trauma hospitals. The doctors fixed me and moved me on.

The washouts took a toll on my mom. She said every morning she'd go back to their room on the military base and cry, thinking about how it would take me all afternoon to recover from the procedure, only to face it again the next morning. And she dwelled on the most dire of the doctors' prognoses: If I walked at all after this, I would likely have a pronounced limp. She wondered how I'd ever be able to return to my job or if I'd need care for the rest of my life. She and my whole family carefully hid those fears from me and only spoke of healing.

In the end the pain from the washouts was more than worth it. Surgeons at Bethesda Naval Hospital later credited those multiple procedures with producing wounds so clean that I'd have remarkable success with my skin grafts. Doctors told me that many of the troops had gangrenous-smelling wounds weeks after arriving in the United States and that their grafts only partially took or, in the worst cases, not at all, necessitating further, more painful operations.

The surgeons at Landstuhl also started on some of the rebuilding work that had to be done to my legs. They literally hammered titanium, which they called "nails," into my femurs or, rather, what was left of them.

The left femur was busted in one place, "cleanly, like an ax hit it," one surgeon said happily. "That's the easy fix"—easy for him to say.

The right femur, which was nearest to where the car bomb hit, was a harder case. It was smashed in three places, one chunk butterflied off to the side, floating in what was left of the muscle.

The orthopedic surgeons were blunt with my family, warning them that the operation would be tricky. Putting in rods is an imperfect science.

The doctors would literally be driving the rods through my bones. They'd have to recreate the alignment so the femurs would rotate properly in my hip sockets. Get that wrong and it could make my knees torque out or in, resulting in a limp, permanent pain, or a host of other problems.

Orthopedic surgeons joke that what they perform is "sterile D-I-Y," as in handymen operating with power tools in a surgical environment. The brute force required for their job is probably part of why other surgeons at the top of the medical totem pole—neuro and heart surgeons—look down on them. But I owe those hammer-and-chisel surgeons every step I now take.

I didn't know how well it would work out then. Unfortunately for me, one of the orthopedic surgeons assigned to me didn't have much confidence in either his ability or my ability to heal after so much damage.

Sweating, tired, and gray in his scrubs after surgery (who knows how many he'd performed that day), he was the picture of despondency.

"We don't know if you'll ever use that leg properly again," he told me.

I dubbed him "Sad Sack." And in that moment, I hated him. His dire prediction made me angry and scared. It would be weeks—actually months—before I'd have any idea whether he was right or whether I could prove him wrong. Ironically throughout my whole reporting career, I've despised the Pollyannas who try to spin me with an overly optimistic line. But just this once, I could have used a man wearing those obnoxiously hued, rose-colored glasses.

Then again, maybe he knew what he was doing, a little reverse psychology at work. To quote Johnny Lydon, "Anger is an energy"—one I would draw on then, and repeatedly afterward, to recover. Like most people in the world, I don't like to be told no, that I can't, or worst of all, that I don't measure up. As the Brits say, it's a "red rag to a bull." And weeks later, once I got past the worst of the surgeries, I charged. There were setbacks, but I kept charging.

In that hospital bed I had many questions in the back of my mind: When would I walk again? How would I walk again? It was too soon for deeper questions, such as whether I would report from a crisis zone again. I was stuck on the immediate. There would be plenty of time during my long rehabilitation for the other concerns.

After almost every surgery, doctors pumped more blood into me. Later I learned that I had lost and then been given an entire adult body's worth of blood, some 40 units, most of which was transfused into me the day I was hit. The blood saved my life, but with every transfusion, my body flipped into minor shock, fighting the new antibodies or whatever it found objectionable in the donor blood. My temperature rocketed, and I burned like a kid with scarlet fever. The nurses iced my neck to bring my temperature down. Next I became too cold, and the nurses took the ice off. Then I burned up again, and the nurses put the ice back on. My body's internal thermostat was unable to keep my temperature level.

Another side effect of all the donated blood was all that edema. My body hung on to the liquid, packing on up to 30 pounds in three or four days. My face was swollen and my hands were mini balloons, a horror my family had to deal with, but I refused to. There were no mirrors in the ICU. And when I was offered one, I turned it down. "You all will be my mirror," I said. "You'll tell me if something needs to be fixed." When I saw the photos of myself at Landstuhl later, I was glad I'd made that call.

Somewhere during that time, a group of congressmen visited the hospital and asked to stop at my room. I reluctantly agreed. I bet they later wished I hadn't.

In their faces I saw what I looked like. They walked in and displayed a rare thing for politicians: unified reactions. They were in complete horror. Tubes up my nose, coming out of my skull, multiple IVs in both arms, face and arms bloated to near twice normal size, hands and fingers still crusted with dirt and blood. I almost laughed as I saw one of them walk in, lock eyes on me, and recoil, trying to backpedal out of the room.

What? No photo with the famous wounded journalist for your constituents, honey? I thought.

Ha. Try living with it.

Other visitors were far more comforting, helping both me and my family cope, as were the hospital's military staff. My parents were at ease at Landstuhl or any military environment. My dad has served as a Marine, surviving the battle of the Pacific in World War II, and my mom had been a Rosie the riveter (the women who worked in government factories to build everything from weapons to airplanes for the war effort). The Marines especially treated Dad with the deference they'd accord a retired general, and the hospital staff included us in the military family, even giving me one of the quilts volunteers make for injured troops. A group of U.S. military spouses in Korea made it. I think Mom hugged mine for a couple days before she told me about it.

Mom and Dad came from the "Loose lips sink ships" generation. Dad says he joined the Marines because Mom wanted to get married to a man wearing Marine Corps dress blues. I think that's the story he tells his two daughters, whereas he reserves a more macho one for his four sons. He tells them he joined because it was his duty and he'd have joined a lot earlier if my mom and his mother hadn't held him back. While Dad fought in Guam and Iwo Jima, Mom was building airplanes in a Baltimore factory. She started on the assembly line and worked her way up to supervising. When Dad came home, they did what all young couples did then. They started having kids.

Their shared philosophy was standard for that era: You show your faith, you do your duty, but you don't make a fuss, and you don't put yourself above others. "Don't break your arm patting yourself on the back" was/is my mom's mantra.

They lived their beliefs, and we breathed them growing up, or we received an old-fashioned tongue-lashing that put us in our place and kept us there.

Together with those old-fashioned values was a small dose of old-fashioned thinking about what girls grow up to do versus what boys grow up to do. Yes, they'd both encouraged their daughters to reach as high and as far as their sons. But that didn't mean working in war zones. They'd always been stunned that after four sons, one of their daughters ended up covering crisis after crisis.

But they had always supported what I did. No matter what they thought of the guy in the White House, in their household you support the men and women in uniform. Long before 9/11 reminded America what the flag stood for, my dad was raising and lowering his American flag on the back porch every morning and evening without fanfare.

For me to end up injured in combat, or rather by ambush, was a crisis of the worst proportions. But in their eyes, I'd been doing the right thing for the right reasons, and that made my injuries in some way easier to take.

Nothing made my family feel more included or honored than the visit from Sgt. Stephen Mapes, a soldier I'd profiled in Iraq a year or so earlier.

When I was hit, Sgt. Mapes was on duty at a U.S. base in Germany. When he heard the news, he and his wife, Elizabeth, drove to Landstuhl. Sgt. Mapes quietly sought out my family to give them his Purple Heart to pass on to me.

Months later I was able to track Sgt. Mapes down at Fort Bliss, Texas, where he was attending the U.S. Army Sergeants Major Academy before heading back for yet another tour of Iraq. He wrote back that he and his wife were thrilled to hear from me. "We hardly know each other, and yet I was filled with such emotion at the news of the attack on your patrol—just as if it was one of my own. I wanted to see you and was invited by your family, but it would have been too emotional. And I didn't want to take anything away from your wonderful family. I knew you were on some pretty strong drugs and wasn't sure if you'd even remember me. I tried not to bring any attention to myself when I gave the medal to Michael."

When Mike handed the medal to me, I had no trouble remembering the man who'd earned it. Sgt. Mapes had been wounded by a rocket attack in the Green Zone in Baghdad, the shrapnel shredding one of his arms. He then fought his way through physiotherapy in double time so he could get back to Iraq and back to his men. They absolutely revered him.

When I'd gone to interview him, one of his men took me aside and pointed to a mountain of bright blue Gatorade bottles. "See that?" he asked. "The sergeant found out the men were getting dehydrated on patrols, some of them coming down with heat stroke. So he bought that Gatorade out of his own pocket so we'd all come back in one piece." The men guarded the stuff like it was Fort Knox.

A year later, in a grim hospital waiting room, the sergeant told my brother that this time I'd earned the medal, just like any soldier serving in Iraq.

That in itself was an amazing gesture. But Sgt. Mapes had no idea of the depth of its meaning, given our personal family history. My dad had been lightly wounded at Iwo Jima, grazed by a bullet on the back of his leg, when he was caught between enemy lines. He told us about it once, under great duress, during commercial breaks of a PBS special on Iwo Jima. He never spoke about it again until I bugged him to for this book.

After my dad's captain said, "Charge," my dad did, unfortunately outrunning his platoon. He'd had a football scholarship to Cornell but nixed it because of the war. He was still fast. He ended up stranded between the two lines in a flat, rocky no-man's land. He took shelter in a shallow depression, but his backpack stuck out within full view of both sides. Dad fell asleep. (He can sleep anywhere.) The problem with sleeping near the enemy is that Dad snores like a pack of wolves. So every time he drifted off, he snored, and his pack rose and fell rhythmically with the motion. The Japanese heard him, saw him, and opened fire. Dad woke to the sound of bullets strafing his pack or hitting things inside it. The pattern continued all day.

After dark, with his leg bleeding and his pack riddled with Japanese bullets, he crawled back to his own lines.

When the medic treating him offered to put him in for a Purple Heart, Dad turned it down. He'd lost almost his whole platoon in the preceding days. He was one of two men in the 70-plus-man platoon to walk off the island. So he didn't think he deserved a medal for surviving.

But then he found out that a Purple Heart would have meant an extra $5 a month in his paycheck, much needed by his mother and new young wife who were struggling on a wartime budget back home, and he kicked himself for his pride.

What he taught us from that is that you can never be too brave, but you can be too proud.

When Mike handed me Sgt. Mapes' medal when I woke from yet another procedure a few hours later, I asked him to call Dad. I handed it over by the purple ribbon, saying, "Hey, Dad, you know that Purple Heart you turned down at Iwo Jima? Can you keep this one safe for me?" His hand closed over it and my hand, and that's the closest I saw my dad come to tearing up. He's keeping the medal safe for me still.

There were other visitors, including CBS boss Sean McManus, who had flown directly from the Memorial Service for Paul and James as their coffins arrived at London's Heathrow airport.

This was a horror he'd never anticipated. In his previous experience, employees didn't die on the job. First he had to try to honor the loss of Paul and James. Now he had to visit me, a foreign correspondent he'd only ever communicated with via email in his few months at CBS News.

And then I made him wait. Just before McManus came into my room, Nancy stopped by with a message that Corp. Potter was in a nearby wing and wanted to speak to me. I seized the opportunity. He had been through what I'd been through, and he could tell me what happened.

I told Nancy, "McManus can wait." (I know he would have agreed.)

Potter came in with his burnt hands bandaged. I remember his blond hair and worried face. That's when he apologized for the rescue taking so long. I asked him how everyone was doing. He outlined who'd been hit and who was being treated for what. Since I'd only met them briefly, I didn't put names with faces. But there was one name that was unforgettable, one he hadn't mentioned.

"How's Capt. Funkhouser?" I asked.

He paused, realizing I didn't know.

"He didn't make it," Potter said.

I sat there stunned—absorbing one more gut-punching reality.

"Oh, God, no," I said, instantly remembering how he'd been talking about his wife and two little girls before we left his base.

Not him too.

Potter left, promising to keep in touch.

That's when I met my boss. He'd been talking to my mom and dad, who bonded with him over sports and their childhoods in Baltimore. Mom and Dad had listened to McManus' dad, sportscaster Jim McKay, for years. It was a comfort and a touch of home for them.

For McManus, talking to me was much harder. The compact, slight man walked into my beeping, blaring, medical-machine-filled room wearing shirtsleeves and tie and looking neatly composed despite more than 24 hours on the road. He gave the impression of a rather intensely focused banker who'd been in the middle of a long, hard day closing deals.

I'd just missed meeting McManus at his new CBS News office in New York five days before the blast. In our last email exchange, I'd promised to catch up for a drink next time I came through. Now we were catching up, about halfway through what would turn into a weeklong stay at Landstuhl.

He walked in to confront the same horror my family had encountered. At his side was Linda Mason, the CBS News Vice President who had stepped on a plane for Landstuhl to be with my family. She'd dropped all day-to-day duties running the news division for seven days, handling everything from how much information CBS gave out about my condition to who in my family would grant interviews to how CBS got me back to the United States, including helping my family decide which hospital to send me to. I had only briefly met her for the first time on my last trip through New York.

She and McManus kept their conversation short. I don't remember much of it, but I remember the effect it had on McManus. As he spoke he teared up and had to pause and compose himself.

I thanked them for coming. And as I often did over the coming months, I deployed humor to try to deflect the emotional intensity and awkwardness of the moment.

"Hey, Sean, next time I'd rather just meet for that drink, OK?"

He and Linda both cracked their first smiles since entering the room, and McManus said, "It's a deal."

At the doorway Linda asked him, "She's all there, isn't she?" He decided to check.

"Hey, you have to promise you'll never tell anyone you saw the CBS News president cry, OK?" he said from the doorway.

"Sure thing." I paused. "I'll just have to remember that for my next contract negotiation."

McManus smiled again. He turned to Linda and said, "She's gonna be fine."

Another visitor snuck in before the hospital staff could spot him—an old friend of mine from Baghdad, Maj. Gen. Mark Hertling. Now he's back in Iraq, but at the time, he was serving as the U.S. Armed Forces Europe deputy chief of staff for operations, based in Heidelberg.

Maj. Gen. Hertling had been the No. 2 in charge of Baghdad in the second year of the coalition presence and the second year of my reporting. I'd gotten to know him well, relying on him to return my urgent, after-midnight-Baghdad-time emails to kill or confirm this or that rumor floating out of Washington, D.C. He wouldn't share much over something as unsecure as email communications, but he'd keep me honest and keep me from embarrassing myself.

From the moment I'd been injured, Hertling's staff had stayed in touch with Landstuhl and tracked my progress. The head of the hospital, Col. Bryan Gamble, had been keeping an eye out for him. Col. Gamble was a constant source of strength for my family, helping them and CBS manage the constant flow of would-be visitors and serving as our spokesman about my medical condition.

Col. Gamble was also vigilant when it came to a two-star prowling his hospital unannounced. "You always like to know what they're seeing," Col. Gamble half joked.

But Hertling didn't much like having to behave like a general, especially on what was a personal visit. More important, he knew it could disrupt the hospital's work schedule, pulling folks off their 24/7 medical tasks to show the top brass around. He'd learned the best ways to wander in and out of the hospital from his wife, Sue, who made frequent visits to spend time with injured troops.

As a military commander-spouse team, Mark and Sue saw it as their duty to support injured troops on behalf of their families back home who couldn't be there. As parents of soldiers themselves, they knew how helpless those families must feel, waiting to get their injured loved one back home from this medical way station. They have two sons and a daughter-in-law in the military, each of whom is serving, has served, and/or is planning to serve again in Iraq.

Hertling himself had been injured in the first Gulf War. And he'd lost fellow soldiers in battle. I was with him on Christmas Eve 2003 when he learned he'd lost one of his best commanders, who was also one of his best friends. We were filming the general and his troops conducting nighttime raids against Sunni insurgents in Baghdad when he heard something over his radio, stopped our conversation, and took a step back to listen again.

When he understood the message, he simply walked away, standing by himself at his Humvee, absorbing the news. A roadside bomb had gone off and killed Command Sgt. Maj. Eric Cooke. Hertling later said that in that moment, he was thinking of Cooke's wife and children, who were about to be devastated by the worst possible news on Christmas Day, a day that would be forever blackened with that memory.

So when Hertling walked into my Landstuhl hospital room, he'd already walked the road I was on. He treated me just like he did any of his injured troops. He told me what to expect and that it wouldn't be easy. He warned me that there would be weeks and months ahead of long, painful rehabilitation and long hours coping with the painful self-examination that comes from surviving when those with you did not.

But he told me, with a confidence no one else could muster at that point, that with hard work and strong faith, I would recover.

"Next year, in Washington, we'll meet up, and I'll ask you for a dance," he said. "If Pete allows it, of course," he added with a grin.

I choked out a smile, thinking to myself, *Dance? I hope you're right.* But after looking down at my shattered body, I also thought, *But I'm afraid you're sadly deluded.*

My memories of all these meetings are snippets of conversations from a dreamlike state. What my mind has shut out is the near constant, soul-wrenching, excruciating pain that throbbed through my body because of my burns and broken bones. I felt like it was hammering me into the bed, especially since I couldn't move my legs or hips and barely even my upper body by myself. I couldn't escape it, my face staring up at the ceiling, my body held down by stabbing pain in my legs and even by the small burns on my arm.

There was a quirky horror to this, specific to me. I sleep on my side and have done so my whole life. For the entire time in Landstuhl, I struggled to fall asleep on my back, feeling all the more exposed and vulnerable. When I finally was able to shift onto my side, maybe three weeks or so after the bombing, I had to create an elaborate supporting fortress of foam pads and pillows to keep me that way and to keep me from falling back on my healing burns.

But at this point the pain was not only keeping me from thinking straight, it was also keeping me from sleeping, and that meant it was keeping me from healing. Sleep is a major part of your body's rebuilding process. Since I was having such trouble sleeping, the anesthesiologists and the doctors decided they had to do something about the problem: increase my painkillers. They told me I needed an epidural, which would feed the painkiller directly to my legs through my spine.

I didn't want it. The very thought was terrifying, a new sensation for me. I dimly remembered that there could be one-in-a-million complications with epidurals, and I was worried about what might happen. I was normally unfazed and quite logical about medical things—but not now. I resisted the procedure until the pain became even greater than my fears. Fear of what might happen was overcome by the agony of what was.

When they mainlined an epidural IV straight to the base of my spine, I felt some relief but also a constant pulse of paranoid terror. As long as that IV was in there, I was terrified of moving left or right (not that I was capable of any movement left or right at that point, at least not without a nurse pushing, prodding, or pulling me).

Over the weeks that followed, the dread I felt over the infinitesimal rate of complications with epidurals only grew stronger, especially when it came to signing release forms for anesthesia, which I had to do before every washout or surgery. Even in my narcotic-ridden state, I had to legally acknowledge with a signature that I understood that surgery involves risk, anesthesia is an imperfect science, and in short that there's a slim, slim chance I might die.

In other words, if I'm one of the unlucky people, when the doctors put me under, I may never wake up.

I didn't feel exactly lucky at that point. I dimly thought, *Aren't I already in a "small percentage of cases"—as in the small percentage of journalists who ended up getting blown up? I don't like these odds.*

I could barely read the forms with my drug-blurred vision. Pete and I pointed out to the doctor that I wasn't exactly completely compos mentis as I signed the documents. The doctor said that nevertheless it had to be done.

Over the weeks and more than two dozen procedures, the fear of dying hit me every time I had to sign the "You might die" form; I almost had. By the time I arrived at Bethesda Naval Hospital, my fear of those forms was so great that I trembled when they were handed to me before surgery. A doctor who'd come in to prep me noticed the quaking and said if I liked, a family member could sign them for me.

Pete didn't qualify as next of kin, so from then on, I left the signing to my dad. That created other complications later. My family became far too accustomed to making major decisions for me. But in the short term, it took away one minor horror.

Together with the epidural, I had a push-powered morphine drip (later to be replaced by another drug, Dilaudid, when my body started reacting badly to the morphine). The doctors wanted me to press a button to give myself extra doses. The self-administered mini dose supplemented the morphine that was already being automatically dripped into my system. And I could actually only give myself six extra doses an hour, no matter how many times I pressed it. But anesthesiologists have found that putting pain control in the hands of the patient produces a twofold effect: It adds more painkiller to the mix and gives the patient a psychological edge over his or her pain.

It works, but it took some getting used to. I was learning the parameters of my new world, primarily how to find the balance between pain and painkiller.

During good moments, I had enough narcotics coursing through my system that the screaming pain in my legs was kept at bay, but I wasn't so dopey that I couldn't hold a conversation.

I heard about Sgt. Mapes and the Purple Heart during one of those sharp, good moments. But sometimes visitors or phone calls came at the wrong time, including when Gen. Casey called my room to see how I was doing. Nancy came into the room to tell me that his aide was on the phone for me.

But I knew I was on a downward slide at that moment, the excruciating pain in my bones and legs building. I'd already sent an extra dose of morphine coursing through my system, and that meant I wouldn't be fit for conversation with Casey until the drugs wore off.

I already knew what would happen when the dose hit me. An otherworldly sense of warmth and well-being was already creeping over me, sort of from the back of my head. I would slide into a loopy haze for a while and probably sleep. Then the system would balance out, and I'd have that window where I could talk again.

So I asked Nancy if Gen. Casey could call back. I could see her eyes widen above her mask. She just about passed out, having to deliver that message to a man who was essentially her top boss. Uncensored, it should have gone something like "I'm sorry, Kimberly's busy right now dealing with copious amounts of pharmaceuticals. Can you call back?"

I imagine Nancy put it more diplomatically.

Even when he did call back, I was a little confused. I thanked him profusely for insisting I wear ear and eye protection on embeds, something his then No. 2 in Iraq, Lt. Gen. Peter Chiarelli, had actually done. In an earlier incarnation, as one of the field commanders of Baghdad, Gen. Chiarelli had taken me out around the city for a day. He didn't like press much, but he had grown more at ease as the day wore on. When he overcame his wariness, he studied my flak jacket and helmet as if looking for something. He was. "Where are your ballistic glasses? Where are your earplugs?"

He'd pulled out a pair of military-spec ballistic Oakleys he always carried, which were studded with a wickedly sharp-looking piece of shrapnel. "See this piece of metal?" he'd asked. "That would have blinded the soldier and maybe even killed him if it went through the eye to the brain."

I'd gone back to the bureau that evening, had a talk with managers in London and New York, and the next day spent $800 on ballistic glasses for everyone in the bureau. (They quickly disappeared into people's personal luggage, never to be seen again, but the point was made. Everyone wore them from then on.)

On the day of the bombing, I'd had all my protective gear with me, but because we'd gotten out of the Humvees, I'd taken my earplugs out just before the bomb went off, which was why both eardrums were blown out. For some reason I'd kept on my helmet and I'd kept on a brand-new pair of ballistic sunglasses, partly because Pete's kids had helped me pick them out in Auckland weeks earlier. I wanted to make sure they ended up on camera so when Rhian and George watched the evening news that night in New Zealand, they'd see the glasses put to work.

For some reason, probably because I'd realized that if I hadn't been wearing those glasses I might have lost an eye, I bombarded Gen. Casey with my thanks. He didn't correct me.

The shrapnel that did get through apparently entered right between the helmet's rim and the top of the glasses, piercing my right temple.

They'd told me I'd had neurosurgery, but what that meant hadn't really hit me until Nancy handed me a piece of the metal that was about the size of a thumbnail. It doesn't look remotely evil until you consider where it was. I celebrated with a bit of a survivor's bravado, silently singing to the fractured metal bit, *Ha, you failed. My brain works.*

A few inches left or right or maybe a half an inch deeper and who knows what I might have lost. The doctors explained that in brain trauma, penetrating head wounds have the best prognosis for recovery because damage is limited to one small area.

My colleague from ABC, Bob Woodruff, had suffered a different type of damage, including bruising of the brain as it was shaken around on the brain stem from the impact of the roadside bomb that hit him. And although Bob didn't have a penetrating brain injury, his skull was shattered by the concussive force of the blast.

Bob and his wife, Lee, contacted my family when we were still at Landstuhl to offer help and advice. I knew Bob from the field. We'd eaten together each night, both our teams at one long table. CBS and ABC shared a compound in Kabul, Afghanistan, to save money because supplies were scarce in a dangerous, expensive city. I was still a radio correspondent and was in awe of Bob's skill, drive, and—most of all— his devotion to his family in London, who were frequent topics of conversation around the Kabul dinner table.

Because of my head wound, Bob and Lee urged my family to send me to the National Naval Medical Center (the Bethesda Naval Hospital) in Maryland—advice we took to heart. Among the military hospitals in the Maryland area, Walter Reed Army Medical Center tended to specialize in amputees and Bethesda Naval Hospital in neuro-trauma. I'd end up on the same floor Bob had stayed, but because of our injuries, our journeys would end up being very different.

I stayed in Landstuhl for a full week—although it felt much, much longer—instead of the usual 24 to 48 hours. I kept getting bumped from the medical evacuation flights that leave Landstuhl for Bethesda and Walter Reed since there were troops coming in who were wounded worse and needed to get back faster than I did. And those were the rules: Civilian casualties are lower priority on military Medevac flights, as it should be. These were military resources.

The few weeks after I was hit turned out to be a hellish time for soldiers in Iraq, and the Landstuhl wards were filling up to prove it. The nurses and doctors were pulling double shifts, skipping days off, simply working at some level beyond burnout. They'd patch up soldiers as best they could and stabilize them enough to get them on the plane. As bad as I was banged up, I was no longer an emergency.

To get through the delay and growing pain, my mind went into reporter mode, recording everything around me. I saw exhaustion, compounded by the way the nurses and doctors kept putting aside their own pain to deal with later.

Only later never came—just more patients.

The medical staff was watching the evolution of the insurgents' tactics, written in blood on soldiers' bodies. Much of the worst damage was caused by shaped charges, which are sophisticated roadside bombs designed to penetrate the strongest Humvee armor.

Also there was a growing army of terrorist marksmen, some of whom were actually learning to shoot well enough to be classed as snipers.

"The insurgents know that the new body armor is good, so now they're going for the only weak points left," one nurse told me. "We're seeing more and more troops hit in the head and the eyes."

She was having nightmares about eyes and was trying to force herself to look at pictures of injured eyes to inure herself to the shock so she could hide her own revulsion and horror from the next injured soldier or Marine she'd treat.

"Some days," one nurse told me, "the only way I get through a shift is hearing the lullaby over the loudspeaker," which played every time a baby was born in the Landstuhl civilian wing. I started listening out for it too, a magical fairy chime that would, for a moment, remind everyone that somewhere close by, something had gone right in the world.

The upside of my long stay for the doctors and especially the nursing staff was that for once, they were getting to care for a patient long enough to see her improve and to see their work take root. Landstuhl, the Baghdad CSH, and the military hospital in Balad are normally such high-turnover factories that medical staffers rarely see their successes. It's just a steady drumbeat of "get them in, get them stable, and within 12 to 24 hours get them on a plane."

I got to know my caregivers, and they got to know me and my family. As I prepared to leave, Nancy, who was one of a team of nurses who'd been watching me round the clock, came in on her day off to prepare me for the journey.

She and Army Specialist Alyssa Dunaj changed my bandages with occasional help from medical technician S. Sgt. Taryn Young, the same procedure I'd woken up to some five days earlier.

Pete stayed with me, and we put on some music for them to pass the time, trying to make the process seem normal. Pete thought he could handle seeing my wounds, and I thought it was time I saw them too.

I now know that no time would ever have been right for me or Pete to see something like that.

We both looked down as the bandages came off. Across my right leg were huge red, raw openings, like a foot-wide bleeding steak. I shuddered and squeezed Pete's hand so hard he gritted his teeth, or maybe he was already gritting them over the sight of my legs. It was something out of a horror movie.

I looked at him and said, "I'm sorry. I shouldn't have asked you to watch this." He said, "It's OK. It's fine." But he turned his back to my legs, and during the rest of the procedure just peered into my face, not once looking downward again. He cradled my hand to his chest and kept me talking, blocking me from looking that way too.

Nancy knew both what we were going through and the hell that was coming. She'd written me a letter and had given it to Pete, saying I should read it when I got frustrated. She warned us that arriving in Bethesda would feel like starting all over again, partly because I'd be so exhausted from the journey and because a whole new host of doctors would have to put me through innumerable tests to get to know my case. She was right about the hell to come, as I was about to find out, but she was also right about the recovery I'd end up making.

Nancy's letter brought me to tears but also fulfilled the morbid curiosity that comes from surviving something like this. I wanted to know every detail, especially those I was too narcotic-dosed to take in at the time or those that people hadn't shared with me because they were protecting me or thought they were protecting me.

Months later, when I was wall-punching impatient with my slow progress, Pete finally handed me her letter.

June 2006 Captain Nancy Miller, U.S. Air Force
Kimberly,
As you read this note in the future, I doubt you will remember my name, face, or role that I have played. But these are things I think are important to express.

During the past five months while here at Landstuhl Medical Center, I have seen many injured young sailors, soldiers, and airmen. The majority of these young men and women have sustained life-threatening injuries. To be able to care for them and somehow help put them on the road to recovery has been a life-changing event for me. This experience reinforces why I became a nurse: to make a difference. I didn't realize what a difference it would make for me.

Throughout the days and nights of caring for the troops, they, their lives, and their stories touch us. Unfortunately, all too often, their story isn't told. Fortunately, we have others like you to help the story be told.

Over the last 36 hours, I have grown from seeing the face on TV and hearing reporters discuss "the injured reporter" to meeting, knowing, and being touched by "Kimberly." Your personal resilience, outlook, fortitude, and attitude are to be admired! I have heard stories about you from your family and friends that have both made me laugh and made me cry. But a couple really stand out to tell who Kimberly really is:

1. A card of well wishes and a transfer of a Purple Heart from a soldier whose heart and life you touched (I'm sure only one of many . . . !)

2. The look on your face when I told you we were trying to organize a meeting for you and one of the soldiers injured with you. Your face just lit up, and it gave me chills. Then later, to say, "Let the CBS president wait. I want to see the soldier." This speaks volumes about you and your priorities. Very admirable, and many of us could learn from you.

At the time you read this, it may be days, weeks, months, or possibly years after your experience. I think it is important that you know how your guardian angel and God are watching over you.

Your injuries are extensive, which is why you underwent numerous surgeries over a short period of time. Extensive bleeding created a need for numerous (around 40?) units of blood to be given to you in these first few days.

First of all, a small scar near your right temple reflects where a piece of shrapnel penetrated your skull but left your brain apparently unharmed. A larger scar encircles this and marks one of the first surgeries to remove this intrusion and evaluate the damage. A small catheter was also in place that we used to closely monitor brain pressures to anticipate and prevent possibly lethal swelling within your brain.

But even more emergent and life threatening is the broken/shattered femurs in both legs. The excessive bleeding from these injuries and the large tissue and muscle injury to your right thigh is what created the need for LOTS of blood products, tourniquets, and surgery (the incision to your right groin) to control the bleeding and hopefully save one or both legs.

Because of the injury and swelling, you began to lose blood flow to your right lower leg. Another surgery created incisions to this area to relieve the pressure and return blood flow to the lower leg and foot.

In addition, you have suffered second-degree burns to your legs. Again the guardians limited the damage to an amount that is small compared to "what could have been."

In 36 hours, I closely monitored your condition and watched as you went from unstable, heavily sedated, unresponsive, and on a ventilator to having you talk to me, breathing well without assistance, coughing, laughing, joking, and asking about events and injuries.

You made tremendous progress in a short amount of time. Now the long journey lies ahead. In your future lies more surgery, lots of rehab, hard work, and there will be frustration.

Hence this note to remind you where you were, reflect on where you are now (at whatever point that is), and hopefully remind you to look ahead to the bright future that awaits.

As you became aware of events, you asked for pictures. Peter and I made a pact. I have taken some pictures of you "at your worst" and your early progress.

Please know that when you look at these, you will feel a sense of disbelief and "Is it really me?" Some may be graphic and reflect your injuries. Others are reflective of private moments of you and loved ones during this crisis.

Kimberly, thank you for what you are doing to support our troops, to let their stories be told. You are an incredible woman with indescribable strength. You have touched and inspired many, and I felt it was important for you to know these things.

May God continue to watch over you, your loved ones, and our troops in the field, whose voices would not be heard without angels like you!

—Captain Nancy Miller, ICU Nurse, Landstuhl, Germany, Landstuhl Regional Medical Center

Nancy was the first in a long line of caregivers who became a lifeline for helping me and my family. The doctors are responsible for the physical fixing, but from my point of view from the hospital bed, it's the nurses, techs (called corpsmen at Bethesda Naval Hospital), and physiotherapists who are in charge of healing. They spend the most time with you, so they're most attuned to your crises large and small, your needs, and your shame over needing them so much. The trauma docs had kept me alive, but this larger army of caregivers would be my long-term lifesavers. Nancy was the first.

Kimberly Dozier interviews Maj. Gen. Mark Hertling, then deputy commander of Baghdad for the 1st Armored Division, at the CBS Baghdad bureau.

Afghan mujahideen helped U.S. forces capture the peak of Tora Bora, but failed to catch Osama bin Laden.

Chris Albert and Dozier after the fall of Baghdad 2003, in what was to become the Green Zone.

Dozier and Agnes Reau visit a Shiite imam in Baghdad. Above: Patrolling Baghdad on Christmas Day.

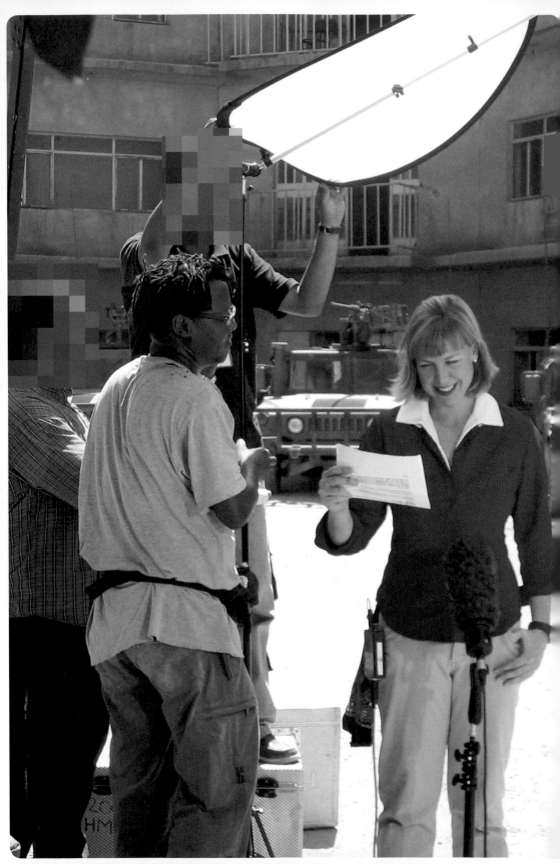

Cameraman Paul Douglas in a Blackhawk and Dozier (above) under fire in Sadr City, both in full gear.
Left: It takes an army to make TV with everyone facing equal risk.

Filming in the streets of Tikrit with Thorsten Hoefle, working with Paul (below and right) and James (far right) in Baghdad, and with producer Agnes Reau on Airport Road (lower right).

Early in 2003—no helmet in sight—during a relatively calm period. Below: At a clinic opening in Baghdad. Left: Kids swarmed U.S. patrols, hoping for candy.

Top: What was left of the Humvee closest to the car bomb on Memorial Day, May 29, 2006.
Bottom: Medics Izzy Flores and Lacye Presley worked on the wounded at the bomb scene. Once th
wounded were rushed to the combat hospital, troops stood guard over the dead for several hours.

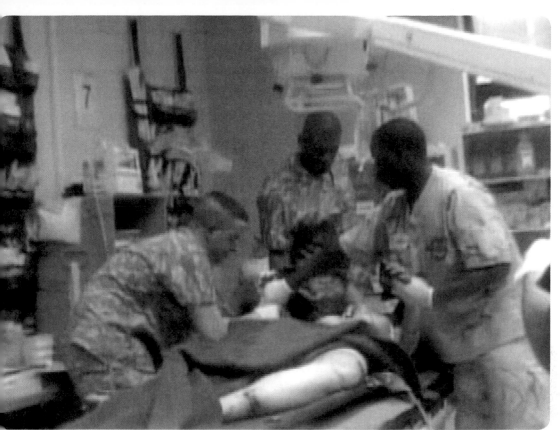

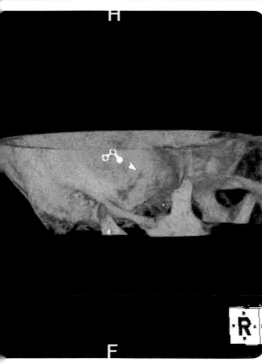

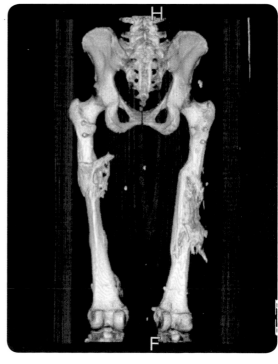

Top: Doctors in Baghdad fight to stop Dozier's bleeding and keep her heart beating.
Bottom left: One of several tiny titanium plates (in white) were screwed in to keep her skull in place.
Bottom right: Dozier's shattered femurs produced bone spurs that had to be chiseled out.

Dozier being stretchered from Balad Airbase, headed for Landstuhl with a mobile intensive care unit strapped on.

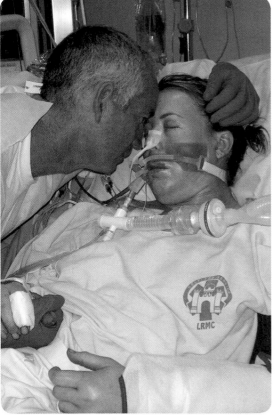

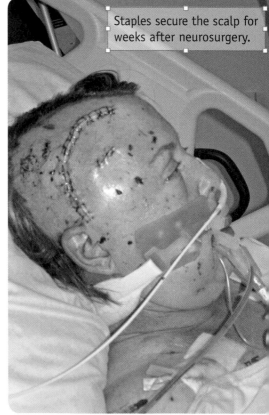

Staples secure the scalp for weeks after neurosurgery.

Top: A rare moment sitting up at Bethesda Naval Hospital with Pete and her mom and dad.
Middle: Everyone entering her room had to be gloved and gowned.
Bottom left: Physiotherapist Becca Shakespeare puts Dozier through her paces
Bottom right: Dozier's sister, MeiLee, with Hahn and kids (from left), Evan, Ryan, and Gracie.

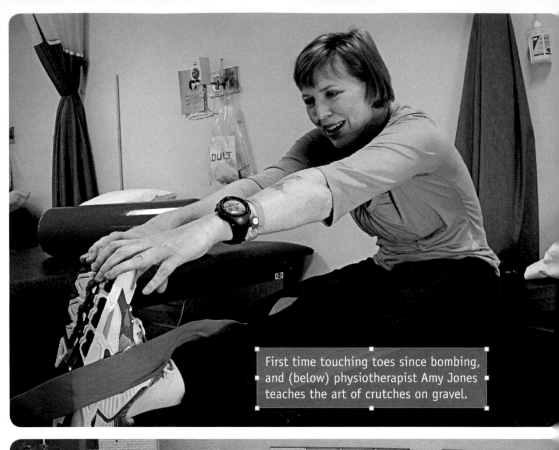

First time touching toes since bombing, and (below) physiotherapist Amy Jones teaches the art of crutches on gravel.

Dozier visits Jeremy Koch after her recovery.

Jennifer Funkhouser's only family photo with Kaitlyn, Allison, and Alex.

Dozier escapes to New Zealand with Pete and (above) testifies before a Senate defense subcommittee with Dr. Andrew Pollak.

CHAPTER 7
hard landing

The last few days at Landstuhl, I was ready to go. The doctors told me they'd exhausted what they could do for me surgically at their facility. The rest would have to be done in the United States. So I knew getting to the National Naval Medical Center was the only way forward, the only way to erase the stomach-churning image of my legs as ground beef. And, of course, the longer I stayed in Landstuhl, the longer I occupied an intensive care unit bed that might be needed for injured troops.

CBS was ready to spring for a private Medevac flight when a space came open on one of the military's Critical Care Air Transport (CCAT) planes, like the one that had brought me and a dozen or so other injured troops from Balad to Landstuhl. This one was bound for Andrews Air Force Base.

I was thrilled, as was my whole family.

Nancy warned us, however, that the trip would be hard and the landing harder—that getting used to the new rhythms of a new hospital would be painful, exhausting, and spirit-sapping. In a surge of hope and optimism over the flight, though, I clung to a different image. I knew the trip would be cold and the military transport engines loud—I'd been on enough military transports to know that.

But I knew the other patients and I would have the best care, a flying hospital in the air. At the other end we'd each be whisked off to our respective military hospitals, some to Bethesda Naval Hospital and others to Walter Reed Army Medical Center.

Then, in my mind, I assumed a team of nurses would slide all of us off our stiff transport gurneys onto proper hospital beds and lull us into sleep after the 10-hour flight. For many of us—there were almost two dozen patients on my particular flight—we'd been awake some 24 hours since our Landstuhl nurses had woken us up at 4 a.m. European time to prepare us for our journey and brief the CCAT team on the complexities of each case.

The first couple hurdles may be particular just to me. The painful dressing change was a hard but necessary way to start the day. The nurses had to ensure I had fresh dressings to lessen the risk of infection as it could take up to 48 hours before the nurses at Bethesda got to the task with all the other tests they'd have to get out of the way.

My next unique hurdle was coping with a surge of paranoid fear during the drive out the gates of Landstuhl, down a public highway to reach Ramstein Air Base, just a few miles away. On that drive I became intimately acquainted with one of the common byproducts of surviving a traumatic attack: hypervigilance.

I thought that drive would be a balm to my soul: beautiful dark pine forests stretching out on either side of the German highway, the first time I'd breathed real, nonhospital-filtered air in a week.

Instead from the moment the ambulance left the hospital compound, my brain went into overdrive, imagining just how easy it would be to ram our transport with a bomb-filled car. All the way there I peered out the ambulance window at the cars driving around us. When one approached I'd tense up, gripping the rails of my hospital gurney. My imagination was stoked by adrenaline and leavened by painkillers.

There was an Al Qaeda cell found in Germany, right? my brain reminded me, working against the logical parts of my brain that were countershouting, *Slim chance. You're not in Iraq anymore. Calm down.*

I later learned that my fears were not so far-fetched. There were Al Qaeda cells operating continuously throughout the country, and a year later, in the summer of 2007, there were several arrests of Al Qaeda suspects alleged to be planning attacks on U.S. targets. U.S. commanders had long war-gamed such attacks and were prepared for them, but the military made the countermeasures unobtrusive to the point of being invisible—or at least invisible to me from the hospital bus.

The 15-minute drive crawled by like an hour. As a soldier saluted us into Ramstein Air Base, I thought, *Back on safe soil.*

Not quite. There was a challenge of a different kind waiting on the tarmac. Again it was more a problem for me than for the injured soldiers who were being carried out of the ambulance around me. Four or five camera crews (maybe fewer; my mind was multiplying threats by the dozen) were waiting about 30 feet from the open end of the medical cargo plane that would be our transport. Linda Mason had spoken with the Air Force, who'd assured her that the cameras would be kept 100 feet back. That's what my doctors were told as well. When we rolled up, the cameras were so close to the back of the bus and plane that my doctor said in annoyance, "What are all those yahoos doing right there?"

I cowered. It's hard to explain my reaction, but Paul and James had started to occupy all my thoughts—why we were there that day, whether we should have been there—questions I was to wrestle with for the next few months. This was the first time I'd faced the public since I'd lost my team, and at that time I felt that I had done the losing, that something I'd done had killed them.

When I saw those cameras, I felt like an accused killer being escorted into the courthouse, trying to put a jacket over my head.

The other reason I cowered was that I felt so horribly vulnerable and exposed. At my feet, in direct line of sight between my eyeballs and the cameras, was every type of medical paraphernalia temporarily doing all the work my insides used to do for me. Frankly, a lot of it was so disgusting it was hard for my family to take, much less a bunch of strangers watching it around the world.

My in-flight doctor didn't want the cameras in his face or filming any of his injured patients that closely. They didn't ask to be on a CCAT with an injured reporter. So with a quick word, he arranged for a military bus to be pulled between us and the cameras.

But even as the cameras were shunted away, my reporter side kicked in. I started feeling guilty, thinking of my colleagues out there filming. *Uh-oh, they won't be able to see anything now,* I thought to myself. I did a mental calculation. It was Wednesday, June 7, around 12 p.m. European time, just an hour before CBS's 7 a.m. *The Early Show.* I thought of my colleague, then-*Early Show* news editor Batt Humphreys, the first man who put me on TV at CBS News.

If Batt tries to do a piece on this, he'll have no tape, I realized. I knew I'd be letting him down.

Okay, I remember thinking. *If this has to be filmed, it's got to be done by people I know.*

I knew that somewhere in that small crowd of cameras were CBS News' Bonn, Germany-based cameramen Kurt Hoefle and his son Thorsten Hoefle, who sometimes did sound for his dad. Kurt, Thorsten, and I had been on a lot of shoots together in Iraq and had survived some close calls. Like Paul and James, they're CBS family.

I asked my in-flight doctor a favor in the middle of his preparations: "When you get a moment, could you walk over to that crowd and shout out for Kurt, the CBS cameraman?" (Pete would have helped, but he'd been relegated to another vehicle for the short trip and was waiting in frustration off to the side on the tarmac. He wasn't sure which bus I was in, and he didn't want to get in anyone's way to find out.)

When he had a moment, the doctor dashed over to the press mob and shouted out for Kurt, whom the other assembled crews screamed at later because they thought he'd planned it.

I had definitely gone into reporter-producer mode, which is single-minded and goal-oriented: Get the shot in the most sensitive, least obtrusive way possible, yes, but get it. Kurt was good at that. I knew he'd almost be invisible. He'd get the shot and stay out of everyone's path. In retrospect I wish there'd been someone else around to ask, not a doctor who was in the middle of a long and complicated job loading some 40 patients and military dependents onto that plane, but let's just say I lacked proper perspective at that point, and that the pictures *did* do some good.

Kurt came onto the ambulance with his eyes a bit misty (surely from the jet fumes) and said, "I don't care about the damned pictures. I just want you to get on that plane."

"If anyone's going to take these shots, it's you," I said.

At that point a young woman Air Force press officer wedged her way onto the now-crowded ambulance and issued an order to us.

"If he takes the shots, then it's pool video."

Uh-oh, I thought, *pool? No way.* Even in my narcotic-addled, preflight, fear-ridden state, I knew that "pool" meant Kurt's camera tape would have to be rewound and fed out as is to every and any media organization who asked for it, from Fox to Al Jazeera. "Pool" meant no editing to remove any invasive or insensitive shots Kurt's camera lens might catch of anyone on that flight. The camera might accidentally capture anything from a closeup shot of a soldier's urine bag going by to another's shredded face.

The more sensitive way to release the video is to allow a good editor a crack at the raw footage to take out anything intrusive before putting it out to everyone. That's how CBS had been doing it, filming such material for the other networks, like the interviews with my mom and dad, and then distributing edited material.

"Kurt will shoot the video," I said sharply to the young press officer. "CBS will decide what to do with it."

But the young press officer was as single-minded in her focus as I was in mine. She kept pushing the point, standing in the narrow bus aisle between the gurneys and obstructing the medical crew as they pushed past her to unload the injured soldiers around me.

In the unspoken honor code of the media (and to those sarcastic about that phrase, yes, we do have one), she'd already broken part of her word to CBS by allowing the cameras so close. Now she was trying to argue with a terribly injured woman who was literally strapped down to a flight gurney with tubes coming out of her mouth, nose, brain, etc. Word to the wise: Do not argue with a woman who is in pain, scared, and grief-stricken, who has had no one to lash out at for at least a week. I didn't have the vocal strength to yell, but I stood my ground (if you can stand your ground when you're strapped to a gurney).

Kurt had already scrambled out of everyone's way and started filming, keeping well back from the parade of gurneys that were moving off the bus, up the ramp, and onto the back of the huge cargo plane.

I didn't understand why the press officer allowed the cameras so close, nor why she insisted on making everything pool until I saw her take her place at the front of my gurney, closest to the waiting cameras. In retrospect I got it. She wanted her family back home to see her doing a job she was proud of, and she represented all the different press officers who'd been working overtime to keep the media informed on this particular story.

But at the time, I wanted to pop her one.

Of course, the other thing fueling my tarmac spat was cold, hard fear. After a lifetime of flying, I was suddenly terrified of the takeoff. Hypervigilance had struck again. As I found out throughout the healing process, anger is a defense mechanism, an outward expression of inner terror.

I didn't tell anyone how I felt, but it was one more crushing blow for me inside. Not only was my body a wreck, but I was scared of my own shadow.

What's wrong with me? I thought as the medical team carried me into the plane.

The positive outcome of the whole affair was that Kurt got some nice shots of the entire medical team, especially one of the woman techs who was talking to me for a bit before helping lift the gurney, which was how all of us were moved from the ambulance buses to the plane. It was rare to have that kind of access, so those shots ended up being used again and again for other stories about the war.

And CBS did release edited, closeup shots of the requisite subject: Dozier on a gurney going home. Linda Mason released a statement, which reflected mostly what she saw that morning at the hospital before departure. "The swelling of Kimberly's face has decreased significantly, she had the first physical therapy session on her legs, and she had her hair washed. She is in good spirits." I can't quite remember any physical therapy, but maybe that was a polite way of describing the skin-shrieking dressings change.

People I barely knew told me later that the shot from Ramstein Air Base was a huge relief to them, especially seeing that U.S. Army woman tech and me in conversation. The last image they'd seen was an unconscious form on a stretcher a week before with a couple hundred pounds of medical equipment strapped to the gurney keeping the comatose body alive. A week later there I was looking pretty normal from the neck up. (My family had combed my hair so it covered the gaping wound and the staples in a 6-inch semicircle on my skull. Sheets covered my shattered lower half.) The image said to people: She'll be OK. And for them that was one bit of welcome good news from the war in Iraq.

Throughout the process I was bewildered by the attention. I kept asking myself, *Why do they want to film me? I'm not a well-known anchor like Bob Woodruff.* But I was to stumble across something later that helped explain it to me. A wide-ranging study seems to show that people have a greater capacity to care about an individual than a group. In tests, one group of people was given a single child to whom to donate money. The other group was given two children or more. Result: The more kids in the group, the less the donors gave. So it seems people can better relate to what happens to an individual. After that the mind goes numb. Maybe that's why so many people were focused on me at that point: I was a single representative showing them in a horribly fresh way something they'd long been numb to.

Maybe journalists are prone to the same syndrome too, and that's why if you read most of the news reports that day, you would think I was the only injured passenger on that plane. The plane was actually packed with people, both troops who were wounded as badly or worse than I was and some civilian military dependents, even a small infant patient who was being flown Stateside for delicate heart surgery.

The cavernous space inside the C-141 cargo plane we were flying on had been turned into a stripped-down trauma ward. Bolted to each side of the plane were bunk beds where gurneys for up to 10 patients (depending on the plane) could be fastened to the metal bunk structure. Each severely injured person would essentially have a mobile ICU attached to a canopy bolted to his or her gurney, with heart rate, oxygen intake monitors, pumps for air, food, saline drips, whatever was needed. Each CCAT team consisted of a doctor, a nurse, and a respiratory therapist, and each team could care for up to three patients, depending on what shape the patients were in. Nancy later explained that sometimes the CCAT team would fly with only a single patient if the person had a life-or-death injury, such as extensive burns.

There were also two rows of canvas jump seats along the center, the rows back-to-back, facing outward toward the gurneys. This is where patients' dependents could sit for the journey.

The doctor and my nurse strapped me onto an upper bunk, with Pete sitting across from me on the canvas seats.

There were at least eight critically wounded troops I could see near me, including a man below me. Ambulatory patients were sitting in another part of the plane. We couldn't really talk to the other patients during the flight. There was no way to shout a casual, "Hello, how are you doing? Yeah, I got bombed too." We could barely make ourselves heard to our flight doctors and nurses, who would lean in close to talk to us over the din of the cargo plane engines. (I assume that many of the other patients, like me, also had one or two shattered eardrums, a common byproduct of blast injuries. I'd be partly deaf for the better part of a year until one side knitted itself together and the other side got a replacement eardrum.) The other barrier to communicating: Unlike me, most of the patients around me, like the one on the lower bunk, were 24 to 48 hours fresh from their combat injuries, so they were still heavily sedated and unconscious.

Pete and I had both been on plenty of military transport planes before, so we knew it would be cold. We had blankets, but I had another idea, borrowed from my camping days. The night before the flight, I asked Linda if anyone had a Therm-a-Rest, a brand name for an insulated, self-inflating air mattress that campers sleep on to keep the cold and damp of the ground from seeping into their sleeping bags and them.

CBS's local driver knew what it was and exactly where to find one in a local camping store and appeared with one at 9 the next morning, moments before my departure. Pete covered the gurney with the insulated mattress just before I was lifted onto it from my Landstuhl hospital bed.

One of the CCAT staffers helping to pack me up for the journey spotted the air mattress. "What's that?" he asked, apparently new to the job.

The rest of my CCAT team chorused, "A Therm-a-Rest."

The new man gave the others a quizzical look. That's how the CCAT team was all sleeping so soundly and warmly on return trips to Iraq in the empty plane. They each had one, yet they hadn't yet shared the secret with the newbie. "OK, I have four hours on the ground when we get to D.C.," he said. "I'll find one." I tried to offer him mine, but the fact that I'd bled on it during the journey made it less than appealing.

Pete had brought other supplies for the 10-hour journey: a movie on his computer (impossible to watch with the noise, but it helped knowing it was there) and a bunch of get-well messages people had phoned in to CBS. He'd downloaded them onto his iPod. His request to people had been: Keep it short and upbeat.

People really did try. But their attempts at optimism only partly covered the shock and the worry in their voices. After a couple I'd get upset and have to stop listening.

The next few months were like going to one long funeral, where everyone I'd ever known or ever met tried to offer wisdom and comfort or later find some wisdom and comfort from me. The process was inescapable and necessary, but as I learned from hearing those first messages, it could floor you.

Luckily there were other more superficial distractions. Pete and I had bonded years earlier over our mutual love of camping, camping gear, and cool outdoor electronic gadgets.

This plane was full of them.

Within moments of boarding we both spotted the most amazing wall-to-wall canvas organizer that was hung on a cargo container that was bolted down in the center of the aircraft's hold. It was stuffed with every type of medical supply conceivable, or so it appeared. I stage-whispered over the engines, "Please, take a picture of that *now*. We *have* to make one of those for the Jeep . . . "

Pete kept saying, "I can't! It's a high-security plane."

"What are they gonna do, throw us off of it? C'mon, just snap the organizer," I pushed. "At least sketch it!"

Yes, these are the things your mind feasts upon when it doesn't want to think about things like *Three hours ago I saw my shredded legs for the first time, and they looked like reject parts from the butcher's shop.*

You think about anything but that.

I was wrapped in blankets, including the quilt I'd been given at Landstuhl. The jangled preflight nerves faded, and I even started guzzling water, the first time I'd done that since waking up in Germany. Eating and drinking had been nearly impossible until then because, like most trauma patients, I had absolutely no appetite. I couldn't even force the food, which shocked me. I was one of the healthiest eaters in the world. The Landstuhl doctors had to force liquid into me by IV, and nutrition into me via a tube that went down my nose into my stomach, a practice doctors would have to continue for some time at Bethesda Naval Hospital. And yet I lost some 30 pounds in those first few weeks as my body turned on itself to find the nutrition it needed for healing.

The first step toward returning to normal came on that flight. The CCAT team baked oatmeal cookies, filling the plane with the smell like Grandma's kitchen at Christmastime. It worked. I ate an entire cookie, then paid for it with a churning stomach, but it was worth it. It was the kind of thing I learned was typical of the military's caregivers. They truly put themselves in their patients' shoes, and on so many occasions, they read our minds and knew what we needed and when we needed it.

The flight had taken off at 1:20 p.m. central European time (7:20 a.m. eastern time) on June 7 and landed in the United States at 4:20 p.m. eastern time. Unfortunately, with the din of the aircraft I didn't sleep at all. I regretted that later. I braced myself for the landing and prayed my way to the wheels touching down on the tarmac. "Made it," I said. "All downhill from here." My whole body sank into the gurney with relief.

The best part of landing was meeting up with Army Specialist Snipes, the soldier from my patrol who'd tried to get the radios back online. He'd been flying in another part of the medical plane with the ambulatory patients, those who didn't need constant care like I did. He was the one who'd been hit in the face by the blast. So when I saw him, parts of his lips were missing and his teeth were exposed. It's strange that I can't recall much about that image. I focused on his eyes as he came up to my gurney and stood there mute, or so I thought. I incorrectly assumed from his injuries that he couldn't talk, but I later found out that he'd given an interview to a radio reporter in Landstuhl before taking off. That means he probably just couldn't drown out the noise of the plane or the noise of me talking over him. (That was yet another time when, as Pete often says of me, I wouldn't let a man get a word in edgewise.)

I remember telling Snipes that I hoped he'd recover quickly and telling him I had a world of respect for him and his buddies, especially the six men who survived the deadly attack on their patrol and then went back to work doing the same job a few days later, all the while knowing exactly what could happen to them.

Snipes nodded and looked down, the unspoken equivalent of saying, "Just doing my job, ma'am," which is what people in uniform generally tell you when you offer them praise. Snipes shook my hand and headed out of the plane. He wanted to get home to Texas to fix his face and, more important, to see his wife and—for the first time—his young baby, who had been born while he was away.

Then came the hard part of the landing: The military press officers informed us there was a crowd of media waiting outside to film my arrival. They were in the spot where they normally waited for Air Force One.

I broke out in a cold sweat. "No way," I said to Pete. "Can I go out a back door?" I knew that team of shooters would have long lenses and know how to get that difficult shot.

I panicked for all the same reasons I had at takeoff. I didn't know how to react or what to do. On one hand I was honored by the attention and bowled over by how people seemed to care so deeply for someone they'd never met. But I couldn't wave to the cameras, as if to say, "Look, I made it!" Paul, James, and Capt. Funkhouser hadn't.

Pete couldn't protect me from those feelings, but he could block the cameras. As I pulled on a baseball cap, he scouted the camera positions with the Andrews press officers' help and then took his place strategically next to my gurney. As an honor guard of Marines, Army, Navy, and Air Force lifted me out of the plane and into the waiting ambulances, Pete stood directly between me and the camera crews. The crews got great shots of the four guys carrying me. And they got a pretty good shot of Pete, which Rhian and George later enjoyed seeing back in New Zealand.

But all the cameramen captured of me was a fleeting shot of the side of my face peeking out from under a baseball cap as the team lifted me into the waiting ambulance bus. The cameramen weren't appreciative. I heard later that one of them was swearing loudly, "Her boyfriend's blocking the shot!"—a fact that perversely pleased the press-hating Pete.

As the medics strapped me into the ambulance, I couldn't know that the worst part of the day's journey was to come: the 24 miles on Washington, D.C.'s Capital Beltway. The intensive care patients, like me, were riding in racks on ambulance buses, vehicles that unfortunately looked like school buses from the outside. The masquerading-as-school-bus aspect turned out to be a major problem.

Most motorists will get out of the way of an ambulance in seconds. But when a big blue bus blares sirens and flashes lights, drivers tend to look in their rearview mirror, see what looks like a school bus, and ignore it.

They wait to move until they see the real emergency vehicle.

Despite the ear-splitting sirens wailing above us, which echoed in my ears for the next three days, time and again the ambulance bus driver had to slam on the brakes because the motorists weren't getting out of the way.

I kept getting thrown around on my gurney, sliding forward with every tap of the brakes. The motion sent shriek-level pain shooting through my burned and broken legs. And I wasn't the only one suffering.

Across from me was a soldier so badly injured by an IED that I hadn't seen him speak or stir for the entire 10-hour flight from Germany. The sirens and the constant braking yanked him into semiunconsciousness. His eyes were still shut, but I watched his hands grab at the gurney rails, white-knuckling every time we all were thrown forward.

Our traveling team of doctors and nurses shared our angst for a different reason. They called this the most dangerous part of their mission. "It's fast from Landstuhl to Ramstein Air Base, and we have everything we need to fly over the Atlantic," one of the doctors told me. "The diciest part of the trip is getting from Andrews Air Force Base to Bethesda Naval Hospital and Walter Reed Medical Center." He always feared he'd get his patients all the way from Iraq to Washington, D.C., and then lose them somewhere on the D.C. Beltway by running out of oxygen while stuck in a traffic jam.

For the last leg of the journey in Maryland, police cars joined our entourage and cleared the way. We'd made it, but my already-shattered ears were ringing as if I'd sat at the front row of a heavy metal concert. One of the first things I swore I'd campaign for when I was released from the hospital was a safer way to get the troops from the airport *to* the hospital. I later shared an early draft describing the journey with anyone I thought could help.

From the ambulance I was wheeled to the ICU, which was surprisingly mostly empty, considering the heavy traffic of injured troops that had been ferried to Bethesda of late. It turned out that injured troops were generally quickly moved onto Five East, the long-term trauma care ward, which was soon to become my home.

But first I had to run another gauntlet. A group of doctors was waiting to see their VIP patient. The job of the meet-and-greet team was to thoroughly double-check me head to toe to ensure that nothing was missed in Baghdad, Balad, or Landstuhl.

Unfortunately it was a rare moment in which I had no patient advocate to watch out for me during the check-in. My parents and siblings were still in the air, flying a commercial flight from Germany. And Pete was settling into his lodgings after barely sleeping for almost a week. Pete stayed for the first couple days at Fisher House until he moved out to free up space for the military families. Fisher House was set up early in the war and was provided by private donations to help cash-strapped military families stay close to their loved ones for weeks or months of recuperation.

I was headed first to the ICU to be evaluated by my new team of doctors. They usually start this process by going over the records that have arrived with the patient. Sometimes the records are lost in transit, as some of mine were. It was another symptom at that time of a system overwhelmed by too many patients.

But where records were lacking, the doctors were blessed with one obnoxiously talkative patient, fueled by adrenaline overdrive from the bus trip to the hospital. I briefed them on my injuries and various surgical procedures from my hospital bed in staccato bursts.

The doctors seemed more amused than annoyed as I took charge, something I often ended up trying to do—and something the doctors later told me was common to military patients as well, I assume injured officers especially.

"You're people who are used to being in charge," my Bethesda surgeon Dr. James Dunne later explained. "So asking questions and demanding explanations is absolutely normal."

I think part of it is that we're also trying to deny how helpless we actually are, how we're suddenly dependent on someone else to manage almost every bodily function. It's humiliating. So trying to go alpha with your hospital caregivers turns out to be a natural response.

I started rattling off the procedures I knew they'd completed thus far. "OK, I had one of those *Blackhawk Down*-style cut downs to my femoral artery in Baghdad to stop the bleeding [referring to the graphic operation shown on the battlefield in the movie], and I had something like 30 to 40 units of blood. In Balad they took out a chunk of shrapnel from my skull, here [I pointed to my scar], and they screwed in titanium plates," I continued before a single surgeon could get a word in. As Pete said in military-radio-speak, I was "stuck on send, not receive."

"Then in Landstuhl, I had numerous washouts of the wounds on my leg, and they put titanium nails in my femurs," I went on, using the surgeons' slang for the titanium rods that were now the main structural support in my legs.

"What?" the assembled orthopedic surgeons exclaimed.

They pulled back the sheets covering my legs.

"The X-fixes are gone already?" one of them said to another with visible disappointment. He was referring to the external support structure of metal that had been holding my legs in place with metal drilled into my bones at several points through my skin. The X-fixes went when the titanium nails were put in.

"Darn . . ." one of them actually said. That type of surgery is a challenge they'd looked forward to. Now they'd simply be caretaking someone else's completed work.

"OK, then we'll look at your wounds," said another of the crowd.

"Wait, wait, wait," I pleaded. "I just got my bandages changed this morning. It really hurts to remove any of them. If you *have* to do it, though, I'm going to need a bolus of painkiller." A bolus meant an extra dose or two to numb my pain response before they started peeling back the bandages from the ground beef area of my legs.

"Don't worry, we'll just look at a couple spots. You won't need painkillers," one of them lied.

With that they proceeded to remove or lift every last bandage from the butchery of my legs. And then they had the nerve to act surprised every time I screamed.

"Oh, did that hurt? I'm really sorry," one of the surgeons kept saying, almost like a chant. By the end of the session, I would have strangled Dr. Sorry if I hadn't just had every last ounce of strength tortured out of me.

That was one of my first lessons in "doctors who don't listen."

I quickly learned to identify which ones empathized and tried to weed out those whose eyes would glaze over when I tried to tell them, "This hurts like hell . . ."

A few I learned to dread would say, "Oh, that pain is to be expected. I'm sure it will pass." Some of the most sensitive among the doctors turned out to be the orthopedic surgeons, an observation I later made to a disbelieving Dr. Dunne. He said it was great to hear, as the "men who do the sterile DIY" aren't routinely pegged as the most sensitive of the surgical breed.

The nurses and corpsmen, I learned, always listened. They, too, were adept at learning which of the doctors would heed my (or their) concerns.

Without exception, over the next six weeks every complaint I brought up turned out to have a genuine root cause. But time and again I had to fight my way through some doctors who thought I was exaggerating or that my head was creating phantom pain.

I also learned that there's an art to getting heard, and it wasn't through anger. Clear, calm, and assertive got the point across without leaving bruised feelings or egos on either side. Complaints at a hospital or anywhere else are like salt: Use sparingly or the resulting bitterness will spoil everything.

After the bandage debacle, I lay crumpled and exhausted when the next horror hit. Two very nice but very tired X-ray technicians came to reX-ray nearly every part of my body—my upper and lower legs, my pelvis, and my arms—to make sure the doctors overseas hadn't missed anything. My body was stiff, and my legs were immobile, so the best I could do to help was hold on to the side of the bed as they rolled me left or right and placed the X-ray plates beneath me.

I winced with each new contortion and was praying for the end of it when one of the techs said, "Uh-oh." They'd mixed up their labels of left and right.

And suddenly I was in a human "Who's on first?" routine. "I used the left symbol for the right side," one of the techs said. "I mean . . . the left for some of the right side, and the right for these on the left. Except for those others on the other right. I mean left."

It would have been comical if I hadn't been in so much pain. It was obvious the technicians were so exhausted that they were having trouble thinking straight. They were nearing the end of a 12-hour shift, one of countless many shifts they'd pulled in the short-staffed hospital that week.

On each side of my hospital bed, they debated back and forth over my head about whether they'd have to start the entire 90-minute process from scratch.

"Please, no," I pleaded.

They finally decided they'd just push on and try to figure out which side was which later. With that, they continued, and I shut my eyes and gritted my teeth, thinking, *Just a little bit longer.*

At that moment one of the techs was reaching across my body, trying to wedge an X-ray plate under my hip. It hurt like hell as rolling into each new position meant either putting pressure on the burns on my legs or shifting the stitched skin above my hip where they'd clipped the femoral artery, not to mention how it felt in both broken femurs.

Then came the finale: The tech was leaning his whole weight on the rails of my ICU bed when the bed rail collapsed.

The tech fell, his hand and the weight of his upper body landing full on my burned left knee.

"Get off my leg," I gasped, then drew in breath in such agony it was hard to speak at all. I was still in a numb glaze of pain from the doctors' impromptu bandage-shifting session. The X-ray tech's fall sent my body into pain overdrive, sweat breaking out in response.

The hapless techs finished as quickly as possible, if only to get away from me, as I couldn't fake politeness anymore. (Pain does that.)

The ICU nurse, meanwhile, was fully occupied with a patient who needed one-on-one critical care, like I had needed when I first arrived at Landstuhl. I overheard that his lungs had been burned by a blast, so he needed to be watched every moment to keep his airway free. As I could breathe on my own, I was understandably far down her list of priorities.

Understanding, however, doesn't make the pain go away. By the time I got her attention and she got me more painkillers to numb the double whammy I'd just been through, I had passed the pain point-of-no-return mark.

As I was to learn, you have to "stay on top of the pain," in medical parlance, or rather stay ahead of it. Once it overwhelms you, it takes up to a double dose of painkillers to catch up. Because of all the in-processing procedures, I was already late getting the medicine, and it was only a single dose, which wasn't nearly enough.

Overwhelmed by layer upon layer of agony, I was wheeled across the hospital to my room in Five East.

Good news, I remember thinking. *Get me the hell out of here.*

By now it was well past midnight eastern time. I'd been up 26 hours without being able to force myself to take even the briefest of naps. I was exhausted and numb from the pain of the surgeons' welcoming committee impromptu dressing change, and the ministrations of Blither and Bleary-eye from the X-ray department.

My new floor, Five East, was a 40-bed ward for injured troops and the occasional military dependent who'd come to Bethesda for serious surgery. The walls of the hallways were dotted with long paper banners that were signed by well-wishers who wrote things like "We support you," "God bless," and "No more 9/11." There were brightly colored posters that schoolchildren made with crayons or paint with grammatically incorrect but cheerful phrases like "We love you, soldier people. Get well soon."

The hall was crowded with the injured troops from the day's CCAT flight and those from earlier flights in the week—the even more gravely injured patients who had gone ahead of me from Landstuhl, I supposed. Each nurse and corpsman had up to 11 patients each to care for. Corpsmen are the Navy's version of nursing assistants. The troops called them "docs" because they're also the medics to the Marines, traveling with them on combat missions, like the Army medics who'd helped save my life.

Some of those I was about to encounter were early on in their careers, and a couple seemed overwhelmed by the job, or at least by the job of taking care of a "VIP."

Dr. Dunne later assured me that I received no special treatment. He said everyone on that hall was treated like a VIP, which meant they worked their hearts out taking care of me, like they did everyone else. But this was my first day there, and there were several media vans sitting in the parking lot that first afternoon when I arrived, so I was attracting a certain amount of unusual attention.

I was at the end of the same hallway in the same ward where Bob Woodruff had spent five weeks in a medically induced coma from the concussive force of the blast. Like Bob and almost everyone else on Five East, I had a private room because I was still on isolation after that positive test for Acinetobacter. As for so many injured troops, the potentially deadly bacteria became one of the biggest threats I faced in my recovery.

My nurse settled me in as quickly as she could, setting up all the various pain meds, saline, and nutrition solutions that were pumping into me. Then she rushed off to deal with one of the many emergencies on the hall.

I lay there praying for the painkillers to take hold. I was still "behind the pain," almost gasping out loud from the throbbing in my legs.

I dimly took in the details of my room: window, one bed, a couple chairs, a raised desk with a computer, white walls, and lots of "Fall Risk" notices (i.e., this patient can't walk, so she's at high risk of falling. Don't let her).

The nurse left behind a young woman corpsman, who was finishing up the long process of entering my vital signs into my room's computer.

I politely mumbled some small talk, "Hi, how are you, yes the trip was fine," all the while wishing to myself, *Please, please, can I sleep now?*

I should have kept my mouth shut. She took the small talk as an invitation to start chatting.

"So I heard you were attacked," she ventured, her expression curious. "Were you attacked?"

I was stunned. Her words sent a chill straight to my soul.

I understand that her tired mind blurted out the first question that came to it, the equivalent of "What happened?" But what the young woman couldn't know was how her words set off a cascade in an exhausted, pain-racked, overwrought patient. With one question, she'd sent me right back to the moment after the blast, lying in the dirt, listening to the ammunition cook off.

My mind started turning over the question, considering it angle by angle. *Attacked. Attacked? Well, yes, it was a bomb. That's an attack. But "attack" means combat and live fire. Did someone also fire on us? There were gunshots. But that was ammo cooking off, right? Or was there something else people hadn't told me that the corpsman had heard on the news? Had gunmen hit us afterward or something?* I knew there'd been a bomb, but at that point, I didn't know what type—a massive car bomb or a smaller roadside bomb. So when she asked, I didn't have the answer, but my mind started searching for it.

"I'm not sure," I answered haltingly. "I, umm, I don't really want to talk about it."

She did a swift mental back pedal as if I'd slapped her and stammered back, "Oh," and left the room, looking utterly crushed.

So now two of us were in hell.

For the rest of the night, until dawn lit up the window, my mind obsessed over her question, examining every detail I could remember from the bomb scene again and again. My brain came to rest where it always ended up over the coming weeks: with Paul and James.

Where were Paul and James exactly when the bomb went off? I wondered. *Were they hit right away? Did they die immediately? Did they feel anything? Oh, dear God, their families . . .*

Somewhere in the haze of narcotics and leftover pain, I started hallucinating. This was common, I later learned, for someone who'd been on that many different painkillers for so many days (even though there weren't enough in my system at the moment to do me much good painwise).

Stuck on my back, as usual, I was staring wide-eyed at the ceiling. In the strange haze between sleep and the lack thereof, the sprinklers on the ceiling became demons' heads.

I slipped into a nightmare where the demons started crawling over the ceiling, grabbing Paul and James by the shoulders, and dragging them backward away from me. I wanted to wake up, but I wasn't really asleep.

To make matters worse, sometime during the few hours of darkness left, my epidural drip ran out of narcotics, and a piercing electronic alarm went off next to my head. The sharp sound snapped me out of the hallucinatory state, but it took a good 15 minutes before someone came in and turned it off and far longer to get a narcotic refill from the hospital pharmacy. That happened night after night, robbing me of healing sleep.

The nurses and corpsmen were slammed that night. Too many people were in exactly the state I was in or worse, and too few people on the ward were trying to put out the fires.

In short, sleep proved impossible.

Just after dawn I asked the nurse to call Pete at Fisher House—a dormlike residence on the hospital grounds, provided thanks to private donations to help cash-strapped military families stay close to their loved ones.

Fisher House had no "front desk," so the nurse couldn't reach Pete unless she knew his room number. I hadn't seen him since we landed, so I didn't know what that was.

I wanted to call CBS, to ask someone from the D.C. staff to intervene. But I didn't know that number either. I pondered calling the Foreign Desk in New York (a phone number engraved in my brain), then considered what I might say: *Hi, it's your good friend Kim Dozier who was bombed in Baghdad. I'm having a bad night. The devils are really getting to me. Could you send some help?* Even in my pain- and narcotic-altered state, I had the good sense to know the *Drudge* headlines that would produce: "Bombed reporter bombed on drugs." Or the *News of the World* headline: "CBS Reporter Possessed. Exorcism at Eleven."

I gave up and waited for someone to appear.

By the time Pete arrived shortly after 8 a.m., expecting to find me rested and recovered from the flight, he instead found a blithering wreck. My eyes were red-rimmed and my voice was hoarse and shrunken.

Pete told the dayside nurses the next night had to be better. They nodded sympathetically, but the dayside team had little to do with those on overnight. So as that first night burned off into day and waves of new doctors came in to check me out, Pete and I let the matter go, chalking it up to a bad start.

The second night, I was sure, would be better. The ghosts and demons wouldn't appear. I'd finally rest.

Not a chance.

The night started out well. The corpsmen had rolled me onto my side, the way I normally sleep, propping me up with an elaborate architecture of pillows. They said when I wanted to change sides, I just needed to call.

The problem was that in their rush to deal with so many patients that night, they'd left my call button behind me on the opposite side of my bed, out of my reach. So there was no way to call them when I woke a couple hours later, stiff and sore, with my legs screaming. Staying in any one position too long caused excruciating pain as the blood pooled in one place and the muscles cramped.

I tried calling out for help, but the inner and outer fire doors to my room were shut tight. No one could hear me.

Finally I grabbed anything I could reach on my bedside table and started chucking it, full force, at the inner door. I sent soda cans, water bottles, and finally a huge jar of hospital moisturizer that hit with a satisfying thwack against the door.

No response.

Finally someone came on rounds to check my vital signs and helped me get into a different position. I was so thrilled and grateful that I forgot to remind him about the call bell problem. That meant unfortunately, as the corpsman was trying to settle me in the semidarkness, the call button was moved again to my opposite side, again out of reach.

It was bad enough that I could do almost nothing for myself, not even roll my body or move my legs. But there's little worse than being in pain, unable to move, with no way to call for help.

In addition, like the night before the alarm on the epidural pump kept sounding for no reason. The nurses had to manually reset them, and so many patients were having the same problem over and over that they couldn't catch up. We'd all suffer through a night filled with piercing beeps next to our heads.

When my parents and Pete saw me the next morning, they didn't even have to ask. I stared at them mutely and then started sobbing.

Finally I choked out the words, "Can I go back to Landstuhl?"

They demanded a meeting with Dr. Dunne—as much social worker as surgeon. Families often have legitimate complaints, but they're seldom diplomatic about how they make them. This is a truism proved by the emotional meetings I could sometimes hear taking place in other patients' rooms. Dr. Dunne proved adept at filtering out the anger and solving the problem.

Simply put, because of so many injuries that month in Iraq, the staff on our floor was overstretched, with the ward at near-full capacity. Pete had stationed a chair outside my room, where he'd wait sometimes if I was sleeping (staying inside my room would mean the discomfort of sitting there in one of the bright yellow paper gowns and purple surgical gloves everyone entering my room had to wear because of the Acinetobacter). From his perch he'd watch the whole hallway and report back to me. He told me that some evenings, the entire hallway would be "lit up like a Christmas tree," with every single call bell glowing and the nurses and corpsmen jogging from room to room in a ceaseless, all-night marathon.

But there were things Dr. Dunne saw he could do, like writing orders to get me a working epidural pump and asking the nurses to sort out the call bell situation. That last one proved simple: They plugged two in, one on each side of my bed. That meant one less thing for them, or me, to worry about.

And most important, someone had a chat with all the corpsmen and gently explained to those who didn't know already that there are some subjects to steer clear of unless the patient brings it up.

That night, for the first time since leaving Landstuhl, I finally slept.

CHAPTER 8
fighting doziers

My parents had moved into Fisher House, intending to stay however long it took to get me well. They'd been through many medical crises themselves and knew that what a hospital patient most needs is an advocate to help advise him or her on the tough medical decisions to come and to watchdog the care.

So I started ahead of the game of most of the injured troops on my hallway whose families couldn't afford or weren't able to leave work to be by their side.

My other weapon, one which became key to my recovery, was everything my parents had ever taught me, starting with our family credo, "Put your head down and work. It will likely be difficult to the point of impossible. Do not complain. Just push through." Over the painful weeks to come, this became my most valuable tool, together with the support of my loved ones: a stubborn refusal to bow to setbacks.

Looking at my mom and dad, you can see where my attitude comes from. It's perhaps best described as down-home-Baltimore "You only deserve what you've earned the hard way" pride. They're from what's been called the greatest generation. When people asked me what my dad was like, I'd say cross John Wayne's Marine character, Sgt. Stryker, from the *Sands of Iwo Jima* with his Rooster Cogburn cowboy role, and you'd have my dad: 6 foot with blue eyes, a ruddy face, dark blond hair, bow legs, and a crushing handshake greeting folks with a "Ben Dozier. Damn glad to know ya."

My mom, Dorothy, was more of a cross between a young Judy Garland and Ava Gardner, a gracious lady on the surface with a temper and steel in full measure underneath. She believed, as she was taught, that her role was to be a good homemaker and a good mother. But her sharp intellect and intelligence fought for outlets over the years, and she voraciously read books, tore through crossword puzzles until 2 a.m. every night, worked as a secretary, ran a church gift shop, and took college courses in anthropology and religion, acing every test.

My mom's parents had literally jumped off boats (or so the family story goes) into the Baltimore harbor as they arrived from Germany between World Wars I and II. My grandfather had been a painter in Germany. In Baltimore he hung wallpaper and painted houses while his wife, two decades his junior, raised four children in a row house in the German and Polish immigrant neighborhoods near Baltimore's docks. Mom was the eldest child and had three younger brothers.

She was also probably the smartest kid in school, skipping two grades. She wanted to become a nurse, but when she graduated from high school, they told her that at 16 she was too young. By the time she was old enough, she'd married my dad, and in that era only unmarried women were allowed to train as nurses.

The marriage itself was an act of rebellion, as neither her mother nor her father approved of my dad, a poor high school football star with a heavy Southern accent. My parents eloped, going to the justice of the peace right after Dad signed up for the Marines (this after Pearl Harbor galvanized the whole country and sent ranks of patriotic American men to war). They had a pastor bless the marriage. And then later they had a full church wedding, which means they have three anniversaries each year, making it difficult for their six kids to remember any of them.

My mom's mother, Louise Cavey, never quite overcame her aversion to Dad, but she doted on her grandkids. We didn't get to know her well; by the time I was born, Dad had found overseas construction jobs with Mom's encouragement. I remember meeting my grandmother when I was 10 on my first visit to the continental United States. She was a traditional German lady, i.e., her house was spotless, and her children had been raised to be proper to a fault. Displays of emotion were kept low key: a hug when we said hello and a brief hug goodbye.

Capping her feelings was a stricture she lived by even as rheumatoid arthritis crippled her body, first confining her to a wheelchair and, toward the end, to a bed in a nursing home. As the disease attacked her body, my grandmother's spine bent until her rib cage was resting on her hipbones. Every time we saw her, she seemed to have shrunken further in on herself. Her hands were so deformed that they looked like the gnarled claws of the wicked witch in *Snow White*. But she fought the disease to the end. My lasting memory is of my grandmother sitting in her wheelchair with a physiotherapist's pulley-and-rope exercise suspended from the doorway above her head. She was grasping the wooden handles attached to either side of the rope as best she could in her hand claws, and she was pulling the rope down first with one hand, which lifted the other hand up, then reversing the process. The idea was to keep the inflamed joints from fusing by forcing the joints to keep moving. She was in so much pain during the exercise that she screamed through gritted teeth, but she wouldn't let that defeat her.

Nora Turner, my other grandmother whom we called Nanny in the Southern custom, raised my father and his younger brother. Dad was born in Norfolk, Virginia, where his father died at an early age. Dad became the man of the house.

When Nanny and her two sons moved from Norfolk to Baltimore, Dad worked hard to lose some of his heavy Norfolk accent, and both he and his brother, Tom, took whatever work they could find to help Nanny pay the bills. They lived in a series of apartments that sometimes consisted of only one or two rooms. Nanny found work selling Utz potato chips in the drafty local market, a job I also did by her side for my first full day's work at age 10 or 11. I remember finishing the shift in the early evening, smelling of grease after scooping chips into small, single-serving waxed paper bags. My back screamed from carting the heavy tin cans from store room to stall, and my toes felt like ice blocks from standing on the cold concrete floor and feeling the constant draft from the front door. My grandmother worked that stall year-round, no matter the weather. I looked at her with a newfound respect. She wasn't just the proud grandma who dragged us to the front row to show us off at her Baptist church some Sundays or stuffed us silly with yams and Southern fried chicken. Underneath, she was steel.

Like his mom, my dad did nothing halfway. He and his friends went to high school during the day, then formed their own work gang to shovel and haul coal at the local stockyard at night. The old timers laughed at them, saying they'd barely shift enough coal to earn a few pennies. So Dad and his friends hauled the coal double-time in relay style and broke the stockyard's record for a nightly haul. I doubt they even made $1 each, but on that particular night, it wasn't about the money.

At school Dad was a football star, a quarterback so good that he was offered a football scholarship to Cornell University. But being from Norfolk and then raised in Baltimore made Dad a Navy man, and all he wanted was "to play for Navy" at the Naval Academy. He almost made it. Despite football and wrestling practice and working a job most evenings, he still earned one of the highest entrance scores the Naval Academy had ever seen. But one of the administrators told him (in the days before such comments would trigger lawsuits) that the two Maryland appointments had gone to friends of friends of the governor.

Dad was devastated. He was offered a consolation place at West Point, but he told my sister, MeiLee, he turned it down "out of dumb pride." He also said he didn't want to move up north and be separated from his young wife. "I was in looooove," he told MeiLee.

The war soon came along, so he fought his way through the battle of the Pacific, then came back and worked as a surveyor while taking night classes in engineering at Johns Hopkins University. He eventually worked his way up the ranks to construction engineer and finally to project manager.

My oldest brother, Bob, was adopted after Mom lost her first child, a daughter, at birth. She was told she would never have children again, but sons Michael, Larry, and Douglas followed quickly in succession after that.

When the boys were old enough, Mom worked as a secretary in a law firm and so impressed the partners with her intellect and discretion that they offered to send her to law school. But she couldn't reconcile a law career with her role as a homemaker, so she turned it down.

She later urged MeiLee and me to get as much education as we could so that we'd have more choices than she'd had. But she also simply loved the job she'd chosen: raising kids and making a home wherever we ended up. When we lived in Iran, she spent hours scouring local markets for the ingredients to make English muffins and bagels from scratch. She also tried to learn how to make all the Persian specialties, with various degrees of success.

Outwardly domestic, my mom was inwardly the risk taker who pushed Dad to apply for the overseas jobs in the first place. She spoke regretfully of how they'd turned down the opportunity to homestead in Alaska when the boys were young. So she wasn't going to let opportunities like that slip away again with her second family of two girls.

I was born just as my youngest brother was leaving home, and MeiLee was adopted when I was 9 years old, so my brothers and MeiLee and I are separated by about a decade and a half at least.

I don't know much about my brothers' childhoods except that Mom's wanderlust expressed itself domestically—inside America's borders, as opposed to our international jaunts. With my brothers, the family moved frequently from Baltimore to Virginia to Tennessee and back. So the boys, like the girls, learned to be comfortable on the move. Mom's spirit of adventure stuck.

When Dad first secured a job in Iran, a place we'd never heard of, Mom picked up the maps from the library (there was no Internet then) and researched Iran's history, religion, culture, and traditions. I first learned from her about the Muslim and Jewish faiths, including the differences and similarities to Christianity, as she understood them from her voracious, autodidactic reading. Once in Iran, she was the one who signed the whole family up for every company-sponsored field trip, taking us all over the country to see how Alexander the Great laid waste to Persian King Darius' ancient capital, Persepolis, or how Muslims worshiped in the mosques of Shiraz.

Mom always seemed almost embarrassed by how smart she was, and later in life, both of my parents seemed uncomfortable with some of the privileges Dad's job had afforded them. We enjoyed the perks that came with overseas contracting, like company-provided tuition at prep schools in Hawaii and Guam and great international schools in Iran. Briefly, until Dad left the job, I even had the chance to go to boarding school when Dad worked in Saudi Arabia. (The Gulf kingdom doesn't allow American kids to attend high school there as their tendency toward trouble with drugs and alcohol and the like is a recipe to land them in Saudi jails. Or so it was explained to us at the time.)

MeiLee, five years my junior, is probably the stronger of us two girls. She's certainly the better writer, although she's currently hiding that with excuses of childcare for her three young kids.

MeiLee says that I, in the esteemed role as her "older sister," was a pain in the ass (holding up the proud traditions of older sisters everywhere). I started out as the golden daughter Mom had wanted so badly after almost two decades of raising four boys. Mom painted my baby room pink way before she had any idea what I was. It's a good thing I was a girl.

I responded to the lavish attention by becoming the family loudmouth, dominating every conversation and being doted on in return. When MeiLee joined us, she realized—probably even before she learned to speak English—that I would take and hold the floor at the dinner table with no mercy, using the volume of words and sound to drown all else out. So she let me conquer the discussion with a roll of her eyes. "Here she goes again . . . "

I can't blame her permanent state of annoyance when I consider how our relationship started out—somewhat painfully. The U.S. Navy was evacuating boatloads of Vietnamese refugees to Guam toward the end of the Vietnam War. They were being held at a refugee camp near Agana, where we lived. So at the end of almost every workday, my dad drove to the camp, usually with a bunch of construction workers and spare supplies in the back of his pickup truck. He gave his best Marine salute to the guards, and they didn't dare stop him. He says they probably thought with his short haircut and tan clothes that he was a retired general—that's what he was counting on. So he'd sneak on base and drive around the camp to see what needed to be built: latrines, when he found out refugees had to walk up to a mile to the camp's only bathrooms, or sun shelters for baby pools for mothers to cool off their kids in the sweltering 100-degree-plus heat with humidity to match.

In between construction jaunts, he and Mom visited the "lost children's tent," a pleasant 1970s euphemism for orphans. Every time they visited, Dad said this tiny little girl would run up to him and jump up with her arms outstretched for a hug. She came with the name "Nguyen Gai Thi," which MeiLee later told me translates to "Jane Doe," Nguyen being the most common Vietnamese surname, Thi the most common middle prefix for girls' names, and Gai for "girl." The only name MeiLee could remember being called by her original family in Vietnam was "Be," which means "baby" or "small" and is used to refer to little girls, usually like a prefix to a proper name. (Vietnamese now call MeiLee's daughter Gracie "Be Quynh" for "Baby Grace.") MeiLee said, "Since I was the only girl, they probably didn't even bother referring to my proper name, which is why I didn't know it." From what she remembers, she was from a small fishing village and lived with her mother and father and three brothers in a house on stilts. She remembers that she had one black dress.

At the same time, I'd been campaigning for a sister or brother, and stories from the lost children's tent fueled my campaign during my nightly dominance of the dinner table. "If I had a brother or a sister, I could . . ." I saw a new addition as my personal action Barbie or Ken doll who was capable of fashioning its own dialogue.

That explains my overeager reaction when Dad picked me up from school one day and told me my new little sister was waiting inside the house. I bounded up the path to the concrete cracker box we called home. All the subdivisions were characterless and boxlike with louvered shutters at every window to withstand hurricanes.

Since I couldn't see behind it, I threw the heavy wooden door open in excitement. And I slammed all two feet of my new 3-year-old sister, who was standing behind the door, into the concrete floor. I think her head actually bounced from the smack down.

MeiLee says she doesn't remember this, but later told me, "It's worth holding over you if it makes you feel guilty."

Since that awkward beginning, my sister and I have always loved each other but have circled each other somewhat warily, expressing our affection in a distant way with hugs once a year, if we happen to see each other, and emails every six to eight weeks at best in a good year. I did once beg a diplomat at the U.S. embassy in Hanoi to search for her when she forgot to write me and my family for a nine-month stretch.

Yet despite our distance we've learned a lot about each other through observation and have dealt with our individual idiosyncrasies with merciless sarcasm. I credit MeiLee's entrance into an Ivy League university (University of Pennsylvania) to an early English essay on how I'd spend up to an hour every morning in the shower. I obviously spurred her literary creativity by humid example.

MeiLee also has a vivid imagination. She spent some of our earlier years trying to convince me that I was switched at birth through a hospital error, since I look nothing like either parent. "At least they're not lying to *me*," she'd say.

Although separated by five years (we guess since we don't know MeiLee's real birthday) and a foot in height, our voices' tone and inflection are so similar that on the phone, people often can't tell us apart. We used this to our advantage when we were younger, working the whole adopted-versus-nonadopted thing into a sister act to abuse unsuspecting strangers we'd come across. "Yes, of course, we're sisters," we'd tell a disbelieving audience at a new school or church. "Twins actually. You *have* heard about fraternal twins, haven't you? The ones that don't look like each other?"

If MeiLee dealt with open racism, she never brought it up. And as self-absorbed as I was as a kid, I never thought to ask her until much later in life. As it turns out, we both had much the same reaction in grade school, when we moved from mostly Asian Guam to mostly Anglo Hampstead, Maryland. We came home from our first day traumatized. We'd been going to school almost exclusively with Asian children. "Mom, why are there all these white people?" I exclaimed when I arrived home. You don't look in the mirror a lot when you're a kid. You become a reflection of what's around you, and I guess I thought of myself as Asian.

MeiLee later told me her outward "other" appearance didn't really become a problem until high school, when dates came few and far between. She thinks it wasn't due to race—as there were popular Asian girls in her school—but rather due to height. All her classmates rocketed taller, whereas her genetic makeup kept her well under the 5-foot mark.

After college, MeiLee moved to Vietnam to try to track down her original parents and develop some of the cultural roots Mom and Dad couldn't give her. She published her story in a Vietnamese language newspaper, and several hundred people came forward, convinced she was their long-lost daughter stolen from them as they fled the Viet Cong. She could only remember her family around her when they went to sleep on the beach, on the run from the fast-approaching troops of the Viet Cong. She remembers resisting when they tried to wake her up, then waking fully to find everyone gone, with a little boy pinching her saying, "Ha ha, your whole family left you."

She narrowed the candidates down to four sets of parents, then to two. Eventually she paid for genetics testing, but that ruled both of them out.

But she did find her own family, of sorts, meeting another expat Vietnamese American named Hahn. They have three kids at last count.

In short, I come from a bunch of people who are used to fighting their way uphill and/or making nontraditional choices along the way. When we run into walls, which we expect, we work around them. And that brings me to me.

Like MeiLee, I ended up in the odd group out during middle and high schools. An already disastrous year at Dumbarton Middle School in Maryland had ended with the publication of the school yearbook on the last day, the type you could pay $10 to publish your own ad or picture in. Some of my classmates thought I was worth the investment, and they drew a mournful picture of a hound dog with long drooping ears (as in I looked like a dog), with the caption "Mush Mouth" beneath the picture (one of my many nicknames, which I'd earned by stumbling on a word in class). I had been a favorite target because as a new kid I'd started in an academically "normal" class but was quickly moved to the "Gifted and Talented" class. I was seen as a snob by my original class, an upstart by the smart kids, and I was roundly hated by all. I feared walking through the hallways some mornings, and I hated lunchtime because I had to stand captive in the lines, listening to my tormentors come up with new names for me.

When Dad's company offered to pay for a boarding school, I begged to go. At a prep school called St. Timothy's in Maryland, I was again one of the odd ones out with none of the financial resources to match my peers. But I thrived within its protected confines, where workaholics like me did well with so many opportunities to win adult praise to make up for the lack of my peers' respect.

The school's headmaster, Charles Lord, pushed me to consider universities my mom thought were above us socially and financially. In the end my dad helped me face off with my mom, and I chose Wellesley College, which had offered me fantastic financial aid and grants. From then on Wellesley always came through for me. When it became clear that rising tuition costs meant my family couldn't pay for me to graduate, the dean allowed me to double my courses and graduate in three years.

Some people trying to "find themselves" in college do drugs or alcohol. I did human rights and hair. I coped with my social misfit status by turning punk (or rather pretend punk since I actually bathed regularly). I cobbled together ridiculous outfits from Student Aid's donated alumnae clothing, combining pink-and-green golf skirts with combat boots and a black leather jacket, topping it off with dime-store hair dye in red, purple, or pink.

Academically I was torn between my loves: human rights and the news business. I joined the Latin American activist group and spent a summer as an intern, working for the United Nations-funded Human Rights Internet (HRI). This was before the web. HRI tracked every human rights group on the planet and served as a library for their reports. One summer I found myself using my Spanish skills to translate Latin American torture documents—torture done by regimes that were supported by the Reagan administration. I started joining marches and protest rallies and surely got myself onto some FBI watch lists (or so I rebelliously hoped, as one did at that age).

I finally left that political activist stage for three reasons. First, I found that petty, personal politics drive many nonprofits. Whom you knew often determined whether your human rights report received funding or saw the light of day. (Which isn't to say the news business doesn't work that way sometimes.)

Second, I found that human rights activists spend a lot of time trying to get the attention of major media to get their report picked up by *The New York Times, Newsweek,* or better yet national TV. I decided I might as well be the one putting it on the air instead of begging someone else to do so.

The third reason I left human rights activism was because I couldn't find protestors with a similar patriotic bent. I was in the midst of organizing a march when some of my fellow rabble-rousers announced they wouldn't march under an American flag. I balked. "If not for that flag, we wouldn't be able to march," I said. They stood fast, so I left.

In between school work, protesting, and hair dyeing, I worked three jobs, including cleaning houses and ironing—I still hate ironing.

Socially I was my usual intense, moping self, a bane for my more socially adjusted, long-suffering roommate, Robin Burgess (then Tobins). Not only did she have to dye my hair, she also had to teach me my name. In typical dramatic, college student fashion, I decided to leave my past behind by changing my name and going by my middle name, Garrington, which to my disappointment people shortened to the masculine-sounding Gari. The problem was that I didn't always remember to answer to it, which drove Robin to distraction and to her calling me by my real first name, which drove *me* to distraction.

The whole punk nonsense and the use of my middle name burned away with a trip to Israel my final year of college. I traveled to Israel because I needed extra credit, and my mom had noticed that Wellesley had a three-week winter session in Jerusalem, the land where Judaism and Christianity were born and Islam intersected with its third holiest shrine.

I was a Latin American specialist who planned a career working in human rights in El Salvador, Guatemala, or Nicaragua. I had no interest in the Middle East or the Gulf, but I figured I could capture a much-needed academic credit and finally silence Mom's campaign to get me to the Holy Land.

After three intense weeks there listening to Israeli and Palestinian scholars, diplomats, journalists, and laypeople on the street battle over everything from whether they could sell ham sandwiches to where Christ was born, I was won over. I came back to Wellesley with one clear thought: My home was destined to be the Middle East.

Everything I did from then on was all about getting there: a professional journey that ended up taking almost two decades.

That's something no one knew as they watched my stretcher travel from Landstuhl to Bethesda. They thought I was coming home. In my mind, I was *leaving* home.

So I knew that first I had to get well. Then I would fight to get back.

CHAPTER 9

we can rebuild her

During my first two weeks at Bethesda Naval Hospital, I had a team of surgeons working to reconstruct me and everyone else on that ward. They met every day and went through every case, patient by patient, then briefed each of us and our families, usually separately.

The scope of what they proposed and the number of surgeries I'd need to repair the damage was mind-numbing. They outlined it only loosely at first: It would take several more procedures to clean out the dead flesh from the burned parts of my legs and then seal over the tissue that survived with skin grafts.

My surgical team, headed by Dr. Dunne, also included reconstructive plastic surgeon Dr. Anand Kumar, orthopedic surgeon Dr. Francis McGuigan, and residents-in-charge of Iraq patients Dr. Chris Burns and Dr. Christy Quietmeyer, with the frequent ministrations of anesthesiologist Dr. Carlton Brown. Those are just some of the dozen or so people who were on the team.

I had sustained so much damage to my right leg's quadriceps, the four muscles that cover the femur, that Dr. Kumar had to figure out how to complete a "flap," meaning he had to move the muscle around and sew it together to cover the exposed bone. The combined muscles would also hopefully give me enough functioning muscle to be able to walk again.

"That was my problem child," Dr. Kumar later told me. He kept his fears to himself at the time, but he wasn't sure quite how he and the team of surgeons working on me were going to close the gaping

1×½-foot patch of raw, shredded muscle on my right thigh with all the skin burned away. But he'd had lots of practice figuring out how to piece this kind of puzzle back together again. He had more than 70 flap cases in the hospital when I was there.

Once the doctors stitched the muscle together, they harvested healthy skin in large strips from other parts of my body, using something that essentially looks like a potato grater. They grated off a ½-foot-wide×1-foot-long strip from an undamaged part of my upper left thigh and the other strips off my back, starting just under either shoulder bone and scraping down in two wide stripes to the middle of my backside. These donor sites then had to heal, regrowing from a single thickness of skin back to normal. Essentially a donor site is just like a burn in that the top few layers of skin have been removed. As I discovered, those areas introduced me to brand-new, scream-worthy pain. And unlike bone and muscle pain, narcotics don't numb or lessen the agony in any way. Nothing does.

Before the doctors could even get to the harvesting-skin-and-closing operation, I had two weeks of painful preparatory procedures, including more of the jet-powered water washouts, which were still hurting my mom more than they were hurting me. At least the doctors were giving me painkillers for them.

I wanted to know all the details of what lay ahead, and I quizzed Dr. Dunne mercilessly. He was neither surprised nor offended by my newfound obsession with medical minutiae. As I mentioned, he later told me I wasn't alone. It was normal for all the injured to want to know every detail. The doctors considered it part of the healing process, a way to take back control of one's life, even if it's only the illusion of control. Just like the button I could press on my pain pump, the important part was making me feel like I was taking part in my own care, not just a helpless body on a slab waiting for the next procedure.

Also there was often a choice to be made, with risks for each possible procedure. The doctors couldn't make those choices for me or the injured troops. I soon found that out in my battle against the Acinetobacter infection and then during the healing of my donor sites.

To help me make some of those tougher choices, my family turned into a team of amateur medical sleuths, researching every potential procedure on the web. My mom and dad would report the latest to Mike and Sherry, who'd returned to their home in Nashville. Pete would pound away on his laptop. Dr. Dunne would brief us; my family would research and come back with question after question.

All the medical information—the pros, the cons, the possible risks— also gave me something to turn over in my head, helping push aside the nightmares of Paul and James and memories of the blast.

And, of course, it gave me something to think about other than the ever-present pain, which continued despite a switch from morphine, which we suspected had contributed to my hallucinations, lack of appetite, and nausea, to IV Dilaudid. Dilaudid is technically a far more potent drug, but in my case it produced fewer negative side effects.

The doctors gave me a bolus or two in advance of the dressing changes, and that helped numb the feeling and lessen my anxiety, but it still didn't completely block out the pain. The surgeons were even more thorough (brutal?) than the nurses since they wanted to get as much of the dead tissue out as possible during each dressing change in advance of the closing operation.

My family, meanwhile, quickly settled into a pattern. Mom and Dad would arrive early enough to get to my room for breakfast. They'd walk from Fisher House, where they stayed for about a month. Mom's knees and hips (both of which needed to be replaced but never were) would give out as she leaned on a cane next to my bed. She would hold out until she was at a grimace level of pain and then retreat to the nearby waiting room. Then she'd trade the pain of her legs for the torture of wondering how long my treatment would last, and she'd stew over either what sort of night I'd had or what sort of procedure I faced that day. She'd wait for Dad to return so they could develop a plan of attack: complain to the doctors, question the nurses, thank the corpsmen, etc.

Dad would stay behind and try to convince me to eat. He would reheat the oatmeal on the tray and try to coax me to take a bite or two, and he'd bustle down the long hall and back with cups of ice and cranberry juice, babying me like I was a helpless infant all over again.

If I asked how his knees were holding up (both had been replaced), he'd always say something upbeat, such as how wonderfully they were doing because of the stretch he'd given them by walking back and forth from Fisher House to the hospital. His knees must have been killing him, but he'd never tell me that. I didn't press him on it or try to tell him not to stand so long. I knew he wouldn't listen.

Now I was aware enough to be able to see the toll this was taking on them to see their daughter like that. Then again, even bleary in my hospital bed, I could see that my elderly mom and dad were energized by being so desperately needed. They relished the role of being full-time parents again to one of their hyperindependent daughters. A trauma expert later explained to me that this was common. The parents revert to caring for their child as if the child were the age he or she had been before leaving home. Essentially I was 18 again in their eyes, and they were in charge.

I did desperately need their help. I also found it less humiliating to ask a family member to reach, fetch, or hand me something than to ask the nurses and corpsmen. I tried to put everything within arm's reach, Velcroing pouches of supplies to the rails all around my bed. But there was always something I couldn't do for myself.

When I asked Dad and Pete for something, they jumped to it. It took my going through my mother's illness a year later to understand why. When you feel powerless to save your loved one from whatever ails him or her, you look for any task to make you feel like you're having some effect. Get a cup of water. Buy a balloon. Get another blanket. Each chore becomes a small victory over the helplessness you feel seeing someone you love crushed like that.

So Dad would help feed me breakfast, and later he'd stay by my side during my morning physiotherapy.

Pete would arrive at midday and take over for Dad, who would either sit with my mom or take up his station in a chair outside my room, recovering from sweating all morning from wearing the hot paper isolation gown and gloves.

Pete's self-appointed tasks included ferrying in the flowers and covering the walls with cards that had started to arrive. He spent his mornings running around trying to find anything he thought would help, navigating a city he'd never visited before with a map and a handheld hiker's GPS. His first purchases included a CamelBak canteen to fill with water and clip to my bed so I'd never go thirsty and a large wall calendar. He'd mark off each day so that when I woke disoriented in the fluorescent light-filled hospital room I'd know what day it was.

Then there were the endless forays in search of decent food, under orders from one of my doctors. The perpetually energetic redhead (and it turns out former Navy Seal), Dr. Burns had been blunt the day after I'd arrived. "The food here sucks. You won't eat it. If you want to get better, your family must bring you food from the outside world." Pete welcomed the mission.

My other saviors were the nurses and, most of all, the corpsmen. They did three to four days of 12-hour shifts straight, shifts that always seemed to stretch to 13 or 14 hours. And they'd come in on their days off just to chat. Corpsmen Nicole Shaw and Shonda Waulk included me in their Slurpee mercy mission, bringing in 12 or 15 of the drinks and handing them out to "their guys." Slurpees were a revelation for us, something I could actually stomach in large amounts. Pete had a new mission: find fruit-and-protein smoothies. Again the corpsmen came to our aid, MapQuesting the nearest shops.

When I'd fall asleep, Pete would set up what the hospital staff called the Kiwi Guard Tower outside my room, and no one could enter, not a surgeon, a researcher, or a single visitor. Sleep is the most rare and precious commodity of all in a hospital, and he didn't care whom he offended to make sure I got some. My last vitals check of the night was around midnight. The next was four hours later, with a corpsman trying to ease a pressure cuff on and wake me up just enough to get a thermometer into my mouth. Then somewhere between 5 a.m. and 7 a.m., a grab bag of doctors would stop by and wake me to ask me about my pain, my symptoms, etc., so they could report to the team at their early-morning meetings.

But the hardest job for both Dad and Pete over the next few weeks was standing by me while I cried. And I was crying a lot.

Dad felt awful. His daughter was in emotional pain, and he could do nothing to stop it, except give me a hug and wait for the tears to stop. Dad ended up seeing a lot more tears than Mom because his legs held out longer than hers. He also didn't want Mom to see how much pain I was in either, so he encouraged her to sit in the waiting room, and he tried to absorb my pain on his own. And when Pete took over the afternoon shift, he got the next round of waterworks.

There were a growing number of what ifs I'd started to torture myself with. *What if I can't walk straight again? What if this takes a year?*

With everything the doctors had described, we all somehow just assumed I'd be in the hospital for four to six months. And we assumed it would be several months before I could even try to take my first step, much less walk. The constant pain and the thought of so much surgery ahead shattered any optimism I'd been able to summon.

Even the outcome seemed like nothing to look forward to. Those ground beef areas of my leg would be covered by grafts, yes, but I'd seen those before on bomb survivors in hospital burn units in Israel. They were strange, snakeskinlike dark patches of skin. I shuddered at the thought of that on my body, even as I reminded myself the doctors had to close me up with something.

Pete would just hold my hand and listen, or he'd speak softly and say, "We'll get through it." I was broken in more ways than one. In normal life my emotions were so tightly stoppered that the only way I could make myself cry was to watch *Million Dollar Baby* or see Bambi lose his mother in the forest fire. Now this once-strong woman I'd been when we'd started dating was reduced to a quivering, bawling, half-stitched-together monstrosity, who sobbed so hard that she was almost choking on her nose tube. (They were still feeding me directly to my stomach since I wasn't eating enough.)

When I later asked Pete what it was like, he said I was "fragile." The king of understatement strikes again. But he passed no judgment or ridicule.

Meanwhile, my mom was freaking out, although I never saw it. I only heard about it from family members who were present for some of her waiting room harangues. Like any mother who wants to protect her child, she didn't want to see me like this, and her anger, panic, and fear showed up in everything.

So my parents, together with Pete, asked the doctors to sugarcoat the diagnoses, to dole out what I faced with less grim honesty about the risk, or at least to dole it out a little at a time. And they tried to keep me company for as much of the day as possible to keep me from being alone with my fears.

They were also careful not to show me *their* fears. Like me, they wondered if I'd ever walk properly, if I'd ever work or be myself again.

I had no idea how hard coping with my crises must have been for my mom until the situation was reversed a year later and I was standing over my mother's hospital bed, willing her to pull out of unconsciousness after emergency ulcer surgery. During her long, slow, and to this day incomplete recovery, I was the one forced to stand helplessly and watch her fight the drugs and the depression that came when doctors or physiotherapists told her she might never get better. I got a glimpse into what she, my dad, Pete, and the rest of my family went through the year before when they stood by my bedside, holding my hand and watching me cry.

In how many rooms on that hallway was the same scene being played over and over again? I was blessed to have Pete and my family around me. Often the patients go through this hell alone, but I was my mom and dad's full-time job.

Pete had been between jobs, studying to requalify as an instrument-rated rescue chopper pilot. We hadn't seen each other much in the past year since his time was devoted to studying and job searching in New Zealand, a country that has more chopper pilots per capita than any other nation in the world. I'd supported him through that, and he said he was going to see me through this.

Another luxury military families don't have: a U.S. TV network stepping up and footing the extensive bill. CBS paid for transport and hotel rooms for Pete and my far-flung family, flying in my brothers and sister from Nashville to Ho Chi Minh City.

Amid the endless series of procedures during the first 10 days, there was also the occasional moment of surreal comic relief. Once I was being wheeled out of my hospital room, headed for pre-op downstairs, when I spotted two black-frocked priests in the hallway on Five East. That was normal. Many of the hospital's pastoral team completed regular rounds on the floor, sometimes popping their heads in to ask if I wanted to chat or wanted them to pray with me. I saw the two priests "clock" me as I wheeled past and thought nothing of it.

The corpsmen took me on the usual route down to the basement OR, a ride made more uncomfortable by the speed bumps installed on the long hallways—speed bumps apparently made necessary by earlier ranks of racing corpsmen.

They left me in the usual place, one of the pre-op surgery bays where the nurses would check my vitals and the anesthesiologist would put me to sleep when the surgeons were ready for me.

Usually there was someone around to chat with, and I'd burn through my presurgery nerves by firing 20 questions at my (often male) nurse. "Where are you from? How long have you been here? How long have you been on shift? What's your specialty? You're doing night school too? Yowch. Any time for family? You have a son? Wow, when do ever see him? Does he remember your name? How's the girlfriend handle the shifts? You gonna get married? No? Is she okay with that? Yeah, I didn't think so." etc.

This time the cavernous room was strangely empty. I was suffering the usual chill to the core from pre-op nervousness and the frigid temperature since the basement operating area is kept arctic to keep the germs down.

The door of pre-op opened and I thought, *Relief, some company.* In walked the two priests who had been upstairs. They walked straight over to my gurney, and the inquisition began.

"Who are you?" barked one of them, obviously the senior of the two. "Why are you here?"

It wasn't the bedside manner I'd expected. Taken aback, I kept it basic. "I'm waiting for my doctors."

That wasn't the answer for which he'd hoped. Before my very eyes the priest walked over and started thumbing through the medical charts until he found mine. He opened it up and said, "Oh, Kim-ber-ly Do-zee-er. You're a civilian."

I was a pretty bemused civilian at that moment. I replied, "Yes, I'm a journalist."

I thought my monosyllabic answers and polite brevity would give the two priests a hint, but not so. I should have told him to bug off, but I found it hard to be rude to a man of the cloth.

They questioned me further. "How were you injured?"

Here we go, I thought.

"A car bomb. I was with a U.S. patrol. It was Memorial Day."

A light dawned. "Oh, fantastic, you're the famous one!" exclaimed the second priest, who had a heavy Eastern European accent. He went on, all excited, "I go home to Lithuania tomorrow! I will tell everyone in all my congregations about you!"

Never mind that he hadn't asked permission, or even asked if I wanted spiritual counseling, for that matter, and never mind that meetings with priests and other such counselors are supposed to be kept confidential.

I was dimly aware in the background that another patient had been wheeled in. Working on him was one member of my surgical team, Dr. Brown. He must have caught the tail end of the priestly inquisition because he came to my rescue, which he did a lot in pre-op. He bustled around my gurney until the two priests got the message and went away.

Ironically Dr. Brown was both in charge of the thing I most feared—anesthesia—and the best at dispelling my pre-op fears. He usually got me babbling about journalism. He and his wife are good friends with *The Washington Post*'s Mideast correspondent, Pamela Constable, and he'd also dated a girl who had gone to my alma mater, St. Timothy's.

Before most surgeries Dr. Brown distracted me by telling me yet another story of his youth, when it seems he dated a lot of different, very high-powered young women. "So this one woman I was seeing . . . her dad went on to head the Navy. . . . If only I'd known, my whole Naval career could have turned out differently," he'd chuckle. Somewhere in the babble, he'd quietly put me under.

When I came to after this particular day's procedure, I was freezing as usual. I was about to have my second surreal experience of the day, but first I had to warm up. Patients aren't released from the arctic OR basement area until they return to normal temperature. It always seemed a little counterintuitive to me since the OR's chilled air meant it would take up to an hour to get back to normal temperature, even with the heated bear blankets that were wrapped around me. I always pleaded with my nurses to let me go upstairs where it was warm.

When my temperature finally reached normal, two corpsmen came to take me back upstairs. I'd been chatting with one of the nurses about what our respective partners had to put up with—his girlfriend had to put up with his long, crazy shifts in the OR, and Pete had to deal with my injuries (and before that, my long, crazy shifts in Iraq).

As we passed the OR waiting room, a bald man wearing glasses sprang to his feet and peered at my gurney. "Is that your boyfriend?" one of the corpsmen asked.

"Nope, not from my family," I replied, peering at him from under my baseball cap, which I always wore to surgery to keep myself warm (and to cover my patchy hair).

As we pushed through the outer swinging doors, however, the bald man stalked my gurney and materialized next to me, peering into my face.

"How are you?" he asked.

"Fine," I said, made reticent by my earlier double-priest experience. He kept staring.

"Who are you?" I finally asked.

"What?" he yelped. "I'm your husband!"

With that, he turned to one of the corpsmen and commanded, "Let me see her chart!"

Both young men got a "What the hell?" look on their faces. "Sorry, sir, we can't do that," they said and rushed my gurney down the hall into the waiting elevator.

As the elevator doors closed, I distinctly remember one of us humming the theme to the *Twilight Zone*.

The final closing operation on June 12 lasted for more than 11 hours and involved a team of surgeons, headed by Dr. Dunne. Dr. Kumar was in charge of harvesting skin off my back and the top of my undamaged left leg and moving it around my body to cover the exposed muscle and fascia, where the skin had been burned away. He covered the exposed areas with a dressing called Biobrain, which was supposed to mimic skin, protecting the damaged layers underneath until they could regenerate. The Biobrain dressing failed for some reason, but that was a week or so later.

The good news was that almost all the open areas on my legs had either been covered by the donor skin or Dr. Kumar had been able to take the edges of the skin on either side of a burn and simply pull them together, stitching them into place. He later explained, "It was great! Because your legs were . . ." and he hesitated.

"Chunky," I'd replied? I'd been about 5 to 8 pounds over my optimum weight just before the bombing. It turned out to be a blessing.

"Yeah, you said it. I didn't!" Dr. Kumar replied gleefully. "Because your legs had been chunky and then you lost all that weight in the three weeks before the final closing surgery, I had lots of loose skin to work with. It was great!"

Gee, I thought, *saved by cellulite—pass the Ben and Jerry's.*

There was one small problem: After 2,000-plus stitches and 11 hours of surgery, they'd run out of the donor skin they'd harvested from my leg and back. Dr. Kumar didn't want to go back and harvest any more at that point since I'd been under for several hours and since he was about to fall over from exhaustion. So he left one fist-size patch open on my upper right leg.

Dr. Kumar didn't break this to me until a week later, by which time my first donor sites were starting to burn because the dressing on them had failed. So when he asked to put me under again and harvest some more skin to cover that spot, I replied, "Hell, no."

The area finally healed, but it took almost four months. It shrank slowly and painfully, requiring visits from a wound nurse every couple of days. It's now a tightly gathered knot of tissue that shows the strains of having to close over such a large gap. Along with the other scars, I massaged it for months to work some give into it, but the area nevertheless unzipped along the stitch line twice a few months later when I pushed my knee-bending exercises too hard and too fast. I butted heads with Dr. Kumar on a couple other issues later on, and I think I made the right choice overruling him, but in this instance I wish I'd heeded his advice.

CHAPTER 10
body battles

The emotional pain that continued to haunt me was not the only thing attacking my blast- and surgery-weakened body, but I wouldn't find that out until the lab results came back a few days after my June 12 "closing" surgery.

At first we thought everything had gone well with my surgery and that my only job ahead was to heal. I would start physiotherapy as soon as the grafts were more firmly established. My legs were covered with strange gray sponge bandages that were attached to tubes and a vacuum pump. The bandages gently suctioned away clear fluid that my healing grafts were producing. I assume it was lymph fluid and sometimes blood. Whatever that stuff coming out of my body was, just looking at the bandages and their various suctioning appendages made my stomach turn.

The suction pressure of the bandages hurt, but according to my plastic surgeon, it was nothing like it used to be. "We used to have to change the dressings on grafts a couple times a day," Dr. Kumar enthused. "You used to be able to hear us coming down the hall by the screams of the patients we treated. That's no more since these babies came along." The bandages cost tens of thousands of dollars apiece to rent, since much of the device is reusable. The company that makes the bandages doesn't sell them or, at least, didn't at that time. I had at least four on me, and considering Dr. Kumar's description of the earlier process, these were worth every penny. But they were still stomach-turning.

"That isn't me," I shuddered. In between prayers and trying to meditate, I tried to concentrate on something Pete's dad shared from the Buddhist tradition. "Tell her she's not her body," he said.

I tried to fixate on that, but with every ache or stab of pain, my body brought me back to the physical realm with a screaming vengeance.

Meanwhile, my family was in the next room receiving bad news. The lab results taken during the big closing operation had come back positive for *Acinetobacter baumannii*. We knew the bug was on the surface of my skin, hence the isolation procedures doctors had already put in place, but this meant the bug was populating inside my body. The doctors had tested my wounds, especially near the titanium rods in my legs, and found that the bacteria had dug in deeply.

So I joined the roughly 10 percent of U.S. troops who came back infected with what we called Iraqi-bacter, although the bacteria exist worldwide. (The current literature says it has a 10 percent prevalence, but almost every military patient I've met so far mentions having to fight it too.)

There's debate over where the infection comes from. Initially doctors thought it came from the Iraqi soil and was blown into troops' wounds by blasts. But recent research at the Army's National Trauma Institute in San Antonio indicates the bug became virulent by being exposed to antibiotics in combat hospitals and spread from there to patients. Adding weight to that theory: Researchers found the strain all over medical equipment from some key combat hospitals and traced the infection back to a contaminated batch of equipment from a European military facility. That's convinced some military researchers that we created this bacteria-resistant strain ourselves by exposing it to antibiotics in those combat facilities, unwittingly training it to be stronger, the same way the superbugs staphylococcus and streptococcus evolved.

However Acinetobacter developed, it's potentially fatal for people whose immune systems have taken a major beating, like mine. It can populate the organs and lead to shutdown. Only a handful of antibiotics treat the bacteria, and the side effects are severe.

"We're between a rock and a hard place," Dr. Dunne told my assembled family members. He explained that the bacteria had to be treated but that the best medicine available had a nasty side effect: It could destroy my kidneys.

Given my recent bouts of uncontrollable tears, my family asked him to break it to me more gently than he had to them. He nodded sympathetically but then walked into my room alone and gave it to me straight, including the "rock and hard place" quote. Dr. Dunne wouldn't coddle me, which I appreciated.

I absorbed the news: My body was in for another battle.

He explained that the Iraqi strain of Acinetobacter only responds to one type of antibiotic: colistin. "It's like pouring chlorine into your system," one of the doctors later told me.

My other options were few, including the drug imipenem, which carries a risk of seizure, and Amikacin, which had limited success against some of the bacteria strains and doesn't work on bone infections, where doctors suspected my case might have been hiding.

Colistin was my best bet. Every day, my blood would be tested to see whether my kidneys were hanging in there. If the kidneys started failing, Dr. Dunne explained, the only other option was to halt the drug, let the kidney tissue grow back, and then try one of the other less-effective antibiotics.

My family went into overdrive trying to research the bacteria to convince themselves there was no other way. Months later, when I asked what they'd found, Pete handed me a thick folder he'd collected of medical research papers from his colleagues in the United States, London, Israel, and New Zealand.

As it turns out, Acinetobacter had been a problem as far back as the Vietnam War and was the second-most-prevalent infection. It hadn't appeared among U.S. casualties in Iraq until Operation Iraqi Freedom, and the new cases were proving much harder to treat than the old versions.

When the first cases started appearing in the beginning of the Iraqi invasion, doctors tried everything before dusting off some old bottles of colistin, which was one of the granddaddies of antibiotics and had long been abandoned because of its kidney-failure consequences.

To me the choice was fairly clear: Take the drug and gamble that it was going to work.

That meant a new addition to the rack next to my bed: a clear bag of colistin next to the saline solution, pain medicine, and a few other tubes. What was worse, this new confirmation that I had Acinetobacter meant the precautionary gowns and gloves stayed. People couldn't touch me unless they were swathed in latex and disposable crepe paper lab coats. It wasn't to protect me from them but to protect all the other patients along the hall from cross-contamination (even though most of them were infected too). I hated that part. People tend not to give you a hug when they've been told you're carrying multidrug-resistant bacteria that can prove fatal to the immune-challenged. Only Pete regularly broke the psychological barrier the gowns presented by insisting on hugging me hello and goodbye—clumsy gown and all.

The corpsmen were best at following and enforcing the isolation rules, as a team of infectious disease specialists had laid out. The worst were the trauma surgeons. One leading surgeon, who shall remain nameless, actually poked around some of my exposed wounds wearing neither gloves nor gown, and a visibly dirty white lab coat. Then he walked down the hall to see someone else. I was stunned.

When one of the hall's most experienced corpsmen, Leon Garland, walked into the room, I asked what to do the next time that happened. He said, "You give the surgeon my name and my rank, and you tell him that *my* commanding officer demands that anyone entering this room glove and gown up. I don't care what your rank is. That's what you'll do on my ward." For emphasis he added, "If you don't do that, you could contaminate another patient, and he or she could die."

My resolve thus fortified, I became a glove-and-gown enforcer, demanding that entire groups of visiting doctors cover up and refusing to shake outstretched hands until they gloved. Some were amused to be issued orders from the hospital bed. Others applauded.

I've found it's a divisive issue for medical teams. One doctor griped to me that the attitude among some of the Bethesda Naval Hospital staff was so lax that he believed it had caused the cross-contamination of "Iraqi-bacter," between military and civilian hospitals. He said the Iraqi strain of Acinetobacter had shown up in nearby Maryland and Virginia institutions among the civilian population—people who'd never been anywhere near the Middle East, or Europe for that matter. The only common factor was the surgical staff doing rounds both at Bethesda Naval Hospital and the other hospitals.

He told me that at a staff meeting, he suggested that all Bethesda medical personnel get tested for Acinetobacter. The response from the doctors assembled, he said, was ferocious and near unanimous: No way.

It's easy to see why. They'd have to take infectious disease precautions for every surgery they performed, and with every patient they saw, from then on as most medical institutions have a "once positive, always positive" presumption. The same applies to patients. The institution forever presumes a patient infected. Even after I tested clear, I have to be treated as contaminated in all future surgeries for all time.

History aside, I had my own battles to fight with the bug. Two weeks into treatment the blood tests start showing telltale signs of renal failure. My kidneys weren't going to last for the six-week course of treatment. That's when the debates began.

Dr. Dunne asked the nephrology department to join the team and add their wisdom to the mix. My mom and dad happened to be in the room when a young doctor from the department stopped by to deliver the kidney specialists' pronouncement. We listened, stunned, as he gave his stark assessment, his bedside manner nil: I had no choice but to stay on the colistin to defeat Acinetobacter, even though it was obvious my kidneys couldn't go the distance.

"We'll just sign you up for dialysis and put you on the list for donor kidneys," he concluded matter-of-factly.

I sat in shock, wondering if I'd keep my legs but lose my kidneys.

Immediately we reached out to Dr. Dunne for a second opinion. When he heard about my morning nephrologist's visit, Dr. Dunne wasn't pleased. As it turns out the young doctor hadn't yet shared his grim assessment with my medical team. And he apparently received an earful later about protocol, something along the lines of "Don't scare a patient like that without consulting her team first, and don't issue ultimatums."

Dr. Dunne told us that giving up on my kidneys wasn't my only option. He'd planned to consult with a number of doctors on the subject, including the infectious disease team, at a meeting later that day.

So I was surprised when the young nephrologist returned to my room a bit later, this time with some backup. He'd brought the head of his department, who was apparently upset that one of his team had been dressed down by my trauma surgeon and even more upset that I wasn't automatically following his recommended course of treatment. The doctors stood at the foot of my bed, angrily insisting that I had no option but to continue colistin until renal failure and beyond.

At this point my main reaction was bemusement. I hadn't witnessed a surgical pecking order face-off before. Apparently my main team was led by the surgical hotshots, whereas the nephrology doctors were behaving like the chip-on-the-shoulder B team. To me, it closely resembled kids duking it out in a sandlot. So I thought, *Why not put them in the same sandlot?*

"Well, now I'm getting two different points of view," I said. "Why don't you go join the big meeting with all the specialists discussing my case. It's at 1:30 p.m. downstairs."

"We're not invited to that," the chief nephrologist snapped at me. "They don't talk to us down there."

"Well, I'm inviting you," I said, not quite believing we were having this conversation. "Go share your opinions with all the other doctors discussing my case so together you can battle out the options." In other words, I told him to stop bullying me and talk to my team. He refused and they stomped out.

I never saw any of the nephrologists again.

In the end Dr. Dunne's team advised me to let my body fight it out, so that's the option I chose. He took me off colistin, monitored my white blood cell count, and hoped for the best. If my white blood cells went up, that would mean Acinetobacter was still floating around my system.

The gamble paid off. After two weeks my kidneys slowly repaired themselves and came back online, and my white blood cell count returned to normal. That initial two weeks on colistin had apparently been enough to kill the bug. If there was any Iraqi-bacter in my system, it was dormant. The doctors warned me that the bacteria could come back in a month, a year, or 10 years. The key was to stay healthy and hope for the best.

Months later, when I was on my own recuperating in New Zealand, I had a scare when my right leg turned red and my temperature soared for two straight days to 103 or 104 degrees. I tried to ignore it, and there was no one around to tell me otherwise. Pete was back at work in the Middle East, so I was on my own in his house. Finally it hit my fever-addled brain that this could be Acinetobacter. I panicked and thought, *I could lose my leg*. So weak I could barely stand, I called a friend and said, "Get me to the ER."

The New Zealand doctors had seen a few cases of Acinetobacter before, so they put me through a battery of tests, but also immediately put me on massive IV doses of a type of penicillin. My body promptly reacted and my temperature dropped within hours. I was told the good news: It can't be Acinetobacter, or you wouldn't be sitting up drinking tea right now.

But they warned me to never let an infection get that far again. I discovered that I couldn't ignore illness as I'd always done, just pushing through until it went away (as everyone in my family does or tries to). My body isn't up to that—at least it wasn't within the first year.

As I'd focused on the bacteria wars, my grafts had been healing—well enough to take off the vacuum bandages and start physiotherapy. Even as Dr. Dunne said the word "physiotherapy," I looked at him like he was nuts. That meant moving, and I thought my legs were too damaged to do much of that yet.

Not so. Doctors have found that the best way to ensure a patient gets back at least some of what he or she used to have is aggressive therapy as soon as the body can handle it.

The first item of business for my physiotherapist, Lt. Com. Carol Petrie—henceforth known as "Carol"—was to get my knees to bend. They'd been in one position for so long that the muscles and joints had atrophied, and movement was blocked by all the scar tissue that had formed where the surgeons had pounded titanium rods through my knees into both femurs.

And there was another wrinkle: heterotopic ossification. Put more simply: My bone was responding to the injury by healing like mad and sprouting rogue bits of bone that were sending sharp fingers into the soft tissue of my right and left upper thighs. My doctors feared it might also be growing near my knee joints, where the titanium rods had been driven through into my broken femurs. Carol and I had to work to break those strands of bone before they thickened and fused my knee into immobility.

When Carol took the first measurement on my legs with a protractor-like instrument called a goniometer, my left knee bent just 50 degrees and my right knee bent only 32 degrees. That was June 19, 2006.

My chief orthopedic surgeon, Dr. McGuigan, put it to me starkly: Get my knees bending past 50 degrees in two weeks, or he and his team would have to put me under, break the rogue bone, and tear the scar tissue, forcing the joint to bend. It would be painful and damage the muscle, but keep the knees from fusing.

With that threat hanging over our heads, we started working on my knees as savagely as possible, or rather Carol did. I could barely hold them up, so she'd hold my leg in the air, one knee folded over one arm, take hold of the ankle, and start bending. Blonde and around 6 feet tall, Carol looked a bit like tennis champ Chris Evert with killer arms, sculpted by lifting broken people like me all day. I didn't understand how strong she was until she asked Pete to hold my leg for a moment, and he started flagging after a couple minutes, sweat breaking out across his forehead.

The only way I got through the early sessions was with double or triple doses of painkillers. Still I fought back tears and gritted my teeth, trying to muffle my screams.

My dad was there for almost every session. He'd had both knees replaced and had one operated on seven times because of complications. He'd had to do exactly what I was doing over and over again. So he knew exactly what kind of pain I was in and exactly how necessary it was if I was ever to walk normally again.

Outside the room my mom complained that this was too much too fast, and my dad would agree. But next to me he'd simply hold my hand and carefully record every degree of movement I gained.

Dr. McGuigan would stop by himself and take up to an hour out of his rounds to help force my knees to bend. Some doctors were doubtlessly annoyed by my chatty manner, but Dr. McGuigan made it work for him. As he bent the knee farther than I thought possible, he distracted me with stories of things like backpacking through Northern Ireland before he went to med school and accidentally tangling with the Royal Ulster Constabulary. (He tried to take a picture of an RUC police station, not realizing that's what the IRA does when they're casing a joint for an attack. The RUC was not impressed.) I was so riveted that I barely noticed the pain.

Dr. McGuigan soon realized that he had a kindred spirit in Carol Petrie. She was going to push me relentlessly, so he let her take over with his blessing, especially after we surpassed his prescribed 50-degree mark a week before Dr. McGuigan's deadline. According to my dad's notes, on June 27 my right leg bent to 55 degrees, my left to 76 degrees.

Physiotherapy was the most painful part of my day but also the part to which I most looked forward. It felt like I was actually accomplishing something. Seven days a week, sometimes two hours a day, Carol worked on my knees, willing them, and often forcing them, to bend. Carol's family was a plane ride away in the Connecticut area. With her 24/7 schedule working with injured troops, she only saw her husband and kids about once a month. The rest of the time she worked through holidays and weekends visiting her patients. She always said for those who pushed and worked their guts out, it was worth it—standards I sometimes met and kicked myself when I didn't.

Every session ended with an attempt at changing my worldview from horizontal to vertical, or at least semi-standing. I had been lying down for so long that the first time she told me I'd be getting out of bed and standing with a walker, I scoffed.

She helped me to the edge of the bed. Actually it took several people to do that, including one to catch me in case I fell forward as I slid my feet to the floor.

It felt as if the world tilted. The blood drained out of my face instantly, and I broke out into a cold sweat. I stood for about 10 seconds (we counted), and then I spent the rest of the day recovering.

Simply put, my heart had grown accustomed to pumping the blood only around my body at rest. All of a sudden it had to work twice as hard to get the blood from my legs to my head.

Each day Carol pushed me a little further. She helped me to go from leaning on a walker to taking two steps with the walker to five steps the next day before letting me collapse into a wheelchair. I'd have to sit and recover from all the effort, getting over the wooziness by sipping the ever-present hospital ginger ale (something I only crave when I'm ill, like I'm 11 staying home from school again with the flu).

Before I could leave my room, I had to put on a new gown and sanitize my hands to keep the world at large from catching the dreaded Acinetobacter, and I'd cover my legs, trying to save other patients' loved ones from the sight of my healing grafts and all the tubes attached to me. This was my little ritual of trying to make myself look normal in a place where absolutely no one expected me to look so, and besides, no one was looking.

I also had to wrap myself up against the cold. With all the drugs I was on and all the operations my body had been through, my internal thermostat functioned erratically at best. One minute I was so cold that I literally shook and my hands turned blue. The next moment I was boiling with my temperature spiking so high that the nurses had to give me ice packs for the back of my neck. (Early on, one of the nurses suggested my family bring me a fan to help. She called the fan the nurses' best friend for temperature control.)

So there I'd be, rolling down the hall, pushed by Pete or my dad, with a baseball cap and a sweatshirt on over the hospital gown, a quilt over my legs, and brightly colored fluffy socks on my feet.

This was my rare chance to get out of isolation and see other faces, even to leave the hospital doors and feel the baking outside air in the hospital's garden courtyards. I craved the sight of birds and plants and the feeling of the hot summer air without the smell of disinfectant, medicine, or an overly pungent hospital lunch cart. I always pushed myself too far, staying out until my heart ran out of the energy to pump the blood from my dangling legs to my brain. My face would go parchment, and the cold sweat would set in. To head off a full faint, my family would have to grab my legs and lift them up to help my heart move the blood until they could get me back into a full horizontal position.

Many of the soldiers, like me, were too weak to leave their rooms or stay out for long. When I saw some of the other temporary escapees, I'd force a smile and a hello. I'll never forget one young man. He was missing both legs, and his skull was misshapen. I smiled and was halfway through saying hi, when I saw that his eyes were fixed on my legs, just staring. My greeting ended in a croak. His eyes flashed up to mine, and he mumbled a hello and looked away. I felt awful. I saw in him a fellow patient. He saw in me someone blessed with four limbs, a reminder of what he'd lost.

CHAPTER 11
ambushed

With the dozen or so surgeries to close me up now over and all the progress I was making, you might think I'd feel a huge sense of relief: The danger was past, I was out of the woods, except for the healing and recovery.

Instead whenever I wasn't doing physiotherapy, I was ambushed by all the other things I'd been able to silence until then or at least muffle in my psyche.

Now I had nothing but time to think about the bombing, Paul and James, and their families. Images of them repeatedly hit me, and each time my mind said no. I didn't see their bodies at the bomb scene. I hadn't seen their funerals. For me they remained frozen in time, doing a Memorial Day shoot.

And I saw every memory through the fisheye of narcotics, intensely magnified and leavened by the multiple nerve depressants that were meant to control my physical pain. From hour to hour my emotions roller-coastered, mostly crashing down.

Mornings were the worst, when physical and emotional pain would one-two me the moment I opened my eyes. They hammered me my third and fourth weeks at Bethesda Naval Hospital. I never slept much, and the nurses and doctors interrupted my sleep periodically from 4 a.m. to 7 a.m. or so as they did their morning rounds. After their rounds I'd try to catch another hour of sleep before breakfast arrived and I stirred. I'd realize that opening my eyes meant facing the day, so I'd try to shut them and will myself back into unconsciousness.

Finally I would be forced to rise, blinking, looking around at the IVs, the tubes, and the bandages. Reality would hit, and I'd start sobbing.

The nurses and corpsmen were unfazed by my tears. I was just one of many on that hallway who had lost someone. The women corpsmen, especially, told me it was tough sometimes to walk into a room of a strapping, tattooed 6-foot Marine who was bawling his eyes out because he just woke up from a nightmare about his buddies. "You never know what to say," one told me. "When someone who looks that tough and that strong is sobbing like a baby, it breaks your heart."

Or the corpsmen would find a soldier propped up in bed with tears rolling down his face because he'd opened his eyes in the morning and locked on the stump where an arm or a leg used to be. So the corpsmen would walk into my room with my morning meds, catch sight of my tear-streaked face, and ask, "Anything I can do?"

I'd usually mutely shake my head, and they'd nod, walk out, and leave me be.

When the hearing specialist stopped by to assess the damage to my shattered eardrums, she got as far as "I'm the hearing specialist, and I . . . " Midsentence she saw my red-puffed face and stopped halfway to my bed. "And I won't be doing your hearing test today," she said with a small, sad smile. She neatly turned and walked out.

I'd try to muffle the sound since I didn't want the whole hall to know. Sometimes it didn't work. At least once, I cried so hard that the nurses heard me 10 rooms down the hall at the nurses' station, and a disembodied voice came over a loudspeaker. "Are you OK? Do you need something?"

They seldom used the room's loudspeaker, so it took me a minute to figure out where the voice was coming from. I scanned the room for the source of the voice and snapped, "What? What?" When I figured out where the voice originated and that the whole damn hall had probably heard me, I was mortified.

I pictured the nurses and corpsmen looking at each other, rolling their eyes, "Yup, the reporter lady is bawling like a small child again."

I'd think to myself things like *If Paul and James were in the next room, they'd be giving the nurses hell. Paul would definitely be yelling something in a London drawl along the lines of, "Darlin, you're five minutes late with my painkillers!"*

And then he'd surely follow with his favorite un-PC phrase, "It's because I'm black, inn'it?" Then loud bellows of laughter as his quarry would generally first look horror-stricken, then sheepish as they realized he'd been "taking the piss," as the quaint British expression goes.

The "cos I'm black" phrase was a personal trademark of Paul, the huge black man who'd married a white Englishwoman to the horror of his fiancée's family and their mutual friends. After Paul's death Linda reminisced with friends about how the couple turned that struggle into an in-house family joke, which bound them closer together.

James was the only man I knew who could keep up with and sometimes outpace Paul's rapid-fire humor. No one's ego was safe with those two in the room. James had served in the British Army and had done every odd job in between, including painting the homes of some of London's political elite. His wit always made a lasting impression. CBS News correspondent Mark Phillips put it best: "James was the man you wanted beside you in the hellholes we sometimes had to cover because he always made it better."

I kept thinking of Paul's and James' families, wondering if the wives wanted to hunt me down. *Maybe they had a right to*, I thought.

I kept trying to assure myself that it was a "safe shoot." Just two or three hours on a patrol, then back to the bureau for *The Early Show*, then see if we could turn around more of the material for the *CBS Evening News*. See the soldiers hard at work on Memorial Day, eating dust in the streets of Baghdad, while folks back home enjoyed their barbeques.

But I'd also torture myself with questions: *Did we have to go out that day? Should I have seen this coming? Did we push it too far?* And the one that no one could ever answer: *Why did this happen?*

Paul, James, and I were from the pre-Al Qaeda days of reporting. Time and again we'd taken calculated risks, and Paul made sure everyone erred on the side of caution. No one could play that "Who is braver" game with him, to goad him into doing something he'd decided against. Some had tried, calling him a coward on several different occasions in the months before his death, sometimes to his face. I called him cautious to the point of frustrating, but I learned that what Paul especially needed was information: Where's the shoot, what's the security, who knows we're going, why are we going, and will it get on the air? If he thought an assignment was too dangerous with too little planning, he'd turn it down flat.

James was the same way. When he'd questioned a Sadr City, Iraq, embed with anchor Harry Smith the week before our Memorial Day shoot, he'd quipped that he didn't need to prove he was brave to anyone. He was "fine with them calling him a coward." They didn't call him that. They just took his advice and skipped the shoot.

When Paul went on a story, he made sure everyone got out all right, even young, less-experienced radio correspondents, as I was when I tagged along with the TV crew in Pristina, Kosovo, on the first night of the NATO bombing. I'd been in Belgrade, Serbia, and my London bureau chief had forbidden me from taking the risky four-hour drive through several Serb checkpoints down to Kosovo. Then I heard that the TV crew in Pristina had asked for a generator, so I disobeyed orders and hitched a ride down with the delivery.

When I got there I found a couple hundred freaked-out journalists, all housed by Yugoslav government decree in one central hotel. You could feel the city bracing for a fight. We all develop a sixth sense when covering crowds. There's a moment when you can feel a sort of electricity pass through, and a large group of people goes from excited or tense to agitated and dangerous. That's what was happening in Pristina, a city braced for a fight.

On that first night of the bombing, as Serb paramilitaries stormed the hotel in which all the journalists stayed, Paul disarmed the invaders in his usual unconventional fashion. He'd gotten tired of waiting as we listened to the paramilitaries smashing their way through the hotel to our rooms where we were trapped on the top floor, so he stretched out in the crew room and fell asleep.

When the Serbs stormed his room, the sight of a snoring giant completely disarmed them. There's nothing more innocent-looking than a sleeping man. We were the only journalists who didn't get our camera gear smashed. The next morning Serb officials made it clear they wouldn't protect "traitorous foreign journalists" from the coming conflagration, i.e., Serb retaliation on the ground as NATO attacked from above. So along with a couple hundred other reporters, we quickly packed up. During the frantic breakdown of our hotel-room studios, the black-clad paramilitaries came back in force, filling the hotel lobby, perhaps intending to finish what they'd half-started the night before, escalating brute force, vandalism, and gunshots into the ceiling into something deadly.

When we spotted one of them throwing a Molotov cocktail into a satellite truck out front, we knew this could get ugly fast, and we needed an exit route.

While many others in the building were panicking and fleeing straight for the paramilitary-filled lobby, Paul calmly jammed one of the hotel's service elevators on our floor. We filled it in five minutes flat, he started it up again, and we went the back way out to the basement. We crammed our gear into our armored vehicle and slid out a side street to join the other journalists in a convoy to Macedonia and safety.

Paul was the same man who later captured the shot that galvanized world public opinion against what the Macedonians were doing to Kosovar refugees. Macedonians were, for the most part, pro-Serb. They spoke the same language, and many of the Macedonian elite had studied at Belgrade's finest schools. There was a fear that the influx of refugees would add to Macedonia's already burgeoning Kosovar-Albanian population and tip the political balance against those who identified themselves as ethnic Macedonians. There was also a fear, which turned out to be valid, that Kosovars would increase the drug trade in the area.

So the Macedonians were trying to make their country look as inhospitable as possible to fleeing Kosovars. When a train arrived full of Kosovar refugees, having pulled over at the infamous Blace border crossing, the Macedonian guards wouldn't let the passengers disembark at the already packed refugee camp. (Actually it wasn't so much a refugee camp as a field of mud, where Macedonians were allowing international relief agencies to provide aid but were frustrating them by not allowing most refugees to travel any farther into the country.) The train passed all of us, bound inward to Macedonia.

Paul and the team, including CBS News correspondent Allen Pizzey, hopped into their crew vehicles and chased the train. A few kilometers in (and strategically away from the press pack at the border), the Macedonian military had been deployed in force to stop the train and turn it back.

As the CBS team pulled up and jumped out, they saw the guards were using their rifles to threaten the refugees, pushing them back onto the train and chaining the doors. Paul, together with soundman Phil Sparks, captured the scene, including the shot of the train heading back to Kosovo with the men, women, and children inside screaming in fear. That picture and those sounds were reminiscent of the Holocaust—of people who were being sent to their death.

The CBS story hit Washington that night and did what the best stories are supposed to do: It represented those who couldn't speak for themselves. It changed policy overnight. U.S. officials came down hard on the Macedonians, and so did everyone else. After that, more refugees were allowed over the border, and more were allowed to transfer to refugee camps inside the country where there were better services and where the very young, the very old, and the sick had better chances of surviving than in the mud and freezing cold of the border camp at Blace.

In short, we regularly got away with doing absolutely insane things to get to the story and to get the stories out. Baghdad had been different for all of us for quite some time, though. The noose had been tightening in terms of the risks we faced every time we left the hotel even to go to a press conference. And as the danger increased, so did the apathy and general malaise back in the United States toward the entire Iraq war. Simply put, when we put the story on the air, people often changed the channel.

I'd been trying to think of different ways to tell stories we'd already told repeatedly. My editors Stateside were blunt with their eyes glazed as I tried to pitch ideas. They thought, "Not another school opening. Not another kidnapping story. Not another 'soldiers are fed up' story whether the soldiers are fed up with the war or, more often, with the media's coverage of the war." They were right. I started seeing the same stories recycled and traded from network to network. We all did the "Iraqis have become a Prozac nation, medicating themselves from their unregulated pharmacies to help them deal with the constant threat of death." And we all did the "Iraqi children are emotionally scarred for life by the war." (We got past the problem of putting the tiny subjects in danger just by filming them, by giving the children digital video cameras to record video diaries.)

There were also the stories I did once a year, every year since 2003: "U.S. soldiers sit down with Iraqi tribal chiefs to broker local government" or "U.S. forces/contractors train Iraqi police/troops/oil pipeline guards, but the training's going slowly" and finally: "U.S. troops/contractors/ aid agencies pour millions/billions into decrepit Iraqi electricity/water/ sewer/medical systems and yet still nothing works because a) the insurgents attack it; or b) the Iraqis don't maintain it once it's fixed; or c) the resources got stolen as soon as we installed them; or d) the system we chose doesn't work well in this environment."

We'd regularly take chances, going to those sites or going to aid agency or military community outreach missions. But unless we were shot at or something blew up, it was hard to get the day-to-day work the troops, the diplomats, and the Iraqis were doing on the air, simply because our audience had seen it all before.

Sometimes I'd ask myself, *Why are we going out? Is it worth it to leave the hotel today?* When conservative media critics accused us of hotel journalism, it hurt because I believed it was partly true. Three and four days would go by, sometimes even a week, with us never leaving our compound. The risk seemed too high to capture another tape's worth of a relentlessly repetitive story.

When we did venture out, we collected snapshots of daily life in 15-minute bites—the time we thought it would take for insurgents to realize we were there and organize an attack. And even if we were willing to venture into Iraqi homes or places of business, sometimes our would-be interviewees didn't want us there. Just being seen talking to a foreign TV crew or speaking out on TV could get an Iraqi killed.

Increasingly from mid-2004 on, our daily reporting came from gathering second-, third-, and even fifth-hand information from Iraqis we sent to the scene, although it was almost as dangerous for them as for us.

Or we'd try reporting over the phone, an effective technique in Washington, D.C., or New York but just about useless where the insurgents or the coalition is monitoring every phone conversation. There's no such thing as "off the record" over the phone in Iraq.

The only things that would reliably get us on the air were point-of-the-spear embeds—if something dramatic happened—and raids—if someone important was caught. One problem: The most effective raids often happened overnight, and the best units didn't want to take you out on them unless they trusted you, which meant you had to spend a few days with them. But we didn't have the staff to allow me to do that. Running an Iraq bureau was costing each of the networks in the ballpark of a million dollars a month for a story few people Stateside wanted to see anymore. Letting me go on overnight embeds away from the bureau meant keeping two correspondent teams in Iraq at the same time. The networks couldn't leave the bureau uncovered with no one there to report in case a major story broke. And having two correspondent/camera teams doubled our costs. Except for a few special occasions like the Iraqi elections, it simply wasn't in the budget.

The bosses would let me leave the bureau only for things they deemed important or if we were able to get out and back for *The Early Show*, 3 p.m. Baghdad time. That meant to film anything, we had to meet a U.S. unit early in the morning, spend a couple hours with them, then rush back to the bureau, hoping we had gathered something that would make a decent story in that short snapshot of time. It was like newsgathering while wearing a straitjacket.

Paul, James, and I had filmed plenty of dangerous events in Baghdad before. Only a month or so earlier, we'd spent a day with U.S. troops who were training their Iraqi counterparts in the neighborhood of Dora. The next day the very spot we drove over was hit by a car bomb. The exact thing had happened a couple months earlier when I filmed in Dora with another crew. A car bomb was set off and people died exactly where we had stepped 24 hours earlier.

Paul noticed the pattern and had a quiet word with me. He didn't have to say much. "Didja see a bomb went off just the next day right where we filmed?" he asked.

"Yeah, scary," I said. "Like it was a message."

"Something to think about," he said. And then he asked, "How's it going, getting that stuff we shot on the air?" Well, frankly, it was hell getting "that stuff" on air because as dangerous as the trip had been for us, nothing had happened. We were lucky and blessed that day. So the material we shot looked like every other patrol we'd been on.

It was a quiet and measured reminder that we had to weigh every trip on the basis of risk/reward. Why risk if we were never going to get the story on TV? Worse, why put the troops in a position where they feel they must deliver good TV by sometimes actually looking for trouble for the cameras? In the past whenever I'd figured out that was what was happening on a shoot, I'd take the commander aside and say, "Sir, if you weren't going to do this, if we weren't here, then please stop. Try to pretend we're not here." It didn't always work. And of course, we *did* want to see the most interesting stuff they did, and we *did* want to get them on the air.

After that conversation with Paul, I decided to start erring on the side of caution in what I asked for and what I said yes to. I left for a three-week hiatus from Iraq, as did Paul, and the next time we worked together was the weekend before Memorial Day, when I thought I was putting my new, safer, side-of-caution plan into operation.

As I replayed those months of risk/reward debate from my hospital bed, I felt as if somehow my previous risk taking had caught up with me to punish me on Memorial Day.

It took two friends in particular to start pulling me out of the guilt. One was Agnes, whom I'd last seen the morning of the shoot. She visited Bethesda Naval Hospital in person later, but first she spoke to me over the phone from London. I knew she'd met with Paul's and James' wives, trying to help them understand what had happened and what we'd been doing that day.

So Agnes told me what I needed to hear at the time: that Paul's and James' wives understood their husbands died doing something they'd chosen to do—that neither man could be bullied into something he thought was dangerous. She said neither woman blamed me. Months later I found out that wasn't entirely true, although it may have been true at the time. Agnes is the daughter of a diplomat and is a keen negotiator herself. She gave me the point of view she thought I was ready for.

Another colleague chimed in around the same time with a second lifeline—ABC News anchor Bob Woodruff, who'd preceded me on this healing route by four months. I'd put off calling him because I was so exhausted most of the time, physically and emotionally, that I was staying in a near-cocoon state with little contact with the outside world.

But I finally asked Pete to put in a call to the Woodruffs. Bob was still recuperating from his injuries at home, which meant he was relearning English. He beat himself up as he talked, saying he couldn't remember words like he once could, even though the only lapses I detected were maybe three umms in the course of a 30-minute conversation. I chalked his self-criticism up to his ever-present perfectionism.

First he asked me to walk him through the Memorial Day bombing, asking me to clarify points and go over each part I could remember. He wanted to know all the details because James had been his friend. They'd been embedded together for three months during the 2003 invasion of Iraq. Bob knew Paul from running into him in the field—everyone in the business knew Paul.

After listening to my story, Bob had some words of advice. "I know you blame yourself. You think you're the correspondent and you took them there," he said. "But remember this: No one took Paul or James anywhere. They decided to go on that shoot, like they made every other professional decision in their lives."

In a sense, he was saying that if I took the blame, I was also dishonoring their memory in a way, turning them into "yes men" who followed another's orders. They weren't and they didn't. That was a turning point and a life raft to which I clung every time the guilt tried to drag me down again.

CHAPTER 12

handling it

Having a wedge to drive into the guilt helped, but it didn't erase the grief. There's no shortcut for mourning. You just have to go through it.

But my family wanted the tears to stop, just like they wanted all the other pain to stop.

I saw it in my mom's and dad's eyes: "Our daughter can't handle this. She's cracking up."

Their desire to help was about to land us on the opposite sides of one of the oldest debates in mental health: medicate the problem or talk it out.

Psychiatrists believe most maladies stem from chemical imbalances in the brain, according to my layman's understanding. And with my brain injury, it was possible my tears came from misfiring, malfunctioning synapses; ergo psychotropic drugs would help solve the problem.

Psychologists and psychotherapists, however, believe rehashing the original incident and the pain that comes with it is the best way to get through grief—and is a necessary and natural part of the process (again, according to my layman's understanding).

From long personal (and private) experience, I knew that talking my problems to death with a therapist or support group worked for me. I wasn't falling apart. I was doing what I'd been taught: reliving the pain head on by bringing up and revisiting every detail. I wanted to excavate, uncover, dissect, and exorcise the pain from my head and my heart, like all the shrapnel the doctors had dug out of my legs and skull.

I was receiving similar advice from old friends in the military who'd been wounded and lost friends on the battlefield. In emails, they warned that bottling up the pain and the anger to deal with later was a recipe for breakdown. They said "find someone to talk to."

But Bethesda Naval Hospital wasn't able to provide a therapist until the last couple weeks of my stay there. The hospital simply didn't have the staff.

So my parents looked for help from the one person on my medical team who was guaranteed to give the "medicate the problem" advice: the neuropsychiatrist.

She was on my team to help evaluate the extent of my traumatic brain injury (TBI) that I'd sustained from the shrapnel to my brain. Until those synapses could be healed or brought into chemical balance artificially, the neuropsychiatrist told my family, and later me, to avoid the Iraq subject. She also advised me directly to not talk about the incident, which I'd already been doing nonstop from the moment I opened my eyes in Landstuhl.

I didn't take her overall advice, and I later regretted the one small piece I did take. She'd advised me to allow my father to sign my presurgery consent forms because they distressed me. In the short term, it meant less stress in pre-op. But it left my family with the impression that I wasn't psychologically "up" to many decisions surrounding my care, especially coupled with her walk-on-eggshells-around-fragile-Kimberly, don't-talk-about-Iraq advice.

Perhaps a better option would have been to talk about why I was afraid of anesthesia, to help me understand that my fears were mostly irrational. That would have left me more in charge of my own recovery from my hospital bed. Instead for my mom and dad in particular, thinking about my emotional fragility became a habit I later had to tear down.

Of course, I *was* emotionally fragile. I couldn't even stand violence on TV. The cartoon kickboxing in *The Incredibles* made me cringe, and when a seal ate a penguin in the documentary *March of the Penguins*, I briefly hated all seals.

But that didn't mean I couldn't take the pain or shouldn't at least try. I pushed ahead with my own prescription, self-medicating with Mideast music on my iPod (the fusion of *Blackhawk Down* and the Clash being a favorite), absorbing every scrap of news on Iraq, and bringing up memories of the attack with every new visitor. I wondered out loud about the gaps in the story I hadn't yet been able to fill in.

When CBS News anchor Bob Schieffer stopped by, he was happy to oblige on some of the missing details, telling me for the first time how my heart had stopped twice at the CSH in Baghdad. Schieffer had no idea where I was in my arc of discovery but I was glad to have answers. When Pete came in afterward, he found me ashen, absorbing the news. Even though I'd obviously survived the heart stoppages, the fact that I'd come that close to dying disturbed me at some deep, inexplicable level. And I was even more upset that no one had told me about it. As insensitive as it may have seemed at the time, Schieffer, to his credit, was treating me like a reporter, not a victim.

"So my heart stopped twice?" I asked Pete.

"Who told you that?" he asked too quietly. I'm glad Schieffer had left the building by then. Kiwis aren't diplomats. They bluntly say what's on their mind, and Pete would have done just that.

That's when I realized my own family was keeping details from me. They'd been told I wasn't capable of handling it, and they believed it.

So I was on my own, holding the line against the medicate-it, make-it-go-away therapy when a team of visiting psychiatrists came to my room to offer me drug therapy. They wanted to discuss my options regarding which drugs might help and why. I was already on an old-fashioned upper, amitriptyline, but not for mood treatment. Dr. Burns had explained that I was receiving a small dose but not enough to have a mood-lifting effect. He said the drug had a secondary benefit: alleviating nerve or neurologic pain throughout the body that comes from the breaks, the burns, the grafts, etc. But I thought even the little I was getting was enough. I didn't want anything else added to the chemical soup in my system.

"No psychotropic drugs, no antidepressants," I said. "No Prozac Nation nonsense. All it does is hide the pain, not treat it. That's not for me."

"But, but," was their reply. "You should be aware of the options . . ."

I was resolute.

"I want to *talk* about how I'm feeling, why I feel like bawling my eyes out, how freaked out I am by how my body's been shredded, how I feel about losing my friends," I told them. "I don't want to cover it up."

I asked them if I could talk to a counselor or join an injured troops support group, where everyone in the room would understand because we'd all gone through the same thing. The psychiatrists didn't reply. Maybe they thought I was avoiding the issue by avoiding drugs. Or perhaps there are no such support groups. Or maybe there are, but they thought an outsider, especially a reporter, would make it even harder for injured troops to open up.

"Well," one of them began. "You might want to consider antidepressants for a short time."

"No," I said, and I meant it. Now I was going to have to explain. I told them I'd learned that talk therapy worked for me, helping me cope after being beaten, menaced, and threatened both as a child and an adult in the Mideast. Then it helped me figure out my divorce and ultimately gave me the coping skills to survive the ever-present tension of living in Baghdad's Red Zone for three years, without developing posttraumatic stress disorder.

"Ah, our patients don't usually come in with that kind of background, nor those types of coping skills," one of the delegation said. They might not have believed I was making the best decision by rejecting their expertise, but they respected my choice.

Thankfully, two visitors appeared who were of like mind regarding talk therapy. First was Brother David, a Franciscan monk who stopped by in full brown-robed wool regalia and a painstakingly trimmed white beard. I always felt bad when he had to put the disposable surgical gown and gloves over his already hot outfit to visit my often-sweltering room. I wasn't Catholic, and it didn't matter. Brother David had worked with 9/11 victims, and in a former life as a fire chaplain, he'd seen plenty of loss and grief. He'd already guided many others through what I was dealing with. He told me about the people he'd met and how they'd managed. He told me about some of the other troops on my hallway and how they were coping and not coping.

Most of all, he reminded me in the gentlest way possible that "God has a purpose, and you're part of it. You know that." He handed me a Franciscan prayer that basically said: This will pass. And with faith, you'll get through it.

When I doubted my ability to figure out how to turn this experience into something more positive, he said, "After all these weeks of talking with you, there's one thing I know: You have a great internal compass. Listen to it."

And he told me to write as soon as I could. I wasn't ready to step back and absorb the whole story yet, so I started with smaller bites. I answered the 1,500-plus emails, which had piled up since Memorial Day, from friends and hundreds of people I'd never met, except through being on TV.

And then two weeks before I left the hospital, a second lifesaver stepped into the breach: Dr. Victor Huertas, a psychologist I'll call Vic, who came to the hospital on his annual National Guard rotation. (He spends the rest of the year doing things unmentionable for Homeland Security, probably trying to figure out what makes Osama Bin Laden tick.)

He shared my philosophy on saying no to drugs; talking trauma out is the healthiest way to go. He said my tears were an appropriate and healthy sign of grief.

His biggest challenge was usually trying to mentally pry open the Marines and soldiers in his care. Their instinctual response to his queries was "I'm fine, sir," even though their nurses and corpsmen heard many of them quietly crying their hearts out day and night, just like me. The moment someone walked through their hospital room door, they'd clam up and be tough. No problem, not me, sir, I'm not nuts.

The problem Vic foresaw with me was different from theirs: Due to my killer combination of being both female *and* a person who is paid to talk, he was afraid I wouldn't shut up. (Good instincts.)

He warned me from the beginning. "If you're rabbitting on, I won't show mercy. I'll cut you off and move you along to something else. No self-indulgent waffling. Oh, and I usually talk to Marines," he added. "So I'll probably swear a lot."

Right, I thought to myself. *Psychotherapy boot camp.*

Sometimes one-on-one and sometimes during physiotherapy, Vic talked me through the pain. One of the things we talked about was how I coped with a smaller version of this pain when I struggled with acute stress in my first two years in Baghdad.

When I first earned my network assignment just after the war ended, it was almost a letdown. The network glory had already been parceled out, and I was on the reporting cleanup crew. This was supposed to be the downslope after the U.S. military's uphill sprint into Iraq.

Then in August 2005, the bombs began, starting with the massive truck bomb that hit the United Nations compound and killed more than 20 people. It was a horrible signal to all of us that the new enemy considered us all legitimate targets, not just soldiers and coalition contractors but also aid workers, journalists, anyone remotely Western, and any Iraqi who worked with any of those groups.

After that the bombs picked up pace, striking small hotels that Westerners—and media—frequented in the neighborhood. That's when the first sign of acute stress started hitting me, something called hyper-vigilance (like the anxiety I felt on the ambulance ride in Landstuhl). I heard everything: car bombs—distant and close, mortars and rockets hitting the Green Zone across the river or straying to our side when the insurgents failed to hit their mark, as well as the constant rat-a-tat-tat of gunfire, RPG fire, and artillery.

I woke at the slightest combat-related sound. This may seem strange to someone who lives outside a war zone, but trust me, one of the first things you learn early on is to sleep through anything that doesn't sound close or immediately life-threatening. Your subconscious learns to differentiate. For years in places like Ramallah and Tora Bora, I'd had no problem with that. Over months of exposure to bomb blasts and their gory aftermath, which came closer and closer to the hotel in which I stayed, my filter shut down and every sound poured in.

At first I relied daily on prayer, meditation, and, when I could, yoga to cope with a lot of what I was seeing and the stress of living 24/7 with my colleagues in a sort of *Big Brother* house on speed. But the problems persisted. I was getting absolutely no sleep.

I decided to turn to my former therapist in London, the one who had talked me through the aftermath of my divorce. Talking helped, but not enough. My coping skills were growing, but so was the threat.

"I have to get sleep," I told my women's health doctor on one trip outside Baghdad. She prescribed me a mild antidepressant. She said it would help me shut off the hypervigilance. I carried the pills with me for a couple months but refused to take them. I'd pull them out, stare at them, and put them away. I still wasn't sleeping, so I'd tell myself that I'd sleep at the end of the six-week or two-month shift.

I was following the Dozier family motto: Tough it out. We don't need help, especially that kind of help. That same attitude applies to most journalists, aid workers, soldiers, diplomats, and contractors who choose to work in the same situation. We don't have problems with what we're seeing. Problems are for those soft folks who choose the comfort of back home. It's a perverse and twisted point of pride. And for a long time, I lived by it.

Then a car bomb went off on New Year's Eve outside a restaurant that was roughly four blocks from our hotel. Sitting at the hotel's restaurant table, I felt the air suck in and the windows shake. My world shifted.

We got our safety gear together and reached the center of the scene within 10 or 15 minutes, where we found a three-block-long hell, with the bomb still burning and relatives still screaming, searching for loved ones. Iraqi families were trapped in houses shredded by the blast.

This was not a new sight. But this time, it was so close.

The next day we went back to interview soldiers and police investigating the scene and film the aftermath in the daylight. I'd seen body parts before, after covering dozens of suicide bombings in Israel. But there the parts quickly get picked up, down to the last fragment, following Jewish religious law. A volunteer organization called Zaka does most of the work. Such a group doesn't exist in Baghdad. The rescue workers risk their lives just heading to the scene—and also risk getting hit by secondary explosions, intentionally planted to hit them. They get to the wounded—and the dead—and get them out of there as fast as they can. Cleaning up the scene comes much later, once it's clear the danger is past.

So the morning after the blast, I was filming a standup in daylight, looked down . . . and realized I was standing on part of a hand. Next to my boot was someone's kneecap, and near that was a small lone toe, floating in a brackish pool of water.

All of us covering these types of stories see a lot of death—bodies lying where they were killed, or collected in stinking impromptu field hospitals, or stacked in morgues, or stashed in unrefrigerated shipping containers, or waiting to be buried in someone's garden-turned-graveyard. That becomes normal. You chart the horror but keep some part of yourself locked away from it. I'd even seen a Palestinian gunman shot and killed by a sniper just 15 feet from my cameraman and me. The man died in front of us, his brain shot through, as the other gunmen tried to drag him to cover.

But there was something more horrible about accidentally standing on what's left of someone—someone I heard die when that bomb went off the night before. It stayed with me.

Now I couldn't even get to sleep, no matter how exhausted. As I'd lay my head on the pillow, I would start thinking, *What would happen if one of those cars parked beneath my window blew up?*

I would picture a thousand shards of glass from the window exploding inward, straight for my face, cutting me to bits. So I'd quickly flip, turning my face away from it. I used up almost a whole roll of clear packing tape to tape the windows, like you do in case of a hurricane. I wanted to make sure the glass couldn't turn into shards if a bomb went off. I would also draw the curtains tight, as another barrier. (Our bureau hadn't yet learned the trick of sticking adhesive-backed Mylar to all the windows. That did come later, at our security team's insistence.)

But sometimes, none of those measures was enough to lull me to sleep, especially if I'd spent the day rushing off to another car bombing, and the screams and burning images were still in my head.

After a couple hours tossing and turning, I'd drag the top mattress onto the floor and put the rest of the bed between me and the window. It was kind of like a kid building a pillow fort. And it made me feel just about as safe, but at least my brain would say: *Okay, you've done what you can do. Sleep.*

Then, the "waking" began. I'd cracked one end of the night: the make-myself-feel-safe-enough-to-fall-asleep problem—but then I'd wake again, just three to four hours later in the small hours of the morning. I'd listen to the 5 a.m.-ish call to prayer across the city, completely wide-eyed, heart pounding, hyperawake.

This went on for days—then weeks. Exhaustion became a permanent state for me.

There was logic at the root of my fear: Our hotel was a perfect terror target. It was inconspicuous, tucked away on a small side street—which sounds safe. But it faced another small hotel, full of foreign U.N. aid workers. They were definitely targets—that was clear from the U.N. bombing. And as the NBC hotel had been hit with an improvised explosive device left outside—killing one member of the hotel staff—we knew we were attractive to the dark side too.

I kept thinking, *Great: we're a terrorist two-fer.*

An attack would be easy: Between the two hotels was a narrow street, which served as full-to-the-brim parking lot. The hotel's Iraqi security staff only rudimentarily checked those cars parked beneath our windows. The Iraqi guards were vigilant only when our small foreign security staff was watching, but left on their own, they'd wave through their friends or relatives without even checking the passengers in the backseat, much less checking the cars' spacious trunks.

One member of the CBS staff had also brought some of Saddam's top insurgent leaders for a visit to our hotel, not quite realizing the downside: that we taught them exactly who we were, and where we lived, for future reference. Even if we weren't a useful target for them then, we couldn't be sure exactly whom they might be talking to.

As I tried to catch some sleep, all these things would run through my mind: how easy it would be to sneak a bomb-laden car through and set it off, ripping half our building away—or perhaps a suicide bomber would walk into our lobby and blow it away.

I wasn't the only one showing cracks at the edges. As I was trying all my new-age coping tricks, the rest of our team was relying more on the time-honored opiate for journalists in a war zone: alcohol, consumed in copious, drink-until-gutter-drunk amounts. Aid workers and contractors and diplomats also liberally applied this solution.

The U.S. military had General Order No. 1 in effect: no alcohol. There was a good reason for that. The cumulative effect of alcohol was a magnitude worse than the stress itself. I'd already found that even a glass of wine a night was enough to crater my emotions after four or five days in a row.

After that initial six-month-to-a-year assignment after the fall of Baghdad, others on the CBS team slowly came to the same conclusion. The first year people partied like it was Spring Break every other night. If there was a second correspondent in town, and I wasn't on call, I joined them.

But by the second year, the city was becoming more dangerous, and the threat more real. Some of our security guys decided to forgo even a single beer in their six-week rotations. They didn't want to be woken up by insurgents storming our building at night (which had happened to a few foreign contractors') and be trying to see straight while steadying their weapons. A schism formed in our security ranks—those who chose to continue to drink were soon drummed out. There were no "off" hours.

The rest of us got off the sauce entirely too, unless it was for a special, once-every-couple-of-weeks all-bureau dinner. Alcohol in any amount seemed to make us all slightly depressed and waspish—feelings we were already experiencing in spades because of what we were seeing outside, not to mention the cumulative effect of spending so much time with each other.

Desperate for a way to turn my brain off, but not willing to leave Baghdad and not happy with the whiskey and wine solution, I finally tried what I called the "Prozac Nation" solution. In early 2004 I opened that little jar of pills and tried the "normal" dose.

Nightmare. It was like stepping into an alternative universe, where everything is numb. *Fifty people killed in the latest bombing?* I'd think. *Shame, that. What's for dinner?*

Yes, I slept that night, but it felt like I'd been mentally sleeping, all day.

So the next day I thought: *Okay, get creative. Cut the dose.* I sliced the pills in half, splintering bits of them in the process. Swallowed the bitter fragment, gulped some green tea, and waited.

Still too much. Like sleepwalking.

Then a quarter dose (the thing almost dissolving into powder in the process).

Nope. Still too semi-Alice-in-Wonderland.

I got a box cutter and shaved the damned thing into eighths and tried that.

Bearable, I thought. For once, I slept solidly, at peace.

But after a week on the stuff, I started developing head-crushing migraines, mixed with another strange side effect: Sunspots appeared before my eyes. This glowing vision was especially entertaining when they cropped up during a live shot. I had to try to figure out where the camera was, hidden among all the spots.

The next time I got back to Jerusalem, I told my doctor there MUST be another way. I wanted to tackle the problem the way I had other things in my past: find an expert who knew even more about acute stress than the general psychotherapist I'd been speaking to. *A trauma expert*, I thought, *would tell me the ABCs of defeating this anxiety.*

My doctor knew I had an aversion to psychiatrists, so she sent me to a trauma counselor who used cognitive therapy to treat both acute stress and its much-publicized older brother, posttraumatic stress disorder (PTSD). I went to her office, took out my reporter's notebook, and waited to be told how best to slay my latest "enemy."

Her answer was simple, and for me as unthinkable as continuing to swallow those awful pills:

"Leave Baghdad," she said flatly. She went on to tell me that counseling was a waste of time if you're going to remain in the same unsafe environment that caused the fears in the first place.

"Oh," I said. "Well, that's not going to happen." So I wrote down a couple of her "visualize you are safe" exercises, thanked her, and left.

Back in Baghdad, after another couple weeks of not sleeping, I stared at the eighth of a pill again and contemplated risking the migraines and the spots.

This sucks, I thought. So I gulped a cup of warm milk and scarfed down a couple candy bars (the closest I could get to downing a pint of Ben and Jerry's), threw an extra mattress against the window, and plotted a new way out: I'd get us the hell out of that hotel.

If we felt safer, I thought, *I'd go less nuts.*

A few of us started an internal CBS campaign to move locations. For my sanity, and my sleep, I needed something with a very large blast perimeter. Moving would cost CBS tens of thousands of dollars, on top of the already budget-killing enterprise of keeping a bureau open in Iraq. Also the place we were in was comfortable, and the staff wonderfully trustworthy—hard qualities to find in a city where violence and greed were wearing both away.

But I didn't want a single vehicle parked beneath my windows anymore, and I wasn't the only one. Our foreign security team was growing increasingly unhappy with our hotel—and our neighborhood. I don't know if they were having the same thoughts I was when they tried to sleep at night. That was something one simply didn't, and doesn't, talk about.

In the end we found a new hotel, surrounded by gardens and high walls, with windows angled toward the river and balconies covered by metal grates. (Rocket catchers, I called them. And they worked. On one occasion when CBS News correspondent Byron Pitts and I were doing our "handover" as he was coming in to replace me, one of the grates broke the impact when a rocket hit our building. Some of the shrapnel whistled indoors, but the bulk of the rocket was deflected into the parking lot.)

The place wasn't in an ideal location, but there's really no such thing in Baghdad's Red Zone. We were just down the road from the capital's infamous Haifa Street—scene of some of the fiercest battles between U.S. and Iraqi troops pitted against Sunni insurgents and Al Qaeda terrorists. That street has been pacified by U.S. and Iraqi troops, then overrun by insurgents, then pacified again—more times than I can remember.

But the new location meant there would be no potential car bomb parked beneath our windows going nova on us before dawn.

The first night I stayed in our new digs, my overactive, ever-morbid imagination was finally at peace. When the fighting on Haifa Street roared on the other side of the hotel from my room, I would simply turn the volume up on the "Ocean" soundtrack on my specially-imported "soothing sounds" alarm clock and drift off to sleep.

The only time hypervigilance and sleepless nights would strike after that was any time I flew into Baghdad, and any time before I went out with U.S. troops. As Vic later told me in Bethesda: That fear was healthy. I was openly acknowledging that what I was about to do was dangerous as hell. It's only when you deny that, or ignore that, that you go nuts.

So I'd fall back on "talk therapy" in that I'd call Pete. Once I had someone in my life who knew the environment, and the risk calculations you make before going out in a war zone, it was easier to open up about it. I'd defuse the fear by naming it out loud.

It's the same method commanders now use with their troops in the field. You battle the fear first by being prepared: You have a careful plan of attack, and a plan if something goes wrong. You fortify your safety gear and check your vehicles so you know you've done everything in your power to protect yourself and those with you. Then you acknowledge to yourself and to a trusted confidant like a battle buddy, chaplain, or frontline counselor that the fear and danger remain.

I'd met some of those frontline counselors when we spent Thanksgiving with a U.S. military mental health team at a forward operating base smack in the middle of Sunni territory, between Tikrit and Mosul. The forward operating base's commanders had experimented with having a mental health team embedded with their frontline units, as chaplains have been doing for generations. People trust those they're fighting alongside. The guys trusted these mental health professionals because they were going on the same patrols, living through the same firefights and roadside bombs. If a soldier had a problem, he or she didn't have to ask to be sent to one of the main bases (provoking questions about his or her mental fitness and possibly damaging his or her career). Instead the soldiers could chat with the counselors over lunch or dinner or hang out in their hooch in the evenings. The counselors would prescribe antidepressants and other drug therapies in only the most severe cases. They found their greatest success was to get people talking about the hell they were seeing every day.

As I found in my own experience, talking made all the difference. The unit I visited was one of the only ones in Iraq at that time that had dropped its mental-health-related attrition rate from the Iraq-wide rate of 11 percent to zero.

At CBS we all kind of talked to each other, but nothing specific. The media lags just as far behind the military in dealing with combat stress, as I was to find it does in dealing with loss and grief.

CHAPTER 13
advice, welcome and otherwise

As I dealt with the grief, my bouts of crying grew less frequent. With each day I was returning to my prebombing independence.

But my parents were still in their mode of trying to protect me, and that meant a clash of wills. They were accustomed to the freedom of asking my doctors anything. Mom, sitting alone in the waiting room, had plenty of time to think up all sorts of ways the bombing might adversely affect the rest of my life. Instead of sharing some of those fears with me, she asked my doctor. In one case she asked Dr. Dunne to assess the health of my reproductive system and whether any of the damage from the bombing would affect my ability to have children.

When Dr. Dunne came up with the answer, however, he delivered it straight to me. I looked at him, saying, "Thank you, but what are you talking about? Why would I even think something was wrong?" That's how I found out how normal it had become for my parents to ask everything and anything about me without my knowledge or input. I realized later that Dr. Dunne had seen this with overprotective parents and their injured loved ones plenty of times before, which explains why he made a point of always briefing me directly.

At last I convinced my mom and dad that they should move back to their condo north of Baltimore and give up their bedside-and-waiting-room vigil. But they surely felt hurt and rejected. It took months for us all to realize that it was just something we had to go through.

Meanwhile I was strong enough for some of my other close friends to visit, including CBS News Radio correspondent Cami McCormick and cameraman Chris Albert. Since they were friends Pete also knew from the Mideast, it also meant some support for him, a chance for him to let his guard down in front of people who weren't part of the daily tug-of-war to help me heal.

Cami was now radio's go-to person for hot zones, as I'd once been. She was also one of the most awardwinning radio anchors in the business. She was their star from 9/11 to New Orleans, bringing the story home to some 30 million listeners a day, with a deep, cigarette-jagged Southern drawl that springs forth after a decent bottle of red wine, or when she's chatting with American troops. (Anyone in the military knows what I mean. You may enter the Army or Marines with a straight, East Coast twang, but after a few years, everyone seems to speak in a Southern/Midwestern fusion I call Army speak. Around the troops, I—like Cami—tend to slip into my dad's old Southern patois, dotting the conversation with y'alls. Cami came by it even more naturally than I did.)

Cami and I had met when I was struggling at the affiliate TV job in Jerusalem. The West Bank, including the Church of the Nativity in Bethlehem, was under siege. The only way to get to it was to sneak past the Israeli military blockade. I remembered well what it was like to be the radio person with a limited budget to hire a driver and translator. People hired on the cheap weren't likely to bust an Israeli military curfew for you, so I invited Cami to come along in our TV vehicle. Halfway to the hotel overlooking the Church of the Nativity, we were caught by an Israeli tank, which was patrolling the curfew-emptied streets. The soldier popped out of the top and yelled at us to leave. Luckily for us the tank was too wide to escort us to the edge of the town, so we turned and walked back the way we came.

As soon as we rounded a corner, I pulled Cami and a freelance cameraman I was working with into an alley and told them to wait. The tank moved off to patrol elsewhere. When the engine noise died off, we kept walking toward Manger Square.

The freelance cameraman shot the standup I'd need and some of the standoff between Israeli troops on the outside and the Palestinian gunmen who were using the church as a refuge. I had to get back to Jerusalem to put the story together and go "live," but my cameraman was going to stay and record the siege. We had rented the last room that overlooked the square.

Cami decided to stay too but realized she had nothing warm to wear or even a toothbrush. I had all those things (including a brand-new toothbrush) in a jump bag I had kept in our crew car since I'd suffered wearing the same clothes for five days after opting to stay inside Ramallah when the Israeli military shut it down in 2002.

I hiked back to the car and picked up the spare clothes, sneaking through the Israeli lines. I also had learned to keep a spare bottle of wine in the trunk, which was useful in thanking certain (non-Muslim or nonobservant) officials for favors. Then I snuck back, dodging the circling tank again, to turn over the supplies. Cami didn't know me very well, but when I came back with all that stuff and then handed over the bottle of wine as a pièce de résistance, our friendship was made.

In Iraq we'd overlapped in the Baghdad bureau time and again, trading story ideas, frustrations with the military, frustrations with our bosses, etc. We also traded stories about our crazy romantic lives. We were two independent-as-hell women who took orders from no one and were getting more stubborn as we grew older. We'd also both been successful professionally, and we both spent as much time as possible on embeds with the troops. She actually went on more embeds than any other reporter I know in Iraq.

From the moment she heard about the bomb blast, she hurt to the core. She'd been in New York. I heard from friends at the U.S. embassy that she'd called them desperately and repeatedly, trying to get an update. Would I live, or would I die?

She'd also been so close to danger so many times that she must have been thinking, "But for the grace of God, there go I."

Cami rushed in and over to my bed to hug me, but I had to stop her because my donor sites were in screaming pain at that point.

But just seeing her helped bring my old world back into focus, and I immediately rattled off the story of what happened and where.

I later asked her what she remembered of that first meeting; she said I was positive and upbeat, not something she'd expected, considering what I'd been through. She said I also wanted my earrings, another sign that I was starting to see myself as a normal person again and actually care how I looked.

Pete had the earrings among the personal effects the trauma team had taken off me in the Baghdad casualty hospital. We had to scrub the blood off them to restore them to wearability.

Cami had brought a DVD player as a gift from my old employers at CBS Radio and a stack of DVDs that I wasn't emotionally ready to watch, including *The Constant Gardener*, a bloody tale about conspiracy and killing in Kenya. I didn't know that when Pete and I started watching it a few days later. We got to a scene early in the movie where Ralph Fiennes has to identify his dead wife in a morgue, and I covered my eyes tightly. I didn't even need to tell Pete. He was already reaching for the off button.

My next visitor, cameraman Chris Albert, also brought a stack of DVDs, but this time Pete did due diligence to avoid another *The Constant Gardener* incident. From the stack he pulled out George Clooney's *Syriana*.

"What's that about?" Pete asked.

"It's great. It's about everything we cover," Chris started out enthusiastically. "Political conspiracy in the Middle East, the violence, the bombing." Then Chris thought about it for a moment. "In the end, the good guys get killed by a car bomb."

Pete looked at him for a beat.

"Maybe not right now, mate," he said quietly, tucking the DVD away in his backpack.

Chris and Pete had already bonded when Pete had visited me once in Israel—two antipodeans with attitude. Whereas Pete is a quiet enforcer of his will, Chris is a mouthy, rangy Australian who believes he's always right even when he's wrong. (Kiwi Pete says this is a typical Aussie trait.) Chris grew up on a farm outside Melbourne, Australia, with a father who was a firearms dealer and a mom who was a nurse. She once threatened to use said firearms (actually, a 12-gauge Virginia State Police riot shotgun) on unwelcome Mormon missionaries. Chris obviously takes after her.

In Jerusalem Pete and Chris got along like two kids at summer camp, Chris grilling Pete about the finer points of helicopters, wilderness survival, off-road four-wheel driving, jumping out of planes from high altitudes, automatic weapons, and sniper fire. They also had a wordless understanding of what it was like to be a traditional antipodean male, dealing with a certain high-strung American career woman.

Chris wrote me later about what Pete told him before he met me:

He took me to lunch basically to brief me on what to talk about and what not to talk about. It seemed as though other people had walked into your room and started blundering on about the incident without thinking about it and had shocked you to hell. Case in point was that someone had walked in and told you that your heart had stopped a couple of times, that you had actually died, and that you did not know about it. So it was a full "actions-on" briefing on how to handle the interrogation of the banged-up correspondent.

It was hard to know exactly how Pete was handling it being one of those stoic (military) types. One thing that I realized was that it must have been a stressful time for him, playing bodyguard against everybody. Everybody thought they were doing the right thing by you, the hospital, CBS staff, and others, but they often must have been causing more damage than good. Thus Pete stepped in and took the role and, by the look of the tired lines on his face, the heat of protecting you.

Walking into the hospital room for the first time, [I saw] you were a wreck but not as bad as I thought you would have been, as the main damage was beneath the sheets. You looked tired, skinny, and frankly unwashed and uncomfortable. You had been put through the wringer, and that's what you looked like, your hair clipped short and unkempt, a great big arcing scar on the side of your head, and your face was pale and gaunt.

The next surprise was that you launched straight into a coherent blow-by-blow account of what had happened. Pete had warned me not to bring it up unless you did, and off you went! I can only assume that you felt comfortable discussing the actions on the ground, as we had spent so much time together in similar situations in the West Bank and the early days of Iraq. You kept talking for about half an hour, until I could see you were actually exhausting yourself from the effort, and I suggested we take it up again the next day.

This was the first day that they got you out of the bed and sat you on the floor in the shower so the next time you did not look so unwashed!

Poor Chris was always having to critique how I looked and fix it. He and I had worked together for almost two years in Jerusalem as a two-person team for New York's WCBS. I'd stolen him from the BBC World Service. BBC correspondent Orla Guerin had found me crying on the steps of Jerusalem Capitol Studios because I'd just had to fire my last cameraman/editor and didn't know where I'd find another skilled foreigner in Israel who could travel with me in and out of Palestinian areas. Israelis frequently were barred from such areas (and you wouldn't want to bring an Israeli to shoot a Hamas interview, for instance—that's a death warrant for the cameraman and you), and Palestinians were often trapped in either Ramallah or East Jerusalem by the latest Israeli military crackdown after a suicide bombing or even a high-terror alert.

Guerin didn't know me well, but she knew I didn't get upset this easily. When I explained, she understood. I wouldn't be able to cover anything unless I found someone, and fast. I'd fail, as would my brand-new bureau. "I know someone," she said. "He's just finished a freelance shift for us, and he's really good. He's probably going to grow into one of the best cameramen in the business." I knew I needed someone with this level of skill, as a poorly shot standup (or two or 10) can ruin your career. Your bosses don't say, "Why didn't the cameraman light that properly?" They say, "She looks awful."

So I met Chris, young, brash, opinionated, with more energy than a thermonuclear power plant and just as much firepower when ticked off. He saved my job by saying yes. I rewarded him with a job that meant 12-hour days, Stateside bosses who had never worked with correspondents in a different time zone before and didn't seem to understand our need for sleep. And he had to work with a correspondent who knew journalism but also thought she knew a lot more about TV than she really did. Although many other people contributed, I most credit Chris with turning me into a network correspondent, especially with his key ability to tell me, and anyone around me, exactly what he thought, usually with swearing and sometimes high volume thrown in.

Chris' lens was a harsh, unforgiving mirror. "Your standups are crap," he'd say. "You're too stiff. And I have to put another filter on to hide the wrinkles on your eyes." He's a lighting cameraman, which means he's always studying film lighting techniques to add to the mix. I became a test project for Chris' latest lighting tricks as he tried to figure out how to hide my every flaw.

I'd never felt uglier in my life. And seldom before or since have I looked better on camera.

The criticism continued in the edit suite, where we'd put together the piece we'd shot. He'd read my script, and the diatribe would begin. "What picture am I going to use to cover that line?" he'd say. "The line's too short [or too long]." I'd fix it, and then I'd track the piece, meaning I'd read my script into the microphone. That meant more verbal abuse. "Your tracking sounds like someone's strangling you. You're shouting at the microphone. It sounds ridiculous."

He told me all the things that previous producers and managers were too polite to say. Maybe none of the rest of them thought I was capable of changing any of my habits. But Chris had to work with me every day, and he doesn't suffer fools. And he doesn't "like his name going on crap," as he'd say, though he put it a bit more colorfully.

Chris and I had been promoted to network together, but he'd stayed at the CBS Tel Aviv bureau, while I had gone to Baghdad. Whenever I came back to my home in Jerusalem, we met up for coffee and discussed whichever supermodel Chris was dating at the moment, which *60 Minutes* shoot he'd just wangled his way onto, what cool, new lighting thing he'd found, and my obsession with Baghdad.

"Why the hell do you keep going back there?" he'd ask. "It's going to catch up with you. You can't keep doing this." I'd point out to him that with another staff correspondent already ensconced in Tel Aviv and him barely getting on the air, there was nothing for two correspondents to do in Israel, so I had to make myself useful in Baghdad or I feared I'd lose my job. And he'd reply, "The job's not worth it."

He looked out for me the best he could by keeping in touch with the other cameramen who went in and out of Baghdad, and he'd bail me out over whatever faux pas he'd heard I'd committed. I'd usually annoy Paul, so Chris played mediator. "Don't tell him how to light," he'd say. "Ask for his help on something specific, then let him decide how to solve it." He was right. The next shift in Baghdad, I told Paul about my fear of looking old on camera because of my growing wrinkles, a souvenir of the sun, stress, and pollution of the Iraqi capital. On Paul's next trip in, he brought out a slew of new filters and lights to try.

So I was used to hearing harsh truths from a man who thinks Hugh Laurie's *House* character is modeled after him. When he came into my hospital room, I braced myself for a stream of Aussie "I told you so's."

I beat him to it.

"Hi. Yes, you told me so," was basically how I greeted him. "Here I am, bombed to within an inch of my life. I know, I know, I know."

He just shook his head. I launched into the story of the bombing, and he just kept shaking his head. I think he took Pete out, and they got drunk that night.

When Chris left a day or so later, he left me with some things to think about. "You have no business being here," he said. "Look, this is your second chance. This is the start of your second life."

And then, because heaven forbid Chris should say anything that sounds profound or poetic, he added: "Don't fuck it up."

CHAPTER 14
another setback

A month into my stay at Bethesda, I had made progress. The Acinetobacter was at bay, and I'd switched from the strange gray vacuum bandages to regular ones to cover my grafts. Dr. Dunne said up to 95 percent of the transferred skin had taken, a success rate far better than he had hoped for. That meant that my body had accepted the skin that was scraped from my back and top of my left leg. The new skin had knitted over the burned areas, especially a vast area on my outer right thigh, which the plastic surgeon admitted to me later had been his biggest concern.

Every day I worked with physiotherapist Carol Petrie, my knees bent a little farther, and my system adapted to standing up. I'd graduated to taking between 20 and 30 steps a day to reach my wheelchair. And I could stay sitting for up to an hour before the cold sweat and the light-headedness hit.

But I was about to enter a storm of unexpected pain, the worst of my entire recovery, worse even than the pain that followed the bombing. And the agony was coupled with nightmarish waves of emotion. Looking back I now understand that one opened the door to the other and left me with little strength to fight it.

I was also about to go through another one of those medical tugs-of-war between two paths of treatment, with no easy answers and each side totally committed to the rightness of its choice. I had to "break the tie" with my brain addled by some of the worst pain I'd ever experienced.

It started in a roundabout way. Carol had recommended that I try a machine that would passively bend my legs as I lay in bed, but it would require that I lie back on my still-healing donor sites.

At first it seemed to be working, the constant motion helping my knees to bend. But the skin under the bandages started to itch and then to burn. My theory was that the friction of lying on my back, putting my full weight on the donor sites, produced sweat, and the sweat had nowhere to go. So the bandages absorbed it, becoming gelatinous instead of breathing as they were supposed to.

The nurses weren't sure what to do or even if anything really needed to be done. I'd twist and turn, trying to get comfortable, thinking the discomfort was temporary. It wasn't.

It took a couple days of complaining before the nurses agreed to call for a doctor. However, their pages weren't urgent, so the calls went unanswered for a day or so. Since I was out of danger and there were far worse cases to deal with elsewhere in the huge hospital, my need was a lower priority.

Discomfort, meanwhile, was turning to full-on pain, and after four days of waiting, my attempts at politeness finally exploded into snarling, rage-filled impatience. "I . . . need . . . help!"

Pain can do that.

The torment was worse at night, and so were my complaints. One of the nurses summoned Dr. Quietmeyer, who was in charge of all Iraq patients together with Dr. Burns. They both did endless rotations between Bethesda Naval Hospital and other local hospitals' trauma wards, all part of the sleepless path of young residents. Grafts weren't her area of specialty, but she took one look and didn't hesitate. "No wonder you're in pain. Your dressings on the donor sites have failed," she said. "They have to come off."

A donor site, as I described briefly before, is an area where the doctors have harvested the top two layers of skin, the epidermis and about a third of the dermis, which is the next layer down. (The slice of skin is 0.001 to 0.014 inch thick.) The roughly two-thirds of the dermis that's left must then epithelialize, meaning it must grow new epidermal cells to cover the damage. Essentially it's the surgically created equivalent of a second-degree burn. The bandage the surgeons chose to cover these areas with in my case was Biobrain. It was supposed to come off by itself in strips, sloughing off naturally as the skin underneath healed.

Instead mine had trapped the moisture, turning into a perfect environment for infection, which could destroy the underlying layer of skin that was left on the donor sites. If that happened, more skin would have to be harvested from other parts of my body to cover them.

Here's the thing I learned about burns and donor sites: There is nothing on the planet that numbs skin pain. Narcotics can't shut it off. That's why patients who have more than 50 percent burns on their body are often kept in an artificially induced comatose state, as my doctors and nurses would later explain to me. Modern medicine offers nothing to stop the constant, mind-thrashing, soul-altering, screaming pain.

That's the world I entered as Dr. Quietmeyer pulled off the worst of the bandages, which had essentially bonded to my scraped skin.

When my plastic surgeon, Dr. Kumar, came to look at the bandages on the rest of the donor sites, he concurred with the younger doctor's diagnosis and ripped the rest off. He said there was no point in being gentle because it would end up hurting the same fast or slow. (Dr. Kumar is the Indian-American son of two doctors who never let their child once complain about pain. "You scraped your knee? Too bad. Wash it off." He applied the same tough love to his patients.)

With the bandages off, I was left with huge, raw, constantly weeping patches across my back with the nerves exposed to the air. I felt the smallest breath of air as if it were a gale-force sandstorm ripping across my back. I couldn't lie on the sites, so I could only lie on my right side or on my stomach.

Dr. Kumar said that was how it had to be. He had trained at the Mayo Clinic, and along the way he had tried different methods to heal donor sites. Of the two camps on healing methods, he was a traditionalist: Dry it out. He'd treated an indigent man and for three weeks had kept the donor sites moist. He explained that nothing happened. They didn't heal until he ripped off the dressing, as he'd done to me, and left the man to dry out until he healed.

He ordered incubator lights, also known as fryer lights, to be brought to my room to bake my wounds slowly dry. I asked him how long it would be, wondering how long I could stand the pain and my already stiffening muscles from the two positions I was allowed.

"A few days," he said. I should have pushed for a better answer. By a few days, he actually meant a week or two. I gritted my way through 24, then 48, hours, thinking, *By tomorrow, I can rest.*

Unlike the pain from the broken bones or even all the incisions, this pain never lessened in intensity. I was always at the edge of gasping-for-air screaming. And my neck, hips, and legs first ached and then started cramping from staying in only two positions. I couldn't sleep. I could barely eat.

I was beginning to understand just what both my grandmothers had gone through. They were confined to a couple positions in their hospital beds before they died, especially my maternal grandmother with her arthritic joints grinding one against the other. It was absolute hell.

The agony started changing my personality, or rather wearing away any attempt on my part to be gracious or polite. I no longer worried about entertaining people who came into my room or making a good impression. I simply snapped at everyone. Pain ground away all civility.

After a few days of lying with my back exposed down to the middle of my backside, Pete helped me come up with a way to protect both my privacy and my skin. We kept my curtain drawn between me and the door with just enough pushed back for me to peek out and see who was coming. And Pete rigged a tentlike structure over the bed to keep the air-conditioner (barely perceptible to anyone else) from raking my open skin.

I tried to pull myself together as it just happened to be the week of both the Fourth of July and my 40th birthday, on July 6. I knew a number of friends and family had planned to visit because they'd thought finally, after all my trials, I'd be well enough for company.

My brother Larry and his wife, Dinah, had traveled from North Carolina to see me for our first visit in years. I was in so much pain that I was having trouble forming words, much less sentences. They were family; they understood. But I knew other guests would be by to celebrate my birthday—all the people who assumed I was on the downslope to healing. I knew that CBS had planned to bring in a cake and a special dinner for everyone, and I didn't want to disappoint them. It was my 40th birthday, and I was supposed to be getting better after all.

I asked Dr. Kumar if I could put a dressing on the areas for just an hour so I could sit up and talk to my visitors. He agreed, and the nurses plastered on a petroleum-soaked, gauzelike dressing called Zeroform. I gritted my teeth and rolled onto the donor sites so I could sit up like a normal human being instead of lolling half-naked on my side like a baking chicken.

It was a relief to sit up and have the sites covered from the air, but I was still in pain. I greeted my guests, who stayed only a short time, and the cake stayed untouched, but I'd made an effort.

The nurses peeled off the Zeroform just an hour after they'd helped plaster it on. To my horror the donor sites were completely wet again. Three days of drying out, and all the pain that went with it, for naught—some birthday. I wept.

Pete was just about to leave a day or so later for New Zealand. He'd hoped this crisis was passing, not getting worse, so he tried to downplay my tears.

I asked him to walk around the bed and look at my back.

"Oh my god," he said. "It's like starting from zero."

When Dr. Kumar came by the next day, he agreed. He added that, in any case, he hadn't expected them to dry out for another six or seven days at least.

I looked at him in horror. There was no way I could last that long and stay sane. He said there was no other way and left.

I cried more. I asked the nurses to call for Lidia Garner, Bethesda's one and only wound nurse. She specialized in burns and donor sites and anything that was hard to heal.

Her time was so pressed and her visits so rare that I couldn't risk her stopping by and then politely leaving if she saw I was visiting with family or conversing with another specialist. I asked Pete to write a huge sign and post it outside my door that said, "WELCOME, LIDIA. PLEASE COME IN, NO MATTER WHAT TIME IT IS, NO MATTER WHO IS IN THE ROOM. THANKS!"

Just a couple hours later, she appeared. The nurses had apparently already sent an SOS a day or so before. She was just catching up.

She walked in, took one look at the drying sites under the heat lamp, and said, "No, no, no. This is what we did 10 years ago." Her recommended treatment was the exact opposite from the one that Dr. Kumar and Dr. Dunne had prescribed.

Like the Acinetobacter/kidney debates, there are vast areas of disagreement regarding treating such wounds, and then there's the battleground of opinion between nurses and doctors, although Lidia was too much of a lady to share that part openly. I got the whole story later from other nurses.

Lidia had done a two-year master's program to specialize in wound care, and she kept up-to-date on all the latest bandages and treatments by reading all the new medical papers and going to endless rounds of conferences and trade fairs. Because of her expertise, she'd actually rewritten the rules of wound care for the Navy.

That didn't mean doctors always chose to follow her methods. Several of the things that had been used on me were outmoded and outdated in her book, like packing the deepest of my wounds with the petroleum-covered Zeroform, which had to be replaced every few days. She preferred the new silver-infused, seaweed-derived bandages, which can stay in for at least a week if not longer. Using silver as an antibiotic was one of the many innovations in wound care since 9/11.

Another was that most wound specialists now believed that wounds needed to be kept moist—not dry—to heal quickly. The other key principles: Keep the temperature and the pH stable. That wasn't going to happen with my donor sites open to the air under heat lamps.

"Tegaderm," she said. "That's what you need."

I had no idea what she was talking about. She explained that she was going to clean the area and then cover it from the air. I knew this was the opposite of what Dr. Kumar had ordered, and I was leery of going against his advice. But I feared the pain more, and I knew it could take another 24 to 48 hours to run the idea past him, so I just told her to do it.

Lidia first scrubbed the donor sites with a soapy sponge, proving to me that as painful as the sites were, there was a way to make them hurt even worse. (She and Dr. Kumar did agree unreservedly on one thing: You don't keep an area moist unless you're sure it's clear of infection. So the areas had to be scrubbed.)

She then stuck on 8×11-inch squares of a clear film that had sticky backings. The sticky part stuck to my normal skin at the edges but didn't stick to the wet areas.

The bandages covered my exposed nerves from the air and the constantly changing temperature, so I felt instant relief. But I was still afraid of defying Dr. Kumar, who obviously held a diametrically opposite opinion on treating donor sites.

I told Lidia I'd keep my leg drying out, as he'd originally told me to do.

Ever the lady (I don't think she knows how to swear), Lidia smiled and said, "Certainly. But I'll leave plenty of Tegaderm with your nurse, in case you change your mind."

Smart woman. She left, and I lay back, my head clearing for the first time in days as the pain receptors shut down on my back, or at least dropped back to a dull roar.

But my leg still stung with every movement of air.

I hit the call bell.

My nurse, Eric (who is probably a Navy Seal by now—that was his next plan), walked in, carrying a fresh strip of Tegaderm.

"What, you have ESP?" I asked.

"Lidia's always right," he replied. (An avid motorcyclist, Eric had a fondness for Tegaderm anyway. It's a great way to treat road rash.)

The nurses thought Dr. Kumar was a wonderful surgeon. But outside the operating room, they all listened to Lidia. When any Bethesda surgeon prescribed old-school bandages in a patient's notes, the nurses ignored it and followed Lidia's hospitalwide wound protocols instead.

I later found out that Lidia had immediately called Dr. Kumar to inform him of my decision to go with Tegaderm. He'd explained to her the fear he hadn't explained to me: that my donor sites were so wet that he was convinced they might already be infected and that I was going to lose that skin too. He later told me I was the worst donor-site case he'd seen, and that's saying something in a hospital full of war wounded from Iraq and Afghanistan.

Lidia took his concerns seriously, which is why every couple days, when she stopped by to personally change the bandages, she rigorously scrubbed them down.

Looking back on it I realize there were upsides to both methods. Dr. Kumar's drying method, which I rejected, would probably have meant faster healing if I'd been able to withstand the pain. The wet method took about six weeks before the very last patch was dry enough to go without some sort of Tegaderm or antibiotic-impregnated absorbent foam dressing. (I tried every new bandage on the market.)

But Lidia's method was healthier for my sanity. And as I learned, a patient's mental state plays a huge role in healing.

I was informed of the options, and I made my choices—some good, some bad. I'm glad I didn't take Dr. Kumar's advice on how to treat the donor sites, but as I mentioned before, I wish I had taken his advice of having the extra graft added on the spot where they'd run out of skin on my right thigh.

Within months of my departure, Lidia left Bethesda to run the ICU burn unit at Johns Hopkins University Hospital. Her nurse colleagues firmly believed she left because she was exhausted from the uphill battle of convincing old-school surgeons to listen to a lowly nurse's new-fangled methods. I prefer to think about the great things she's doing for patients at Hopkins and mourn the loss of her skills for the injured troops.

During all the donor-site drama, I'd had a changing of the guard on the caregiver front. Pete had left for New Zealand a couple days after my birthday. As the day of his departure approached, I'd sunk into a depression that had only made all the donor-site debates harder to take. But I hadn't wanted him to leave on a bad note and thinking I couldn't handle his absence. At least Lidia's intervention the day before he left meant I was physically comfortable enough to put on a brave face.

Agnes had made the trip from London to replace Pete, arriving on my birthday. She and my sister, MeiLee, would split the day, as she said, "spending two weeks watching you . . . burning, burning, burning." As hard as it was to be in the hospital bed, it was hell for those watching me go through it.

"Pete was exhausted—the understatement of the year," she said. He'd alternately been my rock, my buffer, and my punching bag. "Pete was having trouble leaving," she added, but for his own sanity, "he knew he had to exit."

For Agnes, our reunion brought both relief and new pain. I later asked her to tell me what it was like seeing me the first time following the blast, since we'd last seen each other in the hallway in the Baghdad bureau on the morning of the bombing.

"The last time I saw you was on May 29 in the early hours. I waved," she told me. "Then Paul and James died," she said. Those four words were as close as she could come to describing the pain of their loss. She still hadn't let herself cry.

"I walked into your room," she said. "I saw you, and you were alive. You looked strangely like KD [Kimberly Dozier]. Gaunt, in pain, distorted, afraid, confused, removed. Bad fucking hair day too. But you looked like KD. You, the hard-arse I'd always known—you. You were alive.

"Then we had a chat," she said, describing the moment we finally talked about the bombing and I told her what I remembered. Agnes had buried the pain to deal with later, but listening to me started dredging it out. "I think I held your hand," she said. "Maybe you held mine."

She said that after I'd sat up for an hour with the disastrous Zeroform on me, I'd collapsed back into bed in pain. All my guests "ended up stuck in the visiting room (tucked away next to your chamber) with lukewarm tacos and guacamole, cake, and all, celebrating your life, gaunt, in pain, and burning."

After Pete left, Agnes emailed him on my progress.

On July 10, Agnes wrote:

hola pete! kd had a real good day today. i arrived at the hosp at approx 1200 only to find an empty room. no kd or anyone else in sight. called mei-lee who quickly informed me that they were all in the Angel garden.

once back upstairs kd scoffed up some mccdonald i had brought over and an ice cream sundae, she had a real appetite. she ate even more for supper where she had 6 slices of pizza!!!

her parents left at 1400 so kd, mei-lee and i spent the afternoon chatting and napping. i watched the world cup, BTW, we lost.

it's 2000 and kd is a bit uncomfortable because of her back wounds . . . but she still has a grin on her face. we are letting her be right now and both mei-lee and i are typing away furiously . . .

i went thru KD's email account today and divided all mails by month MAY, JUNE, JULY. suggested she stay well clear of MAY and JUNE for now, she agrees. also put her baghdad stuff in the hotel safe and spoke to mei-lee about that.

how was your trip back home? how are the kids? kd misses you but is really enjoying the text messages . . . yesterday kd said she may want to speak to Linda Douglas soon . . . she didn't mention it today so i'll play it by ear. i think if she wants to she should, i'll just make sure Linda is up for it too, which i think she will be.

getting along real well with mei-lee and the folks so all is well . . . relax and be sure to know that i will call you at any time of day or night if i think it's necessary, so chill & enjoy your time home. call me if you need to, will write tomorrow.

Pete replied:

ok grasshopper, you done well for my "getting off the plane update." I am relieved. Pity about the world cup!

Really pleased you helping with the email management!! That's brilliant—I was worried.

Speak of the she-devil, I just got off the phone . . . she is good, the KD-moodometer is "in the GREEN" but she is tired.

My "frog" friend, as I called her, had witnessed how Pete had helped me track down doctors and nurses to solve the donor-site problem, so she took her job as replacement patient advocate seriously. When she found me trying to stifle my crying into a pillow, she went into action. A nurse had applied one of the new silver-infused bandages—a type I'd never used before, and it burned me almost immediately. The nurse told me the sensation would go away. I felt I'd done so much complaining lately that I'd used up my quota, so I was trying to suck it up. Agnes felt no such restrictions and raised hell on my behalf.

The nurses called for a doctor to check my back and by the time he arrived an hour or so later, he found allergic red welts spreading steadily outward from the bandage and quickly ripped it off. Agnes was not going to let pain win on her watch.

But she couldn't stop the effect these new bouts of pain were having on my self-confidence. My initial feistiness with doctors and nurses was fading. So was my ability to do things like take a shot without flinching. Now every time the nurses came around with a heparin injection, the anticoagulant I took up to four times a day to keep my blood from clotting, I cringed and fought off tears.

And as time drew near for me to leave Bethesda, the tentative new me balked at the prospect of leaving behind familiar doctors, nurses, corpsmen, and a routine I understood. My mom and dad shared my sense of panic. It was as if we all thought, "She's in pain, so you haven't fixed her, so she can't possibly leave yet."

I was angry with my doctors for telling me it was time to go. When Dr. Dunne picked up on that anger, he was immediately sympathetic and told me I'd only be discharged when I was ready. That eased my mind. And then Lidia, during one of the dressing changes, made a point I hadn't heard before. "Hospitals are where people get sick," she said. "The longer you stay here, the more likely you are to pick up a hospital infection from a caregiver, your family, or just the air. You need to move on."

It was a sugar-coated, polite version of what was being said about my case in the staff room, where many of the doctors felt I needed to soon leave lest I contract secondary hospital infections. I learned later from others in the meetings that there were loud arguments with doctors asking why I was still there and why I hadn't been told to go, and Dr. Dunne countering that my donor sites weren't quite ready. I'm glad no one put any ultimatums before me because I would have dug my heels in and stayed as long as I could.

Instead I welcomed visits by the hospital's social worker, who told my parents and me about rehabilitation hospital options. We asked him to give us four to five rehab centers to choose from, including care in the Washington, D.C., area. But he kept steering us to one in particular:

Baltimore's Kernan Rehabilitation Hospital. We knew Kernan was one of the best in the field for sports and "ordinary" (not combat) trauma, but I thought I might need to go to a veterans' facility where they understood my type of injury. (This was before the coverage of Walter Reed's outpatient care. I now realize the social worker probably knew more than he wanted to share, namely that veterans' hospitals were stretched to bursting because of the current conflict. He just did his best to steer me away from veteran facilities.)

A delegation from Kernan drove to see me to explain that they knew how to fix me. That VIP, full-court press didn't stop me from being scared, though, and my fear filtered through everything I did. As the day of my departure approached, my confidence ebbed further. I felt fragile and off-balance (even more so than usual), and physiotherapist Carol had to give me extra encouragement to get through my sessions.

The day before I departed, however, I became a bit impatient with myself. Like a small child trying to prove something, I pushed my workout too far. Carol had me walking to and from the bathroom sink, an amazing freedom for someone who had to brush her teeth by using a cup of water and by spitting into a kidney bowl for six weeks.

I was so excited that I decided I would stand at the sink and brush my teeth like a normal human being. It worked and my legs felt fine, holding steady. So I pushed it and washed my hands.

"I think you should walk now," Carol said, a note of warning rising in her voice.

"I'm fine," I said, believing it. I passed the three-minute mark of standing still in one place. I hadn't done that in seven weeks, and I was rejoicing at how great it felt.

I looked in the mirror at the ghostly pale, scarred woman with the drawn face and felt faint.

It wasn't the image that was disorienting. I was blacking out. I got as far as "Carol, I'm feeling . . ." and started sinking to the floor. Black literally closed in on my eyes like curtains drawing shut from left and right.

Carol caught me, muttering, "I haven't had a person fall in 15 years, and I'm not starting today." She got me to a chair and lifted my legs up so the blood would rush back to my head, which it had so recently vacated. I slowly returned to normal but felt so shaken that there was no way I was going to do any more walking that day.

As painful as my time had been there and as much as I wanted to get out, Bethesda had become my world. Not to mention that I'd had enough challenges lately, and deep down I suppose I was frightened at facing another one—at least I was the night before my departure. It was a mild version of the fright I'd felt the night before the Memorial Day patrol. But when the "day of" dawns, I'm always ready for whatever's coming. I was almost euphoric as the moment of my exodus approached.

First there was a long morning of goodbyes to so many people I'd come to rely on. In a hospital, especially when people have to help you do all those private things you'd normally do for yourself, you become close to people overnight. Maybe it's a false intimacy, or a survival technique, or just the intensity of the experience, but you tend to open up to people and, in my case, ask people about aspects of their own lives that you'd never otherwise ask them.

I'd heard so many plans and dreams, like the young nurse who wanted to be a neurosurgeon or the young corpsman who had fought his way through Marine boot camp, stunning even his friends who called him a "weakling." He couldn't wait to be deployed to Iraq so he could save lives in the field. I remember every face and every story, but I lost the names quickly. If I'd only had the forethought to write them down or get a card. I realized that some people didn't give me their names or email addresses although I'd asked for them, probably because they had these intense encounters all the time and knew they didn't have the time or the heart left in their 24/7 days to keep in touch. They knew they'd need their energy for the next broken soul who rolled in.

All that was on my mind, but so were all the other things Bethesda represented for me: the locked-down terror I felt before every surgery that I tried to always keep to myself, the feelings of utter helplessness for the first time in my life, and the humiliation of depending on someone else to meet my most basic of needs over and over, all the while knowing there was someone else on the hall who probably needed the nurses and corpsmen as much, if not more, than I did while they were tending to me. And, of course, there was the guilt, the pain, and the nightmares of those first few weeks as I absorbed what had happened to my friends.

All in all it was an awkward leave-taking. As the moment arrived, after the ambulance attendants had moved me to a stretcher for transport, I felt a surge of giddiness, and as is usual for moments like that, I tried to cover it with nervous laughter. As all the corpsmen and nurses waved goodbye as I rolled past the nurses' station, I cracked a supremely bad joke. "I am outta here! Escape from Witch Mountain." Let's just say the joke didn't go over well. Even in my reclined, strapped-in state, I could see a few faces freezing. Ah, well, I can always blame the Dilaudid.

With that, I was wheeled to an ambulance bay.

Agnes and MeiLee had been packing my possessions for Kernan—just as Agnes had to pack all my things in Baghdad. But this time, Agnes was packing for someone she knew was going to live.

"I knew then that KD was on her way to Kernan," Agnes said. "My friend, Kimberly Dozier, excuse me, Kimberly-fucking-Dozier, was now on her way."

CHAPTER 15
zero to a hundred feet– in two weeks

My one request for my new locale: I was desperate to see trees. My room at Bethesda had faced the parking lot and a sea of concrete buildings. I needed inspiration outside my window as I tackled the next chapter of my recovery: learning to walk on my own without someone shadowing me every step of the way.

Kernan Rehabilitation Hospital obliged, putting me in a room looking out at a tall stand of pines on what was an old country estate. A former children's hospital, Kernan was now tucked in a rare bit of green among Baltimore's neighborhoods and nearby urban strip malls. I couldn't see or hear traffic.

Kernan's CEO, Jim Ross, had wanted to put me on the VIP floor, where the hospital treated various football players and political notables. But I'd been in isolation for almost two months, so I didn't want to be tucked away in an ivory tower. I wanted noise and green.

They found me a room on a regular floor that they'd used as a storage area and cleared it out for me. (Yes, at Kernan I really did get the VIP treatment.) The staff also cleared out a second bed, turning the area facing me into a sitting room. They couldn't give me a roommate anyway; I was still—and will always be—considered contaminated with Acinetobacter.

I was right next to the nurses' station. There was a happy buzz about the place, with patients wheeling themselves back and forth along the soothing pastel hallways, some of them in para- or quadriplegic wheelchairs and many with amputated legs or arms. I felt relief. No one here had been hit by a car bomb, true, but other than that, I blended right in.

The hospital's patient population came primarily from the University of Maryland's Shock Trauma Hospital in Baltimore, a city with "more homicides and shootings than small countries in civil wars," according to my new doctor, Dr. Steven Schwartz. "The traumas were from bullets or missiles or blunt traumas from accidents," he said, so while Kernan hadn't rehabbed war-injured blast victims before, they'd dealt with many cases that came close.

I later found out that some of the toughest, most touch-and-go cases of injured troops were sent from Bethesda or Walter Reed to the University of Maryland's Shock Trauma unit, where renowned surgeon Dr. Thomas Scalea used the most modern techniques to keep them alive. Some of the methods they pioneered to stop bleeding, such as the groundbreaking use of the controversial Factor 7 clotting agent, were passed on to the battlefield and had been used on me in Baghdad.

The center also is one of the three hospitals nationwide where military surgeons study trauma before they deploy. That's how Kernan's Dr. Schwartz had ended up working with Dr. Dunne. Both of them had done their fellowship at Shock Trauma. When I realized that, some of my tension eased. I was still in the family, so to speak.

My new orthopedic surgeon, Dr. Andy Pollak, who would nominally be in charge of me at Kernan, was the head of Shock Trauma's orthopedic department and a man the ortho surgeons at Bethesda Naval Hospital worshipped. He spent his spare time working on innovating new ways to treat blast injuries to troops in the field. My confidence in the place rose as I realized that these doctors really did seem to know how to treat my type of injuries.

But then they shattered my newfound faith in them. Just two days later every specialist on my new team evaluated me and predicted that in just two weeks I'd be walking 100 feet with a cane or crutches and would be ready to leave.

When they told me that, I decided they were certifiably nuts.

Just 48 hours earlier at Bethesda Naval Hospital, I'd passed out when all I'd done was try to stand still for three minutes. I felt a sense of panic, as I had when the Bethesda doctors told me it was time to go. Dr. Schwartz had to promise me the hospital wouldn't kick me out until I was ready. That calmed my panic to simmering.

I couldn't be mad at my physical therapist. The perpetually grinning Amy Jones was a blur of blonde, 5-foot-nothing (if that), gymnast-strong motion. She was too irrepressibly optimistic to argue with. I instantly knew I wouldn't win. I just said to myself that it must take a certain degree of insanity and delusion to do her job, and I told myself not to feel bad if I didn't meet her completely unreasonable predictions and expectations. We fell into a dynamic of trying to one-up each other. "Just do 10 reps," she'd say. And I'd do 12. Her reverse psychology worked as well on me as it would on any 3-year-old.

My occupational therapist, Gwendolyn Alexander, was Amy's opposite: a tall, soigné, unflappable African-American woman who immediately made me feel like I needed to comb my hair, put on some makeup, stand up straight, and act like lady. I discovered that each of them had one thing in common: They put their jobs ahead of everything else in their lives.

In Amy's spare time she taught physically challenged kids how to do things like water-ski, or she took new classes to learn other physio skills and specialties. As of her last email, she finished one set of courses and is motoring on to mastering another subspecialty in her field.

Gwen filled every minute of the day with everyone else's needs. Like many strong Christians I met along the way, she was great with the "Do unto others" part, but always seemed to forget to do some good for herself. She'd go from too many hours at work, managing the other therapists and treating her own patients, to a fully packed house: a husband, two sons, and one of her patients. I spied him during one of the occupational therapy group sessions, an African-American man in his late twenties who wore a loud sports shirt and a huge gold cross and sat in a tricked-out wheelchair. He'd been injured in a shooting and had no use of his arms or legs. His family couldn't cope with him as a quadriplegic, so they'd abandoned him. Gwen and her husband had taken him in.

Kernan was full of examples like that. I know Bethesda was too, but since I rarely left my room, I didn't see them or meet them like I did at Kernan.

Now I was allowed to and expected to rejoin the human race. I had to eat my breakfast, wash and dress myself (with an aide's help), and wheel myself to the physio gym every day in time for my 9 a.m. class. Style wasn't an issue. Everyone seemed to wear the same uniform: T-shirts and pajama bottoms.

Then we'd all work out in the same brightly lit gym, each of us learning baby steps particular to our unique conditions. I was learning things like how to lower myself onto a bench by using my upper legs' quadriceps (or rather quadriceps in my left leg, but triceps on my right since one of the muscles had been burned away). Next to me would be a paraplegic who was learning how to lift his leg with his arm or how to use his arms to move his body from his wheelchair to the bench and use his stomach muscles to shift his lower body.

As we started my workouts, the predictions of my rapid recovery seemed even more ridiculous. I could barely do anything. Amy had me practice first with crutches, unevenly loping the perimeter of the room with her ready to catch me the entire time. I'd collapse back into the wheelchair in relief. Sitting was the edge of my comfort zone.

Still ringing in my ears was the dire prediction from Landstuhl from weeks earlier: You might never walk normally again. But every time I wanted to feel sorry for myself, I turned and saw someone who had it harder than I ever would, and he or she was usually smiling. Every time I felt pain as Amy pushed my knee into a deeper bend, I'd grit my teeth and button it up. You can't cry around people like that. At least I could feel the pain, and at least I had a chance to get better.

I was regularly witnessing minor miracles: people with horrific and permanent injuries who refused to bow to them. Sure, some days I saw an amputee so depressed that he or she stopped halfway through a workout, stared glumly into space, and refused to go on. Or sometimes they didn't show up for their workout at all. The amazing part was how seldom that happened.

I was about to be thrown for an entirely unexpected loop, however, and it nearly knocked me flat. On my bulletin board, where the aides jotted down my day's schedule, they had written "speech therapy."

As those around me could attest, there was nothing wrong with my speaking ability unless they were talking about finding a way to shut me up. So I had no idea what to expect.

My speech therapist, Kristin Bertrand, explained the little-known fact that the term "speech therapy" included cognitive therapy, meaning how my brain was working. Kristin had to break it to me gently: My last cognitive test at Bethesda indicated that my intelligence was just average. And considering the job I had done previously and my education level, that meant I might have lasting damage to my brain.

I sat there, stiffening with anger and disbelief. I already felt at a disadvantage, sitting there in pajamas next to the athletic Kristin, who looked more like an American Anna Kournikova than my idea of a brain specialist. *What does she know? I have to prove her wrong like everyone else,* I thought.

I remembered taking the test she was talking about, and I became angrier. I didn't think it had been fair. Two young soldiers in uniform had come into my room at Bethesda at 8 a.m. and stood over my bed—that alone was a departure from the norm in a Naval hospital and slightly freaked me out.

My breakfast had just arrived and was sitting on the bed table on my left with them standing over me on my right. It was one of the rare occasions when breakfast smelled good and all I wanted to do was eat. Instead they took me through an unexpected battery of tests. With half an eye on breakfast, I got through their tests as quickly as possible. I hadn't realized my results were so poor.

So now, in a calmer setting, my self-indignant rage was fueled and I'd have to show my obviously misinformed speech therapist that test was wrong.

"Fine," I said, thinking, *bring it. What test have I ever failed, except calculus?*

I started out confidently, but I couldn't repeat more than maybe 6 of the 10 words she'd read out to me. *Stress,* I thought to myself.

Then we got to a short-term memory section, where she stood up and did four activities around the room, which I had to copy. She moved to her files and pulled one out. She then went to the door and then crossed the room to a chair and then went back to her desk. I confidently stood to copy her, went through the motions, and sat down.

"You realize you missed one?" she asked, again gently, with her eyebrows raised. I hadn't realized. I couldn't comprehend how I could screw up something so simple.

Now I was humbled, a bit embarrassed at my inner indignation, and truly scared.

Kristin was careful not to give me any definite diagnoses. She said we'd meet for an hour every day and she'd teach me how to improve my short-term memory. I'd learn skills to make up for what my brain had apparently forgotten to do.

Still I was in a panic by the time I met with Dr. Schwartz. I asked him what else could cause short-term memory loss because I couldn't face that there might be something physically wrong with my brain.

I was still taking a couple oral Dilaudid pills every day. Dr. Schwartz conceded that the narcotic could be causing memory problems. I wanted to go off them then and there, cold turkey. I'd cope with whatever pain there was to deal with as long as I could get my short-term memory back.

He convinced me to follow a step-down plan to keep my body from going into withdrawal, but he warned me it would take an indeterminate time to show the results if the drug was indeed the cause of my memory loss.

I didn't miss the drug as I started to come off it. The advice from my CBS Washington bureau chief, Janet Leissner, had come true. Janet, who'd been through so many surgeries herself, had told me that when my body didn't need the drug to block the pain receptors, it wouldn't miss it and neither would I.

Still my body did notice. I started sweating every night, soaking through the gown, the sheets, and even the blankets. It never took long to get help, but the aide who responded always had to take a long hike to the linen cupboard to replace everything. It took 20 minutes from waking soaked to getting back to sleep all warm and dry. I learned to keep first two, and then three, changes of gowns, sheets, and blankets beside my bed every night for the soaking to come.

I suspected it came from my body withdrawing from the Dilaudid, but when I ventured that opinion to one of the nurses as she gave me my usual morning round of shots and medicines, she ventured another diagnosis: menopause.

"I'm 40," I said. "That's too young."

She said matter of factly that perhaps the trauma to my body had triggered it. My world fell in. Perhaps she'd already gone through menopause, so she'd forgotten what devastating news it could be to a younger woman who was still considering having children.

As she walked out, I burst into tears. But I was already late for class with Amy, so I pushed myself down the hallway, trying to swallow the tears in huge gulps. If I was any other patient, it's likely no one would have paid attention, but people notice when the so-called VIP is semi-bawling as she rolls by. I made it to class, and Amy saw me wiping my face off but didn't pry.

Later Dr. Schwartz stopped by to see what the fuss was about, and when I told him the nurse's diagnosis, he stopped me in my verbal tracks. "Didn't I tell you not to listen to anyone else about things like that without running it past me?" "Yes," I answered. He agreed the Dilaudid was probably to blame, but now that I was so upset about the other possibility, he ran a battery of tests on me that ruled out menopause. We never figured out definitively what caused the night sweats, but by the end of my stay there, they'd stopped.

My days were exhausting, especially when you consider that the most exercise I'd been doing before this was walking 30 to 40 steps a day and sitting in a wheelchair. I had an hour of physio with Amy, then an hour of recreational therapy with Jenny Johnson, where we'd end up discussing everything from how I could still do the sports I loved if my legs were weak to how we were both coping with our parents getting older and our fears of losing them. Then came speech therapy and then lunch. (The food at Kernan was good, so this was always a high point.) Then I had more physical therapy and also occupational therapy with Gwen in the afternoon. She put me through the paces of doing ordinary things I hadn't done in months, everything from getting from bed to the wheelchair on my own to learning how to put on socks when my legs were still so stiff I could barely reach my toes. It was exhilarating and frustrating. I ended every day trying to simply stand up and stand still. I started with a minute and tried to add at least a minute each day. I'd play solitaire to distract me, which amused Gwen since she didn't know the rules. (She has no spare time in her life for card games, obviously.)

And then, as Dr. Schwartz described it, I held court. "Instead of sleeping, you're having to entertain a roomful of people day after day," he observed by the end of the first week.

MeiLee, Agnes, and CBS courier Amanda Mackaye helped move me to Kernan. As at Bethesda, they stayed for a few days longer to keep me company. So did my parents, especially since Kernan was close to their home.

This was a problem, my doctor explained, although not one of my own making. He said it was common for the family members of trauma patients to cling, especially since they'd almost lost me once that year. But he said it was draining my energy and holding me back. At Bethesda I'd needed constant help. At Kernan the whole idea was to get me to start doing things for myself, not to mention the fact that since my schedule was so punishing, all I'd usually want to do after my last class was sleep.

Dr. Schwartz knew I'd already had a set-to with my parents over physiotherapy. The first day at Kernan, my dad showed up and stayed with me every step of physical therapy, just as he had at Bethesda. I appreciated his steadfast loyalty, and I didn't want to seem ungrateful. But I was no longer the critical care patient confined to a bed who needed encouragement to get through the pain. And no one else in the room had a parent shadowing his or her every move unless the patient was under the age of 10. By the second week, I'd had to gently discourage Dad from coming.

There was another issue, which Dr. Schwartz had to gently referee. When I'd first checked into Kernan, my parents asked him to give them daily briefings on my medical status just like they'd received at Bethesda. He out-and-out refused. He explained that I was no longer a critical care patient under the influence of copious amounts of narcotics, so legally I was in charge of my own medical care. The doctors and therapists would brief me, and I'd decide what to pass on to my parents.

Despite being told this on the first day, my father insisted on trying to catch Dr. Schwartz for private asides in the hospital outside of my earshot. He'd demur. When I expressed my anger over this invasion of my privacy, my parents complained that I was oversensitive and needed counseling. They were right: The counseling I was receiving at Kernan was focused on how to handle the growing tension with them—again, a common theme for trauma patients.

It only grew worse when I told them I wouldn't be coming to stay at their condominium but instead would be staying in a CBS-provided apartment with Pete. There was no space in their two-bedroom condo, and I knew that my parents would coddle me, which would both slow my recovery and drive them into the ground. They were furious—anger born out of rejection and hurt.

Looking back I realize this chasm between the caregivers and the patient couldn't be avoided. It foreshadowed a larger battle to come as I struggled to prove to my friends, then my colleagues, then my company, and the larger public that I was healed and wanted no more pity and no more help. It was part of the healing process, but like so much in this journey, it involved a lot of pain.

It also helped me be a better caregiver when my mother was admitted for several rounds of emergency surgery and long-term care a year later. I remembered how it felt to be treated as if I wasn't up to the challenge of making my own decisions. I also remembered the times I gave in to helplessness and ceded my responsibility to others. It's hard to recover. So when my mom sometimes asked us to make tough decisions for her, I refused. "You can do this. You have to."

The conflict with my mom and dad was the only low note. A few days before I was to leave Kernan, I retook the memory exam and aced it. Either I'd learned short-term memory coping skills in record time or my memory problems had indeed been drug-induced.

On my last day at Kernan, I reluctantly agreed to let CBS send over a cameraman and a still photographer to document my progress. This was the first time I'd allowed cameras to follow any part of my recovery. I'd shunned them at Bethesda. I wasn't willing to have any of that pain captured on TV.

It felt odd to be filmed as the subject instead of the narrator. I fell back into the old habit of interviewing my therapists as we filmed, and I tried to forget that the cameraman was documenting one of the clumsiest moments of my life. During the occupational therapy session, Gwen had me practice pouring water into a pan, then walking a couple steps while supporting myself with a crutch, and putting the pan on the stove.

I managed it, but by the end of the task, I was out of breath with beads of sweat breaking out on my forehead. Doing anything new still had the power to exhaust me, and I was committing this image to video.

I drafted a short statement to thank those who'd helped me get out of Iraq alive and put me back together again. I didn't have all the facts at that point, and the ones I did have came courtesy of a Maryland grandmother— the one whose grandson had stood guard over Paul, James, and Capt. Funkhouser at the bomb scene. When she'd heard I was staying at Kernan, she'd brought me a homemade cake and an Army newspaper account of the bombing with more detail than I'd read anywhere else.

But it didn't mention the role the Iowa National Guardsmen played that day, especially S. Sgt. Koch, who'd tied the tourniquets on that had saved my life. (I later realized I'd put medic Flores in an uncomfortable spot with my poorly reported thank-you note in which I confused him for Iowa Guardsman Koch, but at least the sentiment was right on target.)

It was one of the hardest and most painful things I've ever had to write.

Folks, I'm leaving hospitals behind, ahead of the deadline, or at least ahead of schedule. I've had a couple setbacks, and I still face a couple minor surgeries, but overall, the prognosis is far better than the docs had hoped just after I'd reached Germany. The teams at Balad, Landstuhl, and the National Naval Medical Center in Bethesda, Md., worked overtime—something like a dozen surgeries at least, including one that lasted 11 hours.

Just a few weeks later, I'm up on crutches and can even manage with a cane. It's not pretty, but I'm walking on my own—and that, I also owe to some hard-driving therapists at Kernan Hospital in Maryland, who kept saying, "Now try this . . ."

The next step: continued outpatient rehab to get my body used to being in motion full-time.

Thanks to CBS, my family and friends have been close by throughout. That, together with all the amazing cards and emails from across the country, has really pulled me through. I've told friends it's been like having 10,000 guardian angels on my shoulders.

I've learned slowly how close I came to joining my friends, cameraman Paul Douglas and soundman James Brolan, both killed by the blast. I owe my life to the quick actions of the 4th Infantry Division's Sgt. Mootoosammy—who took charge of the scene, with his commander down and many of his men injured—and medic Spec. Flores, who patched me up. Even with a car bomb cooking off, sending shrapnel through the air just a couple dozen feet from us, Spec. Flores just kept calmly speaking to me and working on my legs—no wavering, no pause.

Not a day goes by without thinking of Paul and James—two of the most remarkable characters I've ever known. My heart goes out to their families, and I know no words to stop their grief. The last I saw Paul and James, they were rushing from their Humvee to "get the shot" of a young U.S. Army Captain, James Funkhouser, Jr., greeting Iraqi locals at a streetside tea stand. The bomb hit all three of them, together with an Iraqi liaison officer, and took all four lives.

I choose to remember them from the instant before the blast—each one of them consummate pros doing a job they loved to support the families back home they loved even more.

CHAPTER 16
baby steps

I moved into a temporary apartment, or rather CBS moved me in. Janet made sure I had all the help I needed, just as she had since I'd arrived Stateside on a stretcher. I'd be on my own for a night before Pete returned from three weeks of catching up with his kids and bills in New Zealand.

As much as I looked forward to seeing him the next day, it was amazing to be completely by myself for the first time in about nine weeks. No one was checking on me, giving me shots, changing sheets, or asking me how I felt.

Of course, I immediately did too much. I unpacked every box, a process that in my weak state took multiple trips back and forth around the tiny one-bedroom apartment. My body had no stamina. I kept having to rest. If I left my crutches leaning against a wall and took a step without them, I'd end up swaying, looking for a piece of furniture to grab on to.

But I was determined that when Pete walked through the door, he'd not only find me standing on my own two feet but that I'd have made the place a home.

I also wanted to look semihuman because the last time he'd seen me, I was immobilized by the donor sites, flat on my back. So I hopped in the shower, planning to style my hair to cleverly hide the circular skull scar. But my still-busted ears meant I had to wear earplugs, so when Pete arrived, and knocked—I didn't hear him. He had to wait in the hallway for 20 minutes.

When I finally turned the water off and heard the knocking, I lurched drowned-catlike to get the door. Forget my plans to put myself together so I looked normal again. I just barely had time to shift my wet hair to cover the shaved side of my head.

I needn't have worried. Pete was just thrilled to see me actually standing on my own (with a cane stashed within arm's reach).

I wouldn't be anywhere near normal for another couple months, and Pete had a lot more confidence in my return at that point than I did.

First of all, I didn't understand how he could look at anything beyond my face and see someone he wanted to hold. Beyond the obvious limping, I was still a bride of Frankenstein under construction. Two of the donor sites still hadn't healed. The dressings needed to be changed and the wounds cleaned almost daily. A terrific wound nurse, Mark, came every few days to do that, but invariably in between I'd jostle a bandage open during physiotherapy or when I was trying to do too much around the house and Pete would step in, part boyfriend, part nurse and medic.

Pete does nothing halfway. When my bandages needed to be changed, he carefully laid out supplies as if for surgery, scrubbed his hands, and donned gloves. The wounds had to be covered with a thin strip of pink foam that was impregnated with antibiotics and then sealed with the Saran-wraplike Tegaderm. The bandage then absorbed the lymph and other fluids that were still oozing out and kept the area moist to speed the healing. The pink foam, however, also absorbed sweat from my physio workouts, so it often became uncomfortable, a waterlogged sponge stuck to the side of my leg and back. It did not make me feel attractive.

Some of the donor-site areas had healed enough that they no longer needed the full bandages, but the thin layers of skin weren't quite done rebuilding. The skin would bubble and break, weep, bleed, and itch. It was like having poison ivy and poison sumac for six months. I had to sleep on a towel at night, and I couldn't wear any light-colored shirts because they'd dot with blood. Worse, the itching intensified in the humid oven of Baltimore's summer.

The heat sent me into a St. Vitas dance of scratching. I tried everything from prednisone to way too much hydrocortisone to ease the itching. Desperate for relief, I bought several ice packs and would strap them onto my back, where the itching was worst, wearing them day and night. I'd rotate fresh ice packs from the freezer when the itching woke me up at night. I ended up using hydrocortisone for a couple months, far too long, until it did more harm than good. My skin suffered rebound from too much steroid cream, meaning the itching came back worse than before. So I switched to natural cures, like rosehip oil and vitamin E. That helped enormously, but by then my skin was also healing of its own accord.

Another problem I faced was stitch rejection. The 2,000-plus stitches throughout my body were supposedly made with a dissolvable thread that my body would absorb. Instead tight knots were fighting their way to the surface. They were rising through my skin in lumps, usually along the thick red scars. In some cases an edge of thread would break through the surface and I could tug it out and the itching would stop. But as I was rebandaging a spot that wouldn't heal one day (and, of course, scratching it, which I shouldn't have done), something completely unexpected broke through the skin: an inch of clear thread, like 10-pound-test fishing line.

"Pete—help!" I yelped.

Pete got a set of tweezers, grabbed the end of the line, and gently started pulling what turned out to be a 10-inch piece of thread. I held my skin down and felt the end of the thread tracing the edge of the graft. This wasn't supposed to happen. Doctors later told me they don't even know how a piece of thread that big ended up under the graft.

When Pete finally tugged the last of it out, we both looked at it and then at each other.

"Oh, God, Pete, I'm sorry," I said, as I did so often. "This is taking intimacy *way* too far."

That gave him permission to react, as he really wanted to, dropping the tweezers and recoiling. "Gross!!" I was also recoiling into a fetal pose, utterly disgusted at what my body had yielded. From that point on when other bits of thread or shrapnel started fighting their way out through my skin, I handled it solo.

The hardest thing to get used to beyond the disgusting science experiment that was my healing body was how long it took me to do everything. Any exertion left me struggling to recover. I couldn't walk more than a couple hundred feet with my cane without needing to sit and rest for half an hour. It didn't help that neither Pete nor I was getting much sleep because the busiest fire station in the state, Baltimore's Fire Station No. 1, was practically under our window. It seems most fires break out between 3 and 5 a.m. We never slept through a single night.

My legs didn't work well enough to operate a car—I couldn't yet count on their reflexes—so Pete was de facto chauffeur in addition to his nursing duties. He started ferrying me back and forth. Three times a week we drove to Kernan's outpatient physiotherapy clinic near my parents in Timonium, Maryland, to see physiotherapist Rebecca Shakespeare, hereafter known as Becca. She became one of the keys to my recovery, not to mention a savior for my psyche.

As I had learned throughout this process, physiotherapy isn't an exact science. Your progress depends on your physiotherapist's personal area of expertise and the amount of time he or she is given to work with you, combined with the therapist's drive (and yours) and how well your personality meshes. At each stage in this process, I had the right person for the right time, starting with the cheerful but relentless Naval Commander Carol at Bethesda, who saw beyond the blood and gore of my burns and pushed me through my strange initial timidity and terror because she'd seen it in patients so many times before. I didn't quite believe in her confidence in me, but just like she caught me when I fell that last day, she'd caught me every time my faith faltered.

Then there was the unstoppably upbeat Amy at Kernan, who made coming back from a tragedy into a game. She had a blind spot for despair, and by ignoring it she helped me fight it. She was truly happy with any and every millimeter of progress.

Then I met Becca, who bookended my recovery before and after I traveled to "Godzone," as Kiwis modestly refer to their land (short for "God's Own Country"). In Auckland the no-nonsense Sandie Alexander took over. Sandie was Becca's twin when it came to understanding biomechanics. In a field where there are vast differences of opinion in how to treat injuries, I found two coincidentally kindred spirits who assigned me similar exercises without ever looking at the other one's notes or files.

After five months of working with Sandie in New Zealand, I went back to Becca to recover after my final bone surgery in February 2006, a procedure that enabled me to go from walking to running.

Becca was obsessed with biomechanics and skilled with an Oprah-level ability to listen to a patient's personal issues, which helped pass the time during scar massage, another of her areas of expertise. She and I started with weight machines for my legs. This was depressing. I could barely lift, pull, or push 10 pounds on anything. Sometimes she had to take the weights off altogether. And, of course, I was still working to get both my knees to bend. They were so stiff, especially the right one, that I didn't walk down steps. I lurched.

The other problem was that my right ankle had just about fused at a 90-degree angle. It was hard to point it or lift my foot upward. My gait was halting and storklike. I looked and felt like an 85-year-old woman with arthritis.

Over the six weeks I spent in physiotherapy in Baltimore, I'd lift, stretch, and lunge over and over again. Becca would have me walk back and forth between parallel bars and examine where my weaknesses were or where the stiffness that didn't seem to be yielding to the stretching and bending exercises was, and then she'd devise new tortures.

Each two-hour session was followed by an hour of scar massage, which sounds oh-so-relaxing. It wasn't. Each scar was stuck down through the layers of healed tissue to the muscle or sinew beneath. Those glued-down areas were keeping my muscles from moving, or at least were holding them back, so they had to be physically unglued.

That meant Becca would jam her thumbs or the heel of her palm into the scar tissue and manually grind the layers apart. Since these were all new scars, and some quite sensitive, the pain was sometimes intense—not donor-site intense but like the knee-bending stretches I'd been through. It was a long period of low-level excruciation, punctuated by the occasional massive, sharp stab of pain.

The therapy worked. Areas of skin that had puckered and stuck in place when my leg moved now started moving more freely atop the muscles. It was a process I continued for the next six months with Becca and then with two different physiotherapists in New Zealand. I only started the massage treatment initially because it happened to be Becca's specialty. I often wondered if injured troops had access to the same time-consuming and ultimately expensive hands-on care.

Away from the gym I was pushing my walking skills in the real world, taking tentative steps from my apartment to Baltimore's Inner Harbor, which was just a mile away. At first I could manage the trip there with a cane (I had abandoned the crutches almost the moment I'd left Kernan). But Pete had to push me for the return journey in a wheelchair.

Then came a day to celebrate. We were late leaving the apartment for physiotherapy. I raced out the door after Pete, pulled the door shut behind me, shuffled quickly to the elevator, and stopped. I looked at Pete and looked down at my feet.

"I forgot my cane," I said. And then I looked up and smiled. "And that means I don't need it." We hugged, grinning like kids, and left it behind.

I learned the hard part about *not* carrying a cane and not being totally normal. When people, cars, or buses see a person with a cane, they don't expect her to rush. They give her space. They don't brush or push past a person using a cane on the sidewalk. As soon as I left the cane behind, though, it was open season. I'm a tall, sturdy-looking person, even in my then-undernourished state. People started treating me as such. But when someone would push past me on the street, I didn't have the balance or the strength to catch myself. My feet didn't move fast enough. What would make someone else stumble made me trip and fall.

A few weeks later when we left for New Zealand, Pete got angry at my refusal to carry the cane, especially when we went through all the airports. My legs ached from even 10 minutes of standing in line, but my pride wouldn't let me pull the cane out. Besides, my balance wasn't good enough to juggle a cane, a purse, and a carry-on.

In the United States I also didn't like that a cane gave people a clue to my identity. My story had been big news, but mostly it had come and gone, and people ignored me. I liked that. But add a cane or take a ride on one of those motorized grocery store shopping carts and people spotted me. FYI, it's nearly impossible to steer one of those shopping carts properly, and I now understand why my mom had refused to use one for years. She must have been humiliated once, as I was when my cart careened into a cereal display. But at least no one knew who she was.

The kind soul on two feet who helped me put the display back together took the last box out of my hand, looked me in the eye, and said, "Welcome home."

"Umm, thanks," I said. *Great—not only do they know I'm a klutz behind the wheel of a shopping cart*, I thought, *they know who I am.*

It wasn't just a pride problem that made these moments of recognition awkward. Seeing me seemed to dredge up a lot of painful events for people, and they'd share them with me within 10 seconds of recognizing me and introducing themselves. They'd tell me about friends they'd lost in Iraq, faith they'd lost in their government, hope they'd lost in ever seeing the conflict turn out right. And I'd stand there with milk or the gas pump in hand and try to come up with something wise or comforting to say.

When they walked away they'd leave me stuck back among old memories: the bombing, the bombing, the bombing. Even if I managed to leave it behind for the day, someone else would invariably bring it up.

At this point I was still having the occasional disturbing dream, no longer nightmares but more long, confusing musings of a brain trying to make sense of recent history. In them, I'd run into Paul and James at the barbeque next to the Baghdad pool. My brain had last seen them alive there and was still puzzling to put those last memories together with the new reality. I was dealing with the psychological pain in small, manageable doses now, trying to do it at times and places of my choosing, except when a stranger unwittingly foisted it upon me.

In between physio sessions and my slow, careful steps to and from the Inner Harbor, I was writing thank-you notes and emails, trying to answer a couple thousand people. They'd written everything from telling me to get well to thanking me for being with the troops to offering stories of how they came back from either war injuries or car crashes or myriad other major and minor tragedies. There were pictures from schoolkids and quite a few veterans who shared their memories and, in some cases, their medals. One sent me his Bronze Star, and another a Purple Heart. But both those medals got lost in the mail. The Bronze Star certificate reached me with a crumpled part of the paper where the medal had obviously rested. The Purple Heart veteran tracked me down, and when he figured out I hadn't received the star, he got another one issued to share with me.

It was easier to write these individuals than it was to write friends. Every note, email, or phone call to a friend was an emotionally charged experience. I had to explain what happened to me, find out how and when the news hit, and what he or she had been doing while I'd been clawing my way back on my feet. I relived the bombing by relating it or being asked about it at least a dozen times every day. Calling Paul's and James' friends was the hardest. I assumed that some of their friends in the London bureau would pass shock and go straight to anger and blame, and I wouldn't know who until I called them. In many cases, I simply copped out and instead sent a short email of condolence.

Friends from CBS, Wellesley, and beyond were flocking to Baltimore to see me in person, which was both wonderful and exhausting because each visit meant more telling of the tale.

And as always, there were the headlines from Iraq as an ever-present reminder.

When at last I was well enough to get on a plane to New Zealand, a place where almost no one knew me or of me and no one paid much attention to Iraq, I practically leapt onto the plane.

Being in New Zealand spelled relief on a number of levels; first among them was that Pete could be near his two kids, who lived mostly at their mother's home in Auckland. We'd given Rhian and George the minimum details about the seriousness of my injuries and about how many times I faced new setbacks in the hospital, so they hadn't understood why I took so long to recuperate. They half suspected their dad had been on a semivacation instead of nursing, driving, cooking, cleaning, and helping me to learn to walk again, not to mention helping me put every aspect of my life back together.

Pete also endured listening to me tell my story over and over again to him, to other friends, to strangers. He didn't budge or flinch, except over the fishing line.

Now his kids needed his emotional support more than I did. And we decided it was also time for them to know just how bad the ordeal had been for both of us, although the scars on my legs helped tell that story without our having to say a word.

CHAPTER 17

finding sanctuary

Leaving the states for New Zealand meant a glorious break from reminders of Iraq. The war didn't come up much in the news. It wasn't woven into TV shows, nor did it stare up at you from every newsstand. And no one knew who I was or what I'd been through, except for Pete's kids and a small circle of family and friends.

I had two monumental tasks in front of me: learning to walk normally and setting down my ordeal in print, partly because so many people told me I should. Writing is a method of processing grief; perhaps Brother David, Vic, and everyone else who suggested I write this story down was simply appealing to my vanity ("Oh, but you're such a good reporter, you have to write this") to get me to embark on one of the most painful assignments of my career.

Just thinking about what was ahead was exhausting, so I tried to think small: *Find a physiotherapist; write a book outline.*

Physiotherapist Sandie Alexander took on my case at a multitrauma rehab center, The Laura Fergusson's Trust in Auckland, New Zealand. I was sold on her when she looked at my battered legs and said she loved trying to figure out what had gone wrong with muscles and bones in "really complicated cases." *Sandie*, I thought, *I'm your gal.*

The center had a comprehensive rehab gym, full of patients who'd been through the wringer, like at Kernan. No one would be staring at me that much, and even when other patients did notice my scars in the therapy pool or when I wore shorts, they just assumed I'd survived a shark attack (given our geographic location), so I didn't have to explain anything.

I worked out with Sandie three times a week. She put me through half lunges, tilts on a balance board, and any other tortures she could engineer. Like Becca, she'd have me walk and then she'd critique my gait. "You're dragging your right foot," she'd point out. Or "you're listing," kind of like the *Titanic*.

I ambitiously planned to follow each session with weight lifting and then cardio on my off days. As usual I'd cut out more for myself than I could chew. I'd go great guns for three or even four days and then collapse in exhaustion with barely enough energy to get out of bed. That's how I ended up staying overnight in a New Zealand hospital on my own as Pete had started back to work in Saudi Arabia. I'd worked myself to the point that my immune system took a nosedive and my leg became infected. In my short 24-hour stay, I learned that New Zealand hospitals have great tea but no TV.

I started a host of complementary therapies, something New Zealand with its European bent has embraced as a nation. I started acupuncture treatment with one of Pete's old military friends, Pete Caughey, who just happened to be one of New Zealand's top acupuncturists. He treated me for swelling in my legs and used needles and herbs to try to spur my battered immune system.

Sandie picked up on Becca's scar massage, and I eventually added appointments with a second physiotherapist, so I was having up to five hours of scar massage a week. My scars were slowly starting to soften under the combined attack, and my legs were moving more freely.

I also went for focused light treatment on my donor sites, which were still partially unhealed three months after the original injury. I'd learned that one of New Zealand's major burn units used a Swiss-designed system called Bioptron to calm and heal both grafts and donor sites.

Such treatment isn't covered by American health providers, so I tracked down the Bioptron sales rep, Lee McInroe, and went for inexpensive treatments twice a week in her garage clinic at her house. Lee, like each of my therapists, became part of my healing team. Each watched my mood and dragged the pain out of me when necessary.

With all the workout time and different appointments, I'd spend 25 to 30 hours in treatment, the rest commuting or writing. I spent slow, unsatisfying weeks working my way through the pain of the gym sessions, making only incremental progress, frequently mired by setbacks. I'd push too hard and a tight scar would split open, sidelining me for at least a week while it healed.

It was hard work, especially with Pete away for a five-week period. New Zealand was still coming off of winter, headed for spring. It seems to rain in Auckland five times a day, whatever the season, so I sometimes felt monastic, wrapped in fleece against the damp and cold, peering into my computer.

I'd bought a Mac and was ready to follow Brother David's orders to write everything down. At a safe distance from the war and the home front, I started trying to track down the soldiers, the doctors, and everyone who'd been touched by that day, trying to piece the story together.

Sometimes the soldiers, doctors, or diplomats wouldn't write back—or they'd write just once—enthusiastic, emotional emails, talking about what those days after the bombing meant to them and what they'd gone through. They'd promise to write more details and keep in touch, but the follow-up emails never came.

I understood. I was doing the same thing. When I finally tracked down the email address of Jeremy Koch, the Iowa Guardsman who'd saved my life, he wrote me back with his phone number and I promised to call. But day after day I didn't and wasn't even sure why.

Other replies gathered in my inbox. But I'd find a thousand excuses to do anything but write back. Vic had told me that grief would crop up in unusual ways. I assumed this was one of them.

I'd turn investigative reporter one moment and excavate another layer of the story. Then I'd sit back, stunned by the emotion of whatever I'd uncovered, and go "turtle" in withdrawal.

My first draft was angry, raw, and incomplete. I could only write a few pages at a time. It was as if I'd walked into a room where a murder had taken place and the sight of blood and death overwhelmed me. Now with my hands firmly clasped in see-no-evil style over my face, I was peering through my fingers at bits of the crime scene, taking in a little bit at a time.

I read my first draft and felt embarrassed and exposed. The second version was so overly self-conscious that it was almost an apology for the first. And it was unreadable.

Eventually I wrote many drafts as much as an exercise in grief as in an attempt to create literature.

For a mental break I ventured out to the nearby high street, hoping to lose myself in some previously enjoyable hedonistic activities, like getting a haircut or a pedicure (since I couldn't reach my toes to do it myself, and New Zealand's summer and sandal weather was approaching). I thought I might even buy some real clothes instead of physio-friendly sweats.

But getting a haircut meant explaining to the hairdresser why half my head was shaved, although I'd combed my hair over to hide it. The shampoo person would also notice the straight edge of the bone and feel the small titanium plates held by rivets where the surgeons screwed one side of the skull to the other. The four bumps, just visible on the side of my forehead, look like four points on a compass. Next to that you can still see the depression in my head where the bone hasn't quite filled in, where the original shrapnel penetrated—literally a hole in my head.

I'd debate before going into the salon as to whether or not to tell. Telling would mean I'd see the hairdresser yank the shampoo person off to the side and whisper theatrically into his or her ear. I'd see the shampoo person's eyes widen, and then he or she would bustle over as if this whole pantomime hadn't just taken place.

Not telling meant they'd discover the stuff accidentally, and I'd sit closemouthed in the chair, wondering if they'd dare to bring it up or ignore it.

A pedicure was even more uncomfortable. It meant showing my huge shark-bite grafts on my right calf, not just to the nail technician but to the customers on either side of me. The wounds had closed, but the two grafts on my right lower leg stretched from my ankle to my knee, with a thin strip of normal skin down the middle. Tissue was missing, so the areas were and are slightly depressed.

People would stare. The technician would try to be polite. But frankly the bright red, snake-skin-rippled grafts are gross if you're not used to them. And frankly they're gross even if you are used to them. But I always remind myself that I at least have my legs.

Sometimes by way of explanation, I would just say, "Car accident," which was partly true (except I wasn't hit by a car going, say 60 miles an hour. I was hit by car parts, traveling at a much faster rate of speed). Other times I'd take the time to explain. But that would open a host of sometimes pleasant but often unwanted conversation. "Does it hurt? Oh, the war is awful, don't you think? Do you have nightmares? I had an operation once . . . Does it hurt?" It was an endless loop of banalities mixed with personal revelations that I frankly didn't want to hear. As I discovered, surviving death turns you into a mother confessor for some people, and the burden was and is often more than I wanted.

Buying clothes was painful, full stop. Several things were now out, including the obvious like dresses, shorts, and bathing suits and the unexpected like any trousers with thin cloth that showed the deep depressions in my flesh, for instance. I tried to avoid short-sleeve shirts since the burns on my left arm would blister from the sun within a couple hours. The burned patches of flesh seemed to have no defense against solar rays. T-shirts became a luxury that only sunscreen made possible.

But there was an upside to all this, I thought. I was no longer defined by my looks. I couldn't be. No one expects "Scar Girl" to be a vamp.

When I thought back to the last thing that had irked me before the bombing, I told myself that no one's going to give me a hard time about being a "news babe" now.

Before I'd been bombed, it seemed the tide in TV news had taken a decidedly old-fashioned turn. Bob Schieffer had taken over Dan Rather's *Evening News*, and one media pundit dubbed his new female hires Bob Schieffer's "news babes."

He proudly sent all of us the article. Astounding to me, I made the cut. I was No. 6 out of the six new CBS news babes, and the reviewer identified my specialty as "covering Iraqi prisons." Never mind the fact that I'd been reporting from the country for three years. The reviewer must have been given a sample broadcast that included a report I'd done on Iraqi prisons, and she presumed the rest.

I gave Schieffer a hard time, emailing him, "Ah, well, so much for my Wellesley degree, my master's in Islamic affairs, and my study of local languages." He wrote back something to the effect of "Hah, don't take yourself so seriously" and added that "at least you made the list, and they spelled your name right." True, that.

But the article had sent a chilling message to women in the network around my age: There was a new glamorous standard we must meet. I'd already been criticized by my bosses when I was in the field for "looking tired," which I took as code for looking old.

I took it personally until a few months later when I watched Katie Couric take up the *CBS Evening News* anchor chair, and the media critics piled on about her appearance, including her hair, her makeup, and her choice of suits. It seemed to matter as much or sometimes more than her story choice. And sadly, the media critics only seemed to reflect the public. When Katie wore makeup people didn't like, letters and emails poured in.

I realized my TV managers were reacting to that when they said things like "You look tired." It was because the public noticed (my mom always did). So, yes, they (we) really are that shallow.

All that aside, I thought that after what I've been through, no one was going to expect me to look like a babe. When I returned to the United States, that turned out to be true. People were just shocked to see me standing there in one piece. No matter how tired or disheveled I was, I only got glowing comments.

When I wasn't writing I kept trying to answer all those letters and emails. Many, if not most, were from people of faith, strangers who had prayed for my recovery in megachurches, cathedrals, monasteries, at the Jews' hallowed Western Wall in Israel, and at Islam's sacred Dome of the Rock, not to mention my Iraqi friends who prayed at mosques both Sunni and Shia. I firmly believe those prayers helped me heal, especially in Bethesda when I became aware they were being said.

I wrote letters back to a few hundred, compelled to respond to these strangers who'd reached out to me, especially when someone had written me multiple times or shared something so personal that I couldn't ignore that a stranger trusted me with his or her story.

Some of the men who'd written me took my reply as an invitation to romance. In retrospect I was naïve that I didn't see those responses coming. I thought to myself, *Hey, didn't you see that man standing by my gurney every step of the way? The position is taken!*

Others took my replies as affirmation that my very survival was proof that their beliefs were correct, and they assumed their beliefs were my beliefs. One grandmotherly lady wrote me back to say she was so glad I had been healed by Christ and that he saved me from the "ugly world of Islam." I sat there looking at her girlish penmanship, shocked by such offhand words of hate.

I never knew what I was going to find when I opened those letters. One of the most inspiring messages I received came accompanied by a red, white, and blue afghan, one of dozens that two women from Waco, Texas, had woven for wounded servicemen and women. They'd decided to include me and explained why.

Dear Ms. Dozier,

It is with much appreciation for your work as a journalist that Mimi and I write you today. . . . I was drawn to your compassion for the military personnel and your clear stance as an advocate for them in their ceaseless commitment toward human security in such a hostile and unforgiving part of our world. . . . My interest in the safety of all concerned, both military and civilian support, was uplifted in prayer, as night after night, I watched the *CBS Evening News*. In particular, a deep concern for your safety while in Iraq prompted me to daily pray for a hedge of protection around you and your crew. We are so saddened by their loss and your loss. . . . I am sure that Mimi and I are not alone in our appreciation for you and your often somber, always nonpartisan, highly ethical journalism.

—Respectfully, Mimi Jasek & Katie Laurens-Bell, Afghans from the Heart

Letters like that made the day easier to get through. I knew they'd been written in the emotion of the moment, and as I'd learned from some of the awkward replies I'd already received, they'd embarrass the writer later. But I still treasured them and revisited them when I needed a reminder that somewhere out there, people were pulling for me to get through this and get back to work.

My rock throughout, of course, was Pete. He'd always been one of my greatest sources of support before my injury. But now he'd seen me at my absolute worst, physically, mentally, and emotionally, and none of that had managed to scare him away. For us and our relationship there was "before the bombing," when battling the baggage in our lives seemed so important. Then there was "after the bombing," when all that went before seemed petty and insignificant next to the wonder of surviving to live another day together.

CHAPTER 18

coming full circle

As I grew stronger and my walking improved, I started planning my return to work and, eventually, to home in Jerusalem. To me, it was a natural progression: Get well, do a TV special on the bombing to help honor those we lost, then go home to Jerusalem where my house was.

It's not what my bosses were expecting, but then America was home for them; I hadn't lived in the continental United States in 14 years. And few of my CBS colleagues had witnessed my two-decade-long struggle to secure a network TV job in the Middle East. I didn't intend to let the bombing jettison all that hard work. And as I recovered in New Zealand, I could only reflect on how learning to walk normally again was just about as hard as getting this job had been in the first place.

I had started my career as an unpaid intern, working in Jerusalem for a features agency. It was a terrifying leap, as all my career leaps would turn out to be. And it was preceded by painful soul-searching, with my parents echoing and reinforcing my doubts.

I started out scared, and I was always broke and sometimes lonely since I was the only Christian I knew, and daily that difference was pointed out to me. But eventually I found good friends and made headway on the job. The problem: I wasn't learning to write or report from seasoned pros. I quickly figured out that if I stayed, I'd end up being a fixer, i.e., the person who sets up a story for a more experienced foreign correspondent. I was also tired of being asked when I was going to convert to Judaism, a question that was posed to me almost every day by everyone from the postman to the baker to the bus driver.

Most Israelis assumed that if I lived there and enjoyed living there, the logical thing to do was to abandon my Christianity. I respected their faith—I'd been raised to respect Judaism, Islam, and all faiths—and couldn't grasp why many didn't seem to respect mine. While I was there the first Palestinian Intifadah, or uprising, broke out, and my travel to Palestinian parts of the country or even Arab sections of Jerusalem was limited. I didn't get to know that side of the country, and at the time, I didn't know how much was missing from my understanding of the situation. That came much later when I moved to Egypt and covered the peace process from the Arab world's point of view.

I went back to Washington, D.C., to try to learn my craft, dreaming of writing the newspaper article that would one day earn a Pulitzer Prize for its depth and, perhaps, bravery. I dreamt big.

But all my resume earned me was an entry-level research job at a trade publication. I started out covering legislation on Capitol Hill for new technology, something I had never in my life been interested in. I tried to treat each day as a writing exercise.

I was progressing, slowly. But then came the annual Christmas party, and my very genial, old-fashioned boss had one too many and (I now realize) threw his arm around me in what (I now realize) was intended to be a friendly, fatherly way. He told me—an extremely intense, fiercely independent young Wellesley woman—that I needed to "loosen up and find myself a man."

There are many ways I now know I could have gracefully and humorously put my semilit boss in his place. But I didn't have that kind of wisdom at the time. Instead I sprang back from his hug as if hit by sulfuric acid spray and sneered at him loudly, with the entire office arrayed around us. "I don't need a man to be successful," I answered and stomped off.

The next morning the boss came into work and said, "She's fired. She does data entry until the end of the month and then she's gone." Or that's how one editor related it to me.

I had loyal friends among the editorial staff who took pity on the youngster who'd dug herself into a hole and offended the tipsy, overeffusive publisher who'd had his pride hurt. So they sent him to a conference in Asia. And they moved me to his flagship paper, gave me a generous lunch budget, and told me I had "a month to make good or lose my job." In terror I pulled out the company Rolodex and resorted to a rather obvious but ultimately successful strategy. I called up all my publisher's best friends and invited them for lunch. And I flattered them into telling me about themselves, the industry, and Capitol Hill.

When the publisher returned from the conference a few weeks later, he was met by a chorus of "Who is that wonderful new reporter you have?"

I'd bought myself time. I started getting to work in earnest, breaking stories. With every scoop, I thought I was getting closer to my dream of working for a "real" newspaper. For me that meant *The Washington Post*.

Veteran *Post* correspondent Thomas Lippman invited me to visit his office. He congratulated me on beating him on a couple stories and asked me what I wanted to do with my life.

"Work here, of course," I said.

"Look around," he said. "See these writers? They're only a decade or so older than you, and they're not going anywhere." And the stack of resumes to fill their spots came from writers at the best newspapers in the country.

"Oh. Right," I said, absorbing the blow.

He told me I had to do something to distinguish myself. "Go back to school or go overseas," Lippman said. I wonder if he even remembers the conversation. I find it indelible because it changed my life. I decided to do everything he recommended: go back to school, get a degree in Islamic affairs, and then go overseas to become a foreign correspondent.

I had to fight the usual round of naysaying. I'd consult loved ones and colleagues about making a risky move and receive an array of mostly negative opinions that naturally made the move even harder. My venerable publisher, who was now a fan of my ability to break stories, told me, "No one hires journalists with advanced degrees. Waste of time and money."

My parents told me, "Where will you ever find a job that pays you $20,000 a year again? How can you give that up?"

I was accepted to the Columbia School of Journalism and the London School of Economics, but I couldn't afford either and couldn't borrow enough to cover the shortfall. Then it hit me: I was living near Virginia, and the University of Virginia (UVA) had some of the best Mideast scholar-professors in the country. Within months I had packed up my life in D.C. and moved to Charlottesville, Virginia.

In the quirky Southern town that gave birth to the Dave Matthews Band, which used to play downtown every weekend, I lived in an unheated apartment in an old Southern mansion at the edge of town. At night, I bartended for rent and food; by day I dodged freshmen and frat kids to get to class. Like most older students who realize what a privilege it is to study instead of working 9 to 5, I loved homework.

As students, we picked apart the differences between Islamic militancy and Islamic extremism, a discussion led by two contrasting individuals: the political department's chief, Ruhollah Ramazani, an urbane Iranian who had fled during that country's religious revolution; and Shiite imam and religious scholar Abdulaziz Sachedina, a Yemeni who once studied with Ayatollah Khomeini. They both pointed out that an extremist isn't necessarily a militant but is often identified as such in the press. That became the subject of my thesis and something I watched for in my own reporting from then on. Just because someone is extreme in his or her beliefs doesn't mean he or she supports violence. To portray it as such is to demonize those whose faith is strong, whether they're Muslim, Christian, or Jew.

My other obsession, which my professors and students shared alike, was the whys and wherefores of the first Gulf War, which was unfolding in front of us on TV. You could say that war destroyed my university experience even as it helped me decide on the course of the rest of my life. I couldn't stand watching all those journalists out there reporting from the front lines while I was stuck in the library stacks at UVA. I'd been teetering between journalism and diplomacy, but now I knew I couldn't stand being away from the news.

One of my thesis advisors helped convince me. Professor David Newsom was once ambassador to Libya, Indonesia, and the Philippines and later served as undersecretary of state for President Jimmy Carter. He'd also been a top journalist, so he knew both sides. He told me, "You'd hate diplomacy. You could never keep your mouth shut."

I prepared for another leap, and Wellesley College helped. I applied for a competitive alumnae grant that was meant to help winners "study truth and beauty" overseas. It was not meant to help advance someone's career. It was supposed to fund a break from cutthroat stuff like that.

In my application I said I wanted to study Islamic extremism versus militancy in Cairo, Egypt, the birthplace of the Muslim Brotherhood, a religious movement that started as a political party but turned violent when the government repressed it.

To win the grant I had to go through an interview process with several mostly middle-aged and elderly Wellesley alumnae staring at me from behind a large semicircular table. Behind them was a floor-to-ceiling plate-glass window through which I could see a vicious, near-hurricane-force snowstorm blanketing the campus. My concentration was shot. I expected to see a cow blow by at any minute.

Then one of the interviewers stuck it to me. She was a little, gray-haired lady I'd thought of as grandmotherly until she asked, "You want to use this grant to become a foreign correspondent, *don't you?*"

I tore my eyes from the snowstorm and thought, *Damn. I might as well go for the truth.*

"Yup, you've got me. That's what I want to do."

I boarded a plane back to Charlottesville, dejected and demoralized. I'd lost. Halfway back, the snowstorm shut down the East Coast, leaving me stuck for a night in Pittsburgh or Philadelphia or some city with an airport and snow.

My answering machine was blinking when I arrived at my unheated apartment. The message said my Wellesley inquisitors had decided to split the grant, giving me half and the other half to an artist who was going to paint scenes of the Rhine. "That's half truth and half beauty, right?" the woman who left the message said. "So we're being true to the spirit of the grant." I cheered.

That's how I ended up in Cairo, Egypt, with $10,000, two suitcases, no job, and not knowing a single word of Arabic. (UVA's Arabic classes were at the same time as a required seminar. In retrospect I should have skipped political science and just studied Arabic, but that's hindsight for you.)

I was terrified.

For the next six months, fear of failure meant I barely slept. A kindly Wellesley alumna had set me up with Monitor Radio, the now-defunct radio arm of *The Christian Science Monitor*. That meant I could at least legitimately apply for a foreign press pass. I found out that one of the major hotels had an old wire machine in it, which would spit out news copy in a dusty corner of the lobby. For the first few weeks, I lived in that lobby. Then I'd go to the hotel telephones and buy enough minutes to file some of the worst radio reports Monitor Radio had probably ever heard. I'd never done radio before in my life, and my heart pounded just trying to read my handscribbled script out loud to some poor, patient radio editor at the other end of the line.

But fear took a backseat to my need to pay the bills, so I kept filing.

I quickly learned that unlike many places I'd visited in the Middle East, almost no one in Cairo spoke English. Some measure of Arabic was a necessity, so I spent my afternoons taking inexpensive Arabic classes at the local British Council. I learned enough to get by.

In my visit to acquire a press credential, a lengthy bureaucratic process that would make the Soviets proud, I came across an English-language newspaper, *The Middle East Times*. I visited the paper and was hired just by walking through the door. They paid something like $20 an article, so the bar wasn't set very high.

What I didn't realize was that every foreign reporter in town read the newspaper. This was the era before Egypt allowed cell phones or cable TV. Foreign newspapers were flown in once a day and were usually a day old. So English-language-starved correspondents ate the newspaper up, which meant that when I arrived at my first press conference, some of the bureau chiefs actually knew who I was. They also knew I needed a lot of improvement to become a top reporter, which I, of course, didn't realize. But as Lippman had predicted, I was a warm body in a place that's tough to find able help, so I was snatched up.

The Washington Post's Cairo bureau chief, Caryle Murphy, mentored me, critiquing my *Middle East Times* reports and helping me write my first features to offer to the *Post*. Again hats off to Lippman for the introduction. Three months after I'd arrived in Egypt, Murphy left for Christmas vacation.

On New Year's Eve Yassir Arafat came to town to talk about peace with Israel—one of the first, historic steps in the peace process. On New Year's Day my story led *The Washington Post.*

I called my old publisher, the one who'd told me that there weren't any freelance jobs overseas anymore. It was around 8 a.m. on New Year's Day, a cruel time to call those who were likely out reveling the night before. "Hi there. Hey, go look at *The Washington Post* on your front porch!" I shouted a gleeful, long-distance "Happy New Year!" and hung up.

Getting published one place gives you overnight credibility everywhere else. Shortly after my work started appearing in the *Post*, both CBS Radio and Voice of America hired me freelance, and I was finally paying the bills. I quickly learned that broadcast pays better than print, and I started becoming more comfortable with it. I'd churn out four to six 30-second pieces a day for CBS News, earning $47 for each one. A well-researched, 2,000-word newspaper feature could take a week to pull together and only paid $200. My economically driven transition to broadcast had begun.

Cairo was crammed full of people—a city of 20 million Egyptians designed for about 5 million—but it was a lonely place for expats. Foreign women, especially, were harassed—just walking by themselves in public was breaking cultural rules.

Trying to avoid the hassling, I wore long-sleeve, high-neck shirts and long, ankle-skimming skirts even in the blazing summer. But my height, skin, and hair color marked me out, and the heckling would begin the moment I left my building. Running that gauntlet every day drove me to a level of culture shock that bordered on depression. I found it hard to want to learn any more Arabic and sometimes hard to even leave the house.

Living in a police state with constant crackdowns on the local insurgency meant I also saw violence and its results up close, from dead bodies to my first riot.

I had a direct clash with the enforcers of that police state when *Post* translator, Fatemah Farag, and I went down to Assiut, a city in southern Egypt, to investigate reports that young men were being taken away for questioning and then returned in sealed coffins. We took a four-hour train ride, then a taxi, and finally reached a tiny village with two-story mud-brick houses and narrow dirt streets.

We found a family who said they'd talk to us. We sat down in their front room, and they rushed to make tea, the usual prelude of socializing before getting down to the interview. But something was wrong. They were taking too long and weren't answering any of our questions. I can't remember whose nerves jangled first, Fatemah's or mine, but one of us decided to go for the door, and the family blocked us.

They'd turned us in to the authorities, who soon appeared, ushering us from one police station to the next. Each time, they told us they'd checked our credentials and all was well, but they'd keep us waiting, locked in various storerooms or jail cells. Then they'd put us in a car to "drive us to the train station," only to drive us to yet another, slightly larger police station.

They drove us out of the last village into Assiut and finally we thought we were free. But instead of heading for the train station, we pulled up in front of the infamous Assiut Police Station—rumored site of torture and extrajudicial killings. If we went inside I thought I'd probably be able to talk my way out, but I didn't know how long it would take to get a message to Fatemah's family in Cairo so that they could get to the right official to spring her.

I said to Fatemah, "We're going. Now." The cops in the front seat heard me and jumped out to block the car door next to Fatemah, facing the sidewalk. I simply sprang out the other one and pulled Fatemah after me.

"We can't go in there," I said. "Let's walk to the train station." Fatemah nodded, now white with fear. I gambled that none of the men wanted to take a chance manhandling a foreign woman who had been throwing around the names of every high-ranking Egyptian official she'd ever interviewed. They thought I might be lying, but they couldn't take a chance.

Instead they stalked us, four armed men in dark suits on the sidewalk telling us over and over in English and Arabic to "Get in the car, get in the car NOW." Their colleagues curb-crawled us to our left, chorusing the same phrases.

We looked neither left nor right.

Fatemah hissed, "Hijabs," and we pulled out our ever-present veils to whip over our heads.

Now the men looked like they were harassing two proper Muslim women, and the other women on the street weren't having that. They started clucking at the men, "Get away from those girls," and took us by the arms and escorted us to the train station. We raced onto whatever train was on the platform and prayed the cops wouldn't follow us. We were on an all-night, milk-run train, and we didn't reach Cairo until dawn, but we were just happy to be out of Assiut.

For Fatemah and me, the flight from Assiut was a baptism. We'd pursued a lead and had almost become victims of the very abuse we were trying to bring to light. But we'd gotten away with it, and we'd now speak for those who could not in a police state. Within 24 hours our terror had been replaced by the exhilaration of achievement: We'd gotten the story, which appeared in the *Post* with both our names on it. A little success is a dangerous thing. Risk becomes habit-forming each time you risk and win.

That was it for Egypt. I'd met and was about to marry Daniel Casson, a lovely British man who was my opposite in every way. Where I was intense, work-obsessed, and socially clumsy, Danny was laid-back, effortlessly the light of every party, and usually referred to as "cuddly," even by the guys he'd smash at Friday night rugby games. He also happened to be a brilliant Arabic linguist. He was the reason, beyond the culture shock, that I'd stopped learning Arabic; he'd become my in-house translator. We moved to London, where Danny had a government translating job that paid a pittance. We were broke. It was like starting in Cairo all over again.

Once again I spoke the wrong language. I had an American accent, so I wasn't welcome at British news venues. I took every freelance job I could get. I worked at CBS Radio on Saturday and Sunday, although $47 per story didn't stretch like it had in Cairo. Monday and Tuesday I processed video and wrote TV scripts at the news video service WTN (now APTN). This was something I'd never done before and wasn't good at. The rest of the week, I learned to anchor at BBC World Service Radio.

Luckily for me World Service launched two coproductions with American public radio, and needed American-accented broadcasters. This was a brand-new exercise in stress control. I'd never broadcast from a studio before, and I'd never had to wrap up a story off the top of my head in time to hit a commercial post at three and five minutes past the hour.

But I needed the money. I'd drink a cup of mint tea, say a prayer and "ommm" in my head a lot, then sit down in front of the microphone and try not to panic. *I can do this, I can do this, I can do this*, I reminded myself. When I finally left the job three years later, I'd done more than 3,000 newscasts, so my mantra worked. By then I'd also graduated to occasionally anchoring an hour-long show. My biggest coup came when Britain's then foreign minister, Robin Cook, cut off the interview in disgust over a tough question. I was thrilled.

I wanted to be assigned to travel for someone, anyone. But I was too low on anyone's pecking order to merit a trip. So I followed the model I'd used a couple times in Egypt when I'd financed my own side trips, for instance to hear President Muammar Qaddafi speak in Libya. I worked like hell, hoping someone would buy my report when I returned.

That's how I ended up in Belfast, Ireland with a slew of important interviews. Something odd happens when you call Irish politicians and political activists and say in your American accent that you're from CBS News Radio, they don't even pay attention to the "radio" part. They just say yes. America is the political ground they most desire to win over.

Because of my ignorance of Belfast's political geography, I'd arranged Protestant and Catholic interviews back to back on the Shankhill and the Falls roads. On my map, the two roads were parallel, so I didn't think it would be a problem. I didn't know that they were two parallel universes, neighborhoods divided by massive peace walls and serviced only by their own unique taxis that wouldn't venture into the opposite area for fear of reprisals, ranging from vandalism to death. I managed to reach every major political party but was running about an hour late by day's end.

Within a couple years CBS Radio hired me on staff. From then on no vacation went uninterrupted, by my choice as much as by my bosses'.

Disasters and crises kept happening, and I "parachuted" to every one. I was working my heart out at the radio to break stories and feed the 24-hour news maw. Sleep was a rarity.

The hardest part was that in the radio medium, there's no one else to share the load; you're on your own. I'd be covering a story and turn around and see a five-man CBS network TV crew. Sometimes they let me tag along, but I wasn't truly on the team.

I went to then London Bureau Chief Marcy McGinnis and said, "I want to be on TV." I learned the meaning of the phrase "Be careful what you wish for." She gave me a shot at *The Weekend Evening News*, and I had little to no experience. I had plenty of support and patience from the show's executive producer, Pat Shevlin, another Wellesley grad who could see potential. But looking back at some of those early pieces, I don't know what she saw. My writing was clumsy; my voice was so tense and stiff that I might as well have been sucking helium; and I am still getting ribbing about my makeup misfires back then.

Eventually the *Weekend News* experiment faded, but I started working for the network's affiliate TV service and CBS' *The Early Show*. My old friend Batt Humphreys, who had first put me on the air in Cairo, was now in charge of the morning news blocks. When I landed in a place the TV side of CBS had decided was too expensive to cover and some huge headline broke, I lucked onto air.

I started flying into war zones, not because of the war but because that's where the news was. Pursuing the center of the story often landed me, quite unexpectedly, in danger. I often didn't take the threats seriously since I was still protected by the illusion that journalists were allowed to go anywhere as long as they were careful not to stand too close to the target of the conflict.

When Saddam Hussein menaced Kuwait in the late 1990s and President Bill Clinton responded with air strikes, I was all set to drive in on my own, but my radio bosses told me no. Instead I joined the next day's news team convoy. But because Iraqi drivers don't communicate with each other, I quickly was separated, and my car ended up on its own, approaching the city at the worst possible time—the next night's bombing was about to begin.

As I reached the outskirts of the city, an Iraqi radio broadcaster reported that the Iraqi Information Ministry had been hit. I was terrified, wondering if anyone in the CBS network team had survived. As we got closer the radio report was corrected: The bomb had landed near but not on the Information Ministry. I bolted up to the roof, where the TV crews were assembled in a row overlooking the city, and took over a satellite phone the TV folks had already set up for me and started reporting as massive bunker-buster bombs hit within a mile of us. I'd gotten to the center of the story, and I'd gotten away with it.

But the travel and the war zones were wrecking my marriage. For me London was a stop in what I'd hoped to be continuing foreign postings. I thought we'd be moving again, but Danny was growing more comfortable at home after his years living overseas. He wanted to stay where he was.

He'd also returned to his Jewish roots in London, culturally if not religiously. And the more horrors I saw overseas, the more my own Christian faith came to the fore. Our original plan for how to handle faith if we had kids started breaking apart. We believed we had thought it out, but when it came closer to reality, everything changed. I wanted Sunday school, Christmas trees, and Easter baskets. He wanted Passover and Hanukkah. We thought it was OK to have both together, and it was when it existed as a concept in our heads in Cairo. The prospect didn't work well in London, where his parents told us, "The other children won't play with your children if Kimberly doesn't convert." Something had to give, and finally we were it.

When people ask me what happened, I tell them that we had a good marriage, and eventually, after the initial pain and anger and grief, we had a good divorce.

The split came just before NATO forces bombed Kosovo, Serbia. I buried myself in the story, spending four months straight in the Balkans and getting run out of Pristina, Serbia, by the Serbs with the network news crew. Kosovo become one of my hardest lessons in news. I became too close to my subjects, my heart breaking as I watched Kosovar refugees struggle to survive. In my mind the Serbs were bad and the Kosovars good. My own Kosovar translator, Arben Kuka, set me straight, saying,

"You don't understand, boss. The moment we 'win,' we will turn on our own. We will transform Pristina into a little Albania, with drugs, prostitution, gambling, you name it." He'd laugh at my indignation. I blamed his pessimistic predictions on depression over the war and his fear that his mother—still stuck inside Kosovo—wouldn't survive.

A few months later Pristina was freed, and everything Arben predicted came true. Kosovo became a drug superhighway for dealers in Albania, Kosovo, Macedonia, and Yugoslavia. Dens of prostitution sprang up, aimed at providing services especially for NATO soldiers and Western contractors. A group of contractors actually raided one of the houses of ill repute, saying they were rescuing the women from slavery. They were, but they'd only met the women because they'd been paying customers.

Kosovar and Serbian mafias thrived on the business, probably laughing at the way foreigners thought they were bringing freedom and democracy to the place. We'd certainly brought them a measure of capitalist freedom.

I was crushed and disillusioned, and then I found out that my soon-to-be-ex-husband Danny had failed to sign and drop off the divorce papers we'd filled out before I'd left London for the war. The moment we were no longer in the same house driving each other nuts, he'd had a change of heart and wanted to give marriage counseling another try. He'd asked acquaintances at CBS how his wife was doing. This was news to me. We'd been living apart for months. Since I thought the divorce papers were filed, I'd started dating again. So my colleagues assumed the gung-ho correspondent was openly cheating on her husband.

By the time I figured out what had happened, the gossip had done its work. When I got back to London, my TV work dried up overnight.

After that I didn't date a soul for two years, turning everyone down. When my marriage cratered, my job followed, and I spent a lot of time figuring out where all my dreams went wrong.

At least the job part was about to turn around. Six months into my exile from TV, producer Lin Garlick took a job to help overhaul Newspath, CBS's in-house affiliate news service at the network's New York headquarters. She called me and asked me to start offering TV stories on top of my regular radio work—for cash. She single-handedly dragged me back onto TV.

She also tried to help me turn my librarian exterior into network presentability. I always cared about the story but was short on polish. It didn't help that I was trying to do two jobs at once, usually with no backup such as a producer or even my own cameraman. On any given assignment I'd be carrying several pounds of radio gear while rushing around trying to break stories to file into the always-hungry maw of radio. Then I'd have to turn around and try to look rested, composed, and presentable for TV.

I once flew from Belgrade, Serbia, where I'd watched Yugoslav forces cart Slobodan Milosevic away for trial, all the way to Hong Kong. I had to get into Hainan Island to cover the U.S. spy plane that had made an emergency landing there, triggering a Cold War-style face-off between the Chinese and the Americans over the fate of the plane and the crew.

I dashed from radio live shots to an Associated Press camera position, where I filed for *The Early Show* and Dan Rather's *Evening News*. Despite being outgunned by the other networks, I broke several stories. I was told I was the first to report that the crew had been released and was on its way to the airport.

My presentation, however, left a bit to be desired. I was an eminently normal-looking woman, now exhausted and overwrought, so unprepared for the on-camera part of it that I didn't even have hairspray. I had to duct tape the back of my head to keep my hair from flying up.

As they say on Broadway: Dance, 10, Looks, 3. I puzzled over it and told myself that it didn't matter, and I'd wrap myself with feminist, Wellesley-stoked indignation. But I was beginning to understand that until I cracked the packaging formula—how I looked on TV—the networks wouldn't hire me, no matter how many stories I broke. And that meant staying solo—no team, no camaraderie, no backup.

Then came 9/11. A tragedy that erased such petty concerns and everything else that came before it. I watched the images on TV from my London radio studio. As I called my mom in Baltimore, telling her to turn on the TV, the second plane flew into the tower.

By the next day I was on my way to Islamabad, Pakistan, along with much of the world's press corps. I'd been on the phone with my radio bosses within an hour of the second tower's falling to say I had to go. It seemed clear we'd invade Afghanistan, and Pakistan was the gateway. Others headed for Afghanistan, where the U.S. bombing of Taliban targets began.

Pakistan represented a coming of age—a dangerous age—for a lot of journalists. When we first started reporting there, we waded in alone among the crowds that were protesting the invasion. My woman translator Rabia and I could walk anywhere, from a crowded marketplace to a late-night restaurant, to canvass public opinion.

After the invasion, Al Qaeda kidnapped *Wall Street Journal* reporter Daniel Pearl and beheaded him. And yet many of us operated just as he had, trusting our lives to covert contacts. I'd found a Taliban official who'd arranged for his driver, Mustafa, to sneak me over the border as Kabul, Afghanistan, fell. But there was a hitch in our plan: We'd taken a cab from the Pakistan border to the small Afghan town of Jalalabad, where we were supposed to pick up a waiting four-wheel-drive vehicle. The problem was that one of the other warlords in the area had helped himself to it.

I went first to the foreign journalists, including the CBS TV team, who were staying in the only decent hotel in town. They were all convoying to Kabul in the morning, but no one had room for me in their vehicle nor in the hotel.

Mustafa took me instead to an Afghan inn where the local mujahideen stayed. I wasn't just the only foreigner in the place; I was also the only woman. So Mustafa pantomimed to me that I had to lock myself inside my room and open it to no one but him.

I soon understood why. Word had spread through the hotel that there was a foreign woman there. Off and on all night, men came to the door, either calling to me or knocking or banging on the door and rattling the doorknob and the lock, trying to open it. I didn't sleep much.

Around 6 a.m. Mustafa banged on the door, an hour before I expected him. I had tried to communicate to him the night before that I wanted our hired cab to join the TV convoy, which was leaving at 8 a.m. I thought to myself, *He didn't get it.* So I shouted through the door, "Eight o'clock, Mustafa, eight o'clock."

But he kept pounding. "Taxis short," he said. "Leave now."

I jumped into clothes and veil and grabbed my radio gear and satellite phone for the ride. It was no surprise then that I dozed on and off, despite the bumpy road.

Something sharp in Mustafa's voice pulled me out of sleep. He was engaged in conversation with the cab driver he had hired. I looked past them to the road, where I saw black-turbaned Taliban fighters armed with AK-47s on either side. They were holding a rope across the road, which they used as a makeshift roadblock for cars they wanted to stop.

The gunmen didn't see me until we drew level with them. Mustafa said something in Pashto, and our driver floored it, racing away from the men even as they raised their guns and their now-futile rope to stop us. We turned a corner and were away. It happened so fast that I didn't really have time to be scared or even realize what almost happened.

When we reached Kabul I forgot to "call in" to tell my desk I arrived safely. Those who greeted us had been desperate to use my satellite phone to tell their relatives back in Pakistan that they'd survived the city's invasion. So by the time I thought to call CBS Radio to check in, my bosses back home were all but convinced I was dead. The TV convoy that had come up the same mountain road, just an hour or so after my cab, had been stopped, apparently at the same place we'd seen the road block. Four journalists, including one Spanish woman, were dragged out of the first car at gunpoint and killed. It so easily could have been us.

In Kabul, Afghanistan, I filed for radio and our affiliate TV service until I lost my voice and had to ask one of the network TV correspondents to file for me. I spent weeks camped with the CBS TV team at Tora Bora as coalition forces tried to bomb, shoot, or smoke out Osama Bin Laden on the peaks a couple miles above our heads. We all knew the "back door" was open, however. Afghan warlords had told us that no one was guarding the mountain passes to Pakistan.

When I came home after four months to a cat who barely remembered I was the one who normally fed her, there was a new job waiting: CBS affiliate WCBS 2 New York wanted to open a bureau in Jerusalem. As then CBS Vice President Marcy McGinnis explained, it was a chance for me to finally leave "radio girl" behind.

It was also the start of some of the hardest work in my life, which I didn't think was possible after the pace of work in London and before that in Cairo. When you work for local American TV where the bosses and the programs aren't in your time zone, sleep becomes rare.

But I didn't care. I was finally back in the Middle East as a genuine foreign correspondent. I was home.

The hours were insane. A two-person team is capable of shooting, editing, and feeding a network-level piece five to six days a week, but when you add requests to appear live on the New York 6 p.m. and 11 p.m. shows (2 a.m. and 7 a.m. Israel time), you start getting into the impossible. I tried to say yes to the requests as often as I could and still be able to function. My cameraman finally said, "No more late nights. An 18-hour day is enough." So I hired a second crew for the 2 a.m. live shot.

I'd go places the network team didn't feel comfortable, so I started ending up on the *CBS Evening News* again. I even talked my way into covering the run-up to the Iraqi invasion at the CBS bureau in Baghdad for all the affiliates. As the time of the invasion approached, the Iraqi authorities stopped extending many journalists' visas. CBS ordered me out to make sure it would have enough visas for the network team. I balked and was vaguely threatened with being fired.

Thus forced out, I went back to Israel to cover the rain of Iraqi Scud missiles that never came. I moved to Jordan and covered the anger there and across the Arab world that was directed at Americans for the invasion. My cameraman was Chris Albert. Before the Iraq invasion, Chris would use his Australian nationality as a passport to defusing tension whenever we filmed angry, screaming anti-American crowds. "I'm not American, mate," he'd say if he got jostled. "I'm Aussie." But when he tried this in Amman, a man shouted in his face, "The Australians are part of this invasion too." We quickly got out of there.

When we cleared the crowd, he whirled on me and said, "See what your damn country has done to us?" In between trying to figure out what we could file, we watched the invasion on TV. That hurt.

As the troops neared Baghdad and it was clear Iraq was crumbling fast, I heard that Dan Rather was trying to get in. His efforts to enter with U.S. troops through Kuwait had been quashed by the Bush administration, as one producer was told. All I knew was that Dan was coming to Amman and then going in.

I volunteered two spaces in our WCBS armored vehicle in return for visas and a spot on the convoy for Chris and me. It was a trip that probably got me a network job, but it also nearly got us killed.

Dan flew in by charter from Kuwait and then did the *Evening News* at 2:30 a.m. local time. Then we all packed our cars and headed for the border, a 12- to 14-hour drive.

We were on the road maybe 12 hours after the Saddam statue was pulled down. Like the rest of the world, we watched it on TV. But unlike the rest of the world, we were kicking ourselves for not being there in person to see history happen and report on it. A certain sense of desperation and wounded pride drove us, or at least some of us—not the sane ones, as Chris would say.

Dan's cameraman had stubbornly chosen to drive after already pulling an all-nighter, first setting up and then shooting Dan's *Evening News* live shot, then taking two hours to break down and pack up the gear. He was exhausted.

So was Dan. That's why, unfortunately, everyone else in his Land Cruiser kept quiet so as not to disturb him. They should have been talking to the driver to keep him awake on the long, straight road across the desert.

There's no mystery as to what happened next. I awoke from my head-bobbing, fitful sleep to a loud thumping sound coming from a plume of dust on one side of the highway. It was Dan's armored Land Cruiser.

Everyone in the convoy slammed to a halt and stared. The dust cleared, and the battered Land Cruiser came into view, miraculously still upright. One of the doors opened, then another. Gingerly the bruised occupants unfolded themselves. Dan, his cameraman, his soundman, and his producer were shaken but uninjured. The Land Cruiser's undercarriage had been tenderized by its 20-yard juddering flounce across a field of boulders the size of watermelons.

If this was a warning, we didn't listen. We regrouped at the border, and Dan moved to our front seat, with his producer and me in the back and Chris driving.

The CBS convoy was now driving unescorted into an active war zone, past Saddam's military strongholds of Fallujah and Ramadi, Iraq. And there was no way we'd make the capital by dark. Yet somehow an ill-informed optimism was winning out over reality. We started driving, racing the setting sun, set to find out in a few hours how very wrong we were.

The only thing that kept us safe was the fact that every time we stopped, our unarmed security guard telephoned producer Megan Towey back in Amman, Jordan, with our GPS coordinates, and she passed them on to a U.S. officer who tried to keep the Air Force informed. Unfortunately we were driving in the same type of vehicles Saddam's officer corps used. From the air we looked like Saddam loyalists fleeing invading U.S. troops for the safety of the Iraqi capital.

There were plenty of other threats on that road. We started seeing burnt-out Iraqi military vehicles that were stopped in their tracks along the highway. And a couple of times, we had to drive around the highway through the desert, skirting a bridge or ramp that had been destroyed by the barrage from above.

With every delay traversing the road to Baghdad, the darkness got that much closer. We started stopping on the roadside and debating.

Among the passengers in the other vehicles were producers Peter Bluff and Mike Solmsen, correspondents Randall Pinkston and Lee Cowan, then-radio correspondent Charlie D'Agata who was on his own personal slog to network TV, the camera crew from Dan's ill-fated vehicle, and our British security advisor. We had four Iraqi drivers and our Jordanian bureau manager, Amjad Tadros. As we approached a city where we knew pockets of fighting were still raging, most of our convoy was vulnerable in the worst kind of way.

Dan wanted and needed to get to Baghdad to be at the center of the story. I understood that. But in our armored vehicle, we faced less risk than our traveling companions, and they were growing more pale with each delay, their mostly mute worry glowing brighter as we moved closer to Baghdad.

As for me, I feared that heading back for the border would be as dangerous as going ahead. Too many Iraqis had seen us drive by. Maybe like pirates after a sea battle, they'd be waiting for us if we retreated.

The tension in our group built every time we pulled over to debate what to do. Something had to give. In the end it was my then 30-year-old cameraman Chris, who actually turned 30 as of midnight that night, April 11. He later said he thought he only had a 50-50 chance at that point of making it to 31. As he recounted it later, he wanted to "drive off the road and sit in the desert with no lights, no noise, no movement to hide from locals and the Iraqi army and mark our position with the infrared strobes you and I had to safeguard against allied air attack."

On a dusty shoulder of the highway as different knots of us gathered yet again in concerned huddles, my Aussie cameraman lashed out at Dan. "If we keep going down that road," he snarled, "we're going to fucking get killed."

I walked up to the huddled group just as Chris was midlash. It was a valid point, but it wasn't expressed in a way that people normally spoke to Dan. Chris later told me he turned, saw my horror-stricken face, and realized my whole career was flashing before my eyes.

Dan was furious and said that if Chris didn't have the guts to go, he'd go with someone else. He started pulling his gear out of our armored. Chris trailed him, saying, "Dan, I'm willing to drive on, but then either the other vehicles have to come with us or we leave them on their own. And either way isn't safe."

Dan asked for a vote. For the others there was no good choice. Like me they didn't know what was worst: moving forward, going backward, or staying put. So we got back into our trucks and drove on.

A few miles later, our Iraqi drivers mutinied, saying they didn't want to go any farther. One said they knew of a mosque a few miles ahead where we could take shelter. It was a relief. We drove forward into the darkness, glad when we saw the green lights of the mosque minarets in the distance, our sanctuary—or so we thought. We drove down the slope off the highway into the dusty makeshift parking lot—essentially a flat patch of desert with a *Mad Max* collection of small ramshackle buildings surrounding a modest mosque. At the front of it was something that looked like a guard hut, where you'd usually find the attendant who took care of the building.

But as one of our drivers approached the hut to look for the mosque attendant, out burst an Iraqi soldier, and he was getting his automatic weapon into position. He started shouting, rousing other soldiers, who started appearing from the doorways of the other buildings.

In the convoy there was realization and then pandemonium. Everyone was shouting at once, and those half out of the cars were springing back in. The CBS Iraqi driver got physically dragged back into the car by one of his foreign passengers. With that, each driver floored it and everyone tried to duck possible incoming shots as we rocketed up the couple ramps from the parking lot, peeling off down the highway. Unfortunately, the direction our car happened to have been pointed meant we sped in the opposite direction from the rest of the convoy, away from Baghdad toward the border. And we had no way to let the others know where we'd gone. Since there were only four radios for the five-car convoy, we had gone without.

When we realized we'd lost everyone else, we had to take some time before turning around. To rejoin our group we'd have to drive right by the Iraqi troop-ridden mosque.

By the time we caught up with our team in the darkness, they were debating whether to call our bosses in New York and report that hostile Iraqi forces had seized Dan Rather.

Now there was no direction to go but forward, deeper into Iraq and deeper into danger.

In the darkness ahead we saw a dirt chicane, so everyone slowed down for the obligatory zigzag. Just before the chicane we saw the flashing lights of a police car rushing through the night on an adjoining road on an intersect course with our convoy. Maybe the forces at the mosque had alerted them.

As we raced toward the chicane, the police screeched to a halt at the mouth of the barrier, and five guys jumped out, ran to the back of the vehicle, sprang the trunk, and passed out AK-47s among themselves.

Chris turned to Dan and said, "If they start firing at our car, I'm going to run them down. OK?" Dan realized what Chris was saying: kill or be killed. He nodded and said "OK." Chris floored the Land Cruiser, and we headed toward the zigzag, picking up speed instead of slowing down.

This wasn't the response the Iraqi "policemen" or whoever they were expected. As we drew level with them, we heard gunshots, but they must have fired into the air, expecting the threat of force to stop us. It didn't. The entire convoy took the turns at top speed, everyone's gear-laden trucks rocking on their axles. We got through it, our hearts uniformly pounding.

The convoy slowed down, perhaps in uniform dread, with all of us wondering what else was waiting for us. We didn't have long to find out. A flatbed truck approached from behind us full of armed Iraqi troops who were staring at us. It was too dark for us to read their faces or their intent. The truck passed our entire convoy, then slowed down and sped up, cruising up and down the convoy like a shark. The truck did this long enough for all of us to wonder if they were going to open fire.

Then as if we were quarry that proved too boring for further play, the truck sped ahead of us toward Baghdad, leaving us alone.

The CBS portion of the ragtag convoy decided once again to stop and debate. It was an opportunity to share with each other that, yes, we were all scared; yes, we all thought now that we should have stayed in Jordan; and no, we didn't have any other option but to move ahead. And we'd better move on while we could still catch up with the rest of the journalists.

We scanned ahead of us for the rest of the convoy we'd lost. Eventually we saw what looked like a parking lot on the road ahead of us. It was the journalists' convoy. In the median there was a smashed-up truck flipped on its side.

As we slowed down we spotted the reason for the logjam. We'd found the invasion. Four American Humvees blocked the road.

The soldiers explained to us that their orders had been shoot to kill at anything driving at them out of the darkness. That explained the truck on its side; it was actually the remains of the truck that was full of Iraqi troops that had passed us earlier.

The journalists' convoy had almost gotten the same treatment, but one of the soldiers had spotted an iridescent "TV" on the side of the lead media truck, so he fired a warning shot instead, giving the convoy a chance to slam to a halt just feet from the Humvee blockade.

The soldiers told us, "You just came out of Indian country, and there's nothing but Indian country in the 10 miles between here and Baghdad. So you better park your vehicle and stay with us for the night."

For once, we didn't need to take a vote.

Dan and I broadcast to our respective programs that night via our WCBS videophone, standing on a cold, dusty highway. The *CBS Evening News* videophone didn't work after the pounding it took when Dan's truck had crashed. So Dan and I shared mine, which unfortunately for me worked just fine for my on-camera, but started jamming when Dan got in position to record his *Evening News* segments. As it turns out, he'd been standing in the shadows waiting for me to finish, his patience fraying. When I got out of his way, and he finally took his position to at last file his report from the outskirts of Baghdad, the culmination of a long, horrible battle to get there, the videophone signal started to break down. Let's just say that he wasn't too happy with me, the videophone, the crew, and perhaps the world in general. And I couldn't really blame him.

If you were a viewer tuning in that night, you might have wondered why Dan was broadcasting in ghostly green, the infrared beam making his eyes shine like a cat's as he stood in front of a nondescript, crumpled Iraqi truck and a couple Humvees. Viewers had no idea what it took to get there. Later Dan graciously apologized to all of us for the fraught trip and the frayed tempers along the way.

The next morning, we thanked our impromptu American hosts and left them at their roadside position, picking our way into the city, skirting the burned-out leftovers of the shattered Iraqi army—tanks, trucks, and gun positions blasted by the American onslaught. Against all reasonable advice and common sense, we'd made it to Baghdad and got the story: from the jubilation of those happy to see Saddam gone to the rampant looting to the first signs of the insurgency Saddam left behind.

This was the start of my network TV chapter, although I didn't know it then. I'd proved myself to Dan and his team, turning out material and story leads, working through the power outages, the scarce food, and the ever-changing security situation.

We even survived a trip to Tikrit, Iraq, when our Land Cruiser broke down on what we called "looters' alley"—the main thoroughfare into Tikrit had a steady stream of cars leaving it, filled with goods looted from Saddam's suddenly abandoned palaces. Our fuel line was damaged, so Chris pumped the fuel pump and together with radio correspondent Charlie D'Agata coaxed it to a U.S. checkpoint that Marines had set up just a couple hours earlier outside the city. Marine armored engineers spent the next 12 hours fixing the vehicle in return for phone calls home on our satellite phone—their first calls in more than two months.

But I, as usual, was worried about filing for WCBS that night. So I left my cameraman and D'Agata in the company of the Marines and hitchhiked on my own from Tikrit to Baghdad so I could get back to a satellite dish with our tapes.

I thumbed a ride in a car I thought was full of European journalists. It took me about five minutes to figure out that they were all Euro-Iraqis, and a couple were actually Saddam loyalists who were taking their prized possessions—gold-plated AK-47s—from Tikrit to Baghdad. They did eventually take me to the CBS bureau after stopping in two of the toughest Sunni neighborhoods in the city to drop off friends and the AK-47s first. I was shaken but was soon busy filing my story.

Within the space of 72 hours, I'd survived three of the most dangerous and half-thought-out journeys of my entire career. I now look back on that time as our golden years of covering Iraq, when we were still able to do stupid things and not get killed for it.

Chris and I drove back to Israel after three weeks in Baghdad. We arrived in Jerusalem after two solid days of driving. Each of us went home to collapse and do laundry.

We did a story the very next day, and then late that evening the phone rang again. There had been a suicide bombing in Tel Aviv. It was "sweeps" back in the States, when they measure ratings, so our station demanded we get to the bomb scene. I called Chris. He swore but grabbed his gear, picked me up at my house, and drove like mad.

Tel Aviv is a complicated city to navigate, so when we saw a police car in the general area of the bomb scene, we stuck to it. The cop car rushed through an amber light. We followed, crossing the intersection as the amber turned red. Bad call. A van was entering the intersection from the cross street, which meant the two cars were on a collision course.

Chris saw the van in time to jerk the wheel left. Instead of T-boning the other vehicle, we hit the front of it, which sent us careening toward the intersection's median and a massive streetlight. We flipped on our side, me suspended in space and Chris trying to stay inside the car as glass flew into his face from the concrete below. We came to a halt, and I was still suspended in the air. Onlookers climbed onto our Land Cruiser and lifted open my door to pull us out.

One of our rescuers from a corner sandwich shop said to me, "Are you OK?" then continued inanely (in my view). "That was the best car accident we've ever seen! It was like a movie." It was a popular corner for accidents.

The other driver, like us, was shaken but OK. Both our cars were totaled.

It was 4 a.m. by the time the police left, and I called WCBS to explain what had happened. They asked if I could still file on the suicide bombing for their 11 p.m. show—7 a.m our time. I said no.

When Chris and I went to work the next day, our boss called to say she was sorry to hear about the accident. Then she told us she was closing the WCBS bureau in Jerusalem. Just like at the intersection in Tel Aviv hours before, I didn't see that one coming.

But she said the network wanted to hire us. So I called my old London boss, Marcy McGinnis, who was now a senior vice president in New York. She said absolutely they had space for Chris. As for me, she said she'd honor the year and a half left on my WCBS contract, but she said quite honestly that she didn't have a "head" for me (head count being all, in a world of dwindling news budgets). I knew I would be corporate deadweight unless I found a way to be useful, pronto.

I called the CBS News London bureau chief, John Paxson, and explained that I now worked for him. John knew what I needed: a chance to prove myself and fast. "Well, I'm having trouble covering Baghdad," he said.

I told him to name a date, and I packed my bags.

On the way into my first Baghdad shift, Pete was one of our two security advisors, keeping us safe as we drove down that same road I'd traveled on earlier on that frantic trip in with Dan. Pete was on his last shift for CBS News anyway, but it became his last job for the media after he met me.

After a week or so in Baghdad, Paxson asked me when I wanted to leave, expecting me to say what most correspondents said: "After a month." Four weeks was the standard rotation.

I said, "Why leave?" And I started spending anywhere from six weeks to three months at a time in Baghdad. I was learning my craft, and Iraq became home.

There were close calls and tough times, like the day Kurt Hoefle, his son, Thorsten, and I were on an armored Bradley patrol that was ambushed by the Mahdi Army in Sadr City, Iraq. We were hit by more than a dozen IEDs, and two of the Bradleys were disabled. We were trapped as RPG gunners moved in and started firing on us while Kiowa and Apache helicopters tried to protect us from above. We actually all shouted, "Shoot, shoot, shoot," when we saw an insurgent through the tank's infrared lens about to fire on us from just a few feet away. Col. Gary Volesky was at the controls of our Bradley. He opened up the 50-caliber rifle and took the gunner out. We finally escaped near dawn.

The video was amazing. Unfortunately it was also two weeks before a major Dan Rather anchor trip to the region. My bosses told me that the material had to be saved for Dan. This kind of thing is the dirty secret of the news business, and it's done for every anchor. There is no way one person can be in as many places as the network needs him or her to be to "brand" the news. So often much of the material is gathered beforehand. I wrote the script for Dan. He was a bit embarrassed about it when he realized just how much danger we'd been in, but he had the pressure on him to make the cost of his trip to Iraq count. So I was a good soldier. But we both regretted it.

While I was recovering from the bombing, Dan referred to the incident obliquely on the CBS website: "Kimberly is widely known among fellow pros for being a team player. She gives of her information, even sometimes her hard-gotten radio tape and/or television footage to CBS colleagues. (She's done it for me any number of times.)"

Dan always struck me as being tortured between his instincts to nurture his correspondents and their careers in a paternal father-son sort of way and fearing their success would eclipse him—the man always haunted by the number-three rating and the knowledge that he'd never matched the success of the man he replaced: America's ultimate media father figure, Walter Cronkite. I mostly got to see Dan's best side. I owe him my air time at *CBS Evening News* those first years in Baghdad—as with all anchors, you did not appear on his show without his say-so. He is ultimately the reason I got and kept the job covering the war in Iraq, and for that I owe him respect and thanks.

Part of the baggage of working for CBS News, however, was that whatever the military or media critics thought of CBS's coverage of things like Abu Ghreib often got applied to the whole team—and the longer I was there, applied to me in particular. This was my first foray into network level exposure and, therefore, my first contact with constant criticism from critics, pundits, and bloggers back in the States—criticism that continued even as I lay in a hospital bed trying to recover from the car bomb. As I researched the bombing online, I found that bloggers had been rating me as a journalist, as an American, and as a human being—some were defending me and some were finding me lacking. That was surreal.

I knew that how you reported on the war in Iraq was a bit of a Rorschach test. Writers with a leftist bent usually saw only failure, the glass half-empty. Writers with a right-wing bent brought their best rose-colored glasses and saw only future success in every American foray.

I thought of my reporting as a field of gray. One day I'd report on a bombing, the hopelessness Iraqis felt, and their frustration with Americans. The next day I'd report on a hospital that American troops had reopened to the joy of the local Iraqi neighborhood.

But people don't like gray. They like black and white. So when critics looked at my reporting, they saw things selectively, depending on their point of view. To some I was a diva-style, liberal-loving TV hotshot out to make a name for myself, and my sole aim was apparently to shred the reputation of American men and women in uniform and those who led them. One website called my reporting bogus and held up one of my scripts from 2003 as proof of my negativism. I had written of

> . . . A growing sense of frustration among top brass here that no measure is enough to protect their soldiers or Iraq's resources . . . Ordinary Iraqis blame Americans for not fixing the damage fast enough, even as the soldiers are risking their lives to do it. America has made new enemies. They're chanting the name of that old foe, Saddam Hussein, and vowing to attack Americans everywhere . . .

In large measure that report held true for the first four years of the war—though after Saddam's incarceration some Iraqis started chanting the name of now-deceased Al Qaeda of Iraq leader Abu Musab al Zarqawi instead.

Or I was portrayed as championing the U.S. invastion—a Dr. Strangelove-like, military-loving gal who was blinded to the faults of the troops I was covering and the damage they were doing. As one blogger put it:

> Dozier has played an important role as a pro-Corporate pimp for the illegal war in Iraq. . . . The misinformation and disinformation of which she and others have relentlessly foisted upon us is significantly responsible for enabling and prolonging the disastrous and criminal U.S. invasion of Iraq.

I didn't recognize either of these reporters. I had plenty of personal opinions on how the war was going, but I kept those to myself, as is the credo of most reporters I know. I'd been taught at the BBC and before that as a trade reporter in D.C. that you didn't express your personal opinions on air or in print.

Dan refused to have opinion in his broadcasts, and scripts were stripped of any vestige of outrage or even gentle sarcasm that we'd all sometimes try to put in. Maybe Dan was so careful because he'd been stung by the constant drumbeat of conservative criticism of his reporting. All I knew was that in the field when I heard a military commander or diplomat go on about my "military-hating boss, Rather," I thought to myself, *You should try to get a script past him with a hint of opinion about the war.*

Whenever I could I stuck with the one thing I found no one could argue with: interviewing people about how they felt about the situation, whether they were Iraqis who were tired of being "helped" to death or American kids who'd left a safe life back home to try to do some good.

I tried to become a clear lens that would distill their reaction and reflect it back. But in Iraq the situation is so complicated and the country so vast that my lens frequently became a kaleidoscope.

I saw Iraqi families who had cheered U.S. troops when they'd arrived but who were now living in fear because of the near-daily accidental shootings of innocent bystanders at American checkpoints or in traffic. I watched generals cry openly over the troops they lost in combat when their tour was extended for three months. I saw American soldiers coming back for a second deployment, terrified because this time they knew what they were in for. They were kicking themselves because, as they'd tell me, "The last time we were here, we really screwed up. We didn't know what the hell we were doing." And they'd hope out loud that they hadn't figured out the formula too late.

People kept asking me then, as now, how I thought it would turn out. I'd think to myself: *long, bloody, messy, and complicated with no clear winners but plenty of losers.* I could see the downsides to both pulling U.S. troops out immediately and staying in the meat grinder and contributing to it.

That isn't a popular answer. Both ideological sides of the equation think I'm a defeatist or a coward for not taking a stand.

But I'm a realist who refuses to be bullied, who has learned a simple lesson: Once blood has been spilled, the grief and the enemies last at least one generation. In the past five years, too much blood has been spilled in Iraq between the Sunnis and Shiites, between Al Qaeda and the Sunni tribes that turned on them, between the Kurds and the Turks to their north, between the Arab world and America and anyone who joined the U.S. in Iraq.

The other thing so many Americans forget is that Iraq has always been a violent place. Other Arabs will warn you, "Be careful, those Iraqis are brutal." Deserved or not, Iraqis have the reputation of being the Cosa Nostra of the Middle East. Everything is tribal, even when everyone's wearing suits and ties. When you put some of the horror stories of Saddam's regime in that context—from the shark tanks Saddam would stuff with a steady diet of supposed traitors to the violent impromptu assassinations at weddings or birthday parties of the loftiest members of the regime—it all makes sense: Iraqis are the worst Godfathers you've ever seen, and they're on overdrive.

Even in Saddam's time, when having an unauthorized weapon could get you executed, every driver kept a handgun under his front seat. I asked why. "In case we get into a traffic accident," one driver stated matter-of-factly. That's the simplest way I've found to explain that Iraq works differently—not just differently from America, but differently from anywhere in the Middle East. And Iraqi men often take pride in it with a Sicilian-style swagger.

But just like my reaction to my translator's gloomy prediction in Kosovo, no one wants to hear that the good guys wear gray hats and that they also change the hat depending on which alliance offers them the best deal.

I summed up the reaction to my reporting in a speech I gave when people asked me to talk about my recovery:

> No one wants to be the bearer of bad tidings, but that's what I was for the three years I reported from Iraq. Liberals have criticized me for "selling the war." My own journalist colleagues criticized me for being too comfortable with the military and too willing to embed. Conservative websites attacked me for being a hotel-bound antipatriot who criticized the war effort and failed to spend enough time with the troops.
>
> Then terrorists attacked my team as we followed a U.S. patrol in Baghdad.
>
> And *since* then, as I recuperated . . . and there was wave of public opinion against the war in Iraq . . . I've seen my Iraq reporting from before the bombing attacked . . . for *not* being negative *enough*.

So I guess I've come full circle.

From all that, I've learned a couple things, which apply to my business . . . and probably to your business as well.

First of all you don't do this job for the "thank you." You do it because you think you're doing the right thing. You will always get criticized, but you can comfort yourself by saying if you're offending everyone equally, you must be doing something right.

If you don't take the risks of telling the unpopular stories or taking the hard route, you are letting the critics win, and you will let people down, which means you just have to get comfortable with risk—to your career and, in extreme cases, to your life.

I've realized that because my job is to hold up a mirror to show us our failings, as well as our triumphs, that my message will never be popular. But if I let the critics be my internal compass and keep quiet, I am failing the American people and that voice in my head and heart, which tells me to do what's right.

And last, on a personal note, surviving the psychological slog of reporting in Baghdad is great training for recovering from a car bomb.

CHAPTER 19

coming to terms

Arriving back in the United States meant a return to a full-on public excavation of the bombing and my part in it, with cameras following me at each step.

It also meant working at the CBS News corporate headquarters in New York—a first for someone who'd spent her life as a foreign correspondent— and finding out how people respond to a walking miracle.

It was a chance to say thank you, but it also meant my experience became a vehicle that enabled people I barely knew to bare their souls or to ask me to reveal mine. It was both an honor and intensely uncomfortable, especially when the intimacy was uninvited. I'd considered a career as a member of the Episcopal clergy. Now I was getting a small glimpse of what that life would have been like. People I barely knew were revealing such private, inner pain. They told me what they went through during the bombing or maybe how it reminded them of some horrible loss they'd endured in their own lives. They wanted and needed my wisdom.

I tried not to stiffen as if from an unwelcome hug; I tried to share what I had learned, but it hurt, and it drained me. I was mostly healed, yes, but not enough to carry others' emotional burdens.

And then there was the uncomfortable public revelation of my own pain, the Oprah-like dissection of my private thoughts and emotions for the entire world to see. I'd already had a glimpse of that when I'd stopped by CBS's Washington, D.C., bureau before I'd left for Auckland, New Zealand, five months earlier. I'd arranged to drop off my CBS computer before heading for the airport.

Bob Schieffer spotted me and said he wanted to "introduce me to a couple people." I tensed up as he dragged me into the large room that housed all the *Evening News* producers. I wasn't ready for a public outing. But mercifully there were only a couple people there.

I found myself politely stammering to three producers, people I was in awe of because of their reputations. But I'd never worked in D.C., so they were strangers to me beyond their names.

I heard rustling and turned. A dozen people were quietly filing into the room. I stammered another awkward greeting.

Then I heard more rustling from a door on the other side of the room, and I whirled that way. Another bunch of people was entering. All the faces were open and friendly, but still I'd never met them and didn't know I'd be meeting them en masse that day.

Bob was wading through the small crowd. He proceeded to dive into the questions that were on everyone's mind.

"So are you in pain? Do you have more surgery scheduled?"

"Umm, well," I stammered. And then I answered. "No, no pain, just some permanent numbness, and one last bout of surgery when I get back from New Zealand."

Then the coup de grace: "Are you planning to go back to Baghdad?"

I froze. "Well, Bob, I'm not exactly ready to go back on a Baghdad foot patrol," I said with a half-smile, trying to make light of it. At that point, I hadn't yet asked myself that question (though he did get me thinking).

Mercifully a young woman intern at the back of the room fainted and fell to the floor. She'd been on a crash diet and had low blood pressure. While listening to me she probably also locked her knees, which often causes fainting.

I tried to skulk out as everyone scrambled to bring her to, but I was stopped by a CBS web person. She wanted to turn my visit into major copy. I reluctantly agreed, and we sat in a private office where I tried to talk to the twentysomething woman about some of the guilt and pain I'd been dealing with and the tough physiotherapy that lay ahead. This was beyond her realm of experience. What resulted was a short piece that made me cringe and shake my head. It centered mostly on how presentable I looked with my new haircut and a fashionable skirt.

I worried that it would infuriate those who'd lost loved ones in this tragedy. From then on I vowed to write my own web pieces.

Five months later I suspected that on my official return to CBS in February 2007, I'd find similar intense curiosity and barrages of questions, always well-meaning but sometimes driving me to annoyance, depression, or distraction.

I was right. I found myself enveloped by an unexpected, cheering crowd in the New York newsroom.

I'd been told I'd be going to the day's televised editorial meeting, which usually consists of about a dozen people, so I could say hello to everyone there. That sounded like a lovely and understated way to come back to work, a quiet reentry from the wings.

Just a couple days before the event, I'd been asked if I minded if a single camera crew followed me. I didn't like it, but I agreed. I told them only one. I reminded them that this was my first official appearance since losing Paul and James. "It can't be triumphant," I said. "You can't have a cake and streamers."

When I arrived at the CBS headquarters, the bosses asked me to wear a microphone. I walked into the newsroom, feeling just a touch apprehensive, behind CBS President Sean McManus.

The place erupted. Instead of the 20 or so people I expected, there must have been a hundred in the newsroom, many of whom I barely knew. The rumor had spread that I'd be visiting the newsroom that day, so people had poured in to see the woman they'd worked with, worried about, and prayed for.

But I'm not good with surprise parties, no matter how well-intended. I didn't know what to do. A blush raced up my face, and I wanted to jump under a desk.

McManus handed me a microphone, and suddenly I felt like I was on *The Price Is Right*. I stammered through a statement about Paul and James that I'd intended to say at the editorial meeting.

And then I messed it up.

I thanked everyone who'd supported me, prayed for me, sent flowers to me, emailed me, etc. And then I had intended to say, "And finally I'd like to pay tribute to Paul and James."

It came out, "I'd like to pay a final tribute to Paul and James."

Oh, hell. I thought. *That's not what I meant to say! Who the hell am I to decide when we'll stop paying tribute to Paul and James?* I couldn't take the words back, so awkwardly I plowed on. Within the CBS family I knew my stumbles didn't matter, but my words were recorded as news and reported far beyond CBS walls, and I worried that Paul's and James' wives must have thought, "Final tribute? Says who?"

Walking through the halls of CBS from that moment on was a bittersweet ordeal. I found myself being a sort of mother confessor for people who were far behind me in the grief process. I'd been at the center of the tragedy, so I'd talked about it, written about it, even blogged about it. To use the language of psychotherapists, I'd processed the incident again and again and again. In the course of the next few months, I processed more by filming the CBS News primetime special *Flashpoint* about the bombing. I met many of the people I'd been on patrol with that Memorial Day and many of the people who helped put me back together.

No one else had that luxury.

In New York old colleagues and people I barely knew would stop me in the hallways to pour their hearts out. By the end of each day, I'd end up hopelessly late for meetings and emotionally exhausted. I learned to skulk around the building, using back stairways and little-known, dusty hallways to avoid being spotted. I begged associate producers at *48 Hours* to pick up food for me so I didn't have to run the gauntlet of the CBS cafeteria, where I was once stopped and told that if I still felt guilty over Paul's and James' deaths, I needed to "talk to someone and get over it."

In London the grief was even more raw. I'd been warned of it just a couple days before my arrival. Many were still stuck exactly where I'd been in Bethesda: blaming me. Others simply didn't want to see the person who reminded them of the good friends they'd lost. So when I stopped in London on the way to film in Landstuhl, I was terrified to enter the bureau.

I needn't have been. Most people were happy to see me, though their happiness was tinged with a certain guilt. They'd look at me, give me a sad smile, maybe a hug, and then look away. I went to embrace one old friend, and as I stepped forward, he crossed his arms and stepped back. I froze, halfway to a hug. That hurt like hell.

Then I ran into one colleague I'd been told blamed me for Paul's and James' deaths. I met his gaze for a moment. I accepted that he'd never forgive me for surviving. *Yes, I'm here,* I thought. *No, I'm not apologizing.*

I went on to Germany to film *Flashpoint* at Landstuhl. It was a high point, revisiting my old room with nurse Nancy and her husband. Now I was standing on two feet.

There was only one soldier there, and I hoped it would stay that way for the rest of the war, but of course it didn't. He'd lost a limb, maybe two. I couldn't see beneath the sheets. He stared at us but didn't really seem to see us. He was drugged, as I had been. He had no one with him except the nurses, the doctors, and the nurse's aides. I wanted to talk to him but thought he'd had enough intrusion. It would take too long to even explain why I was there and why I understood what he was going through. Then again, he was an amputee. How could I understand that?

The film crew I was working with, cameraman Dennis Dillon and soundman Eddy Jones, was sensitive to a fault, having already been present at some very painful reunions.

The most surreal meeting was with the Iowa National Guardsmen—Jeremy Koch and Patrick Flattery, who'd been at the bomb scene, and their commander, Captain Grant Kaufman, who'd been back at base. He'd brought this meeting about by tracking me down. Kaufman had gone on to fight for more than a year to make sure every one of his guys got a Bronze Star for Merit for what they all did that day.

The moment I walked through the front door to Jeremy Koch's home, where we met, I had this awkward sense of déjà vu. I recognized Jeremy's voice from the bombing, but I'd never seen his face.

Now I was confronted by this six-foot-plus blue-eyed, Terminator-like guy and his buddies in their Army uniforms, with Jeremy's wife and extended family behind them, gathered like it was Thanksgiving Day—except they were all tearing up.

My mind grappled to put him in context: *Iraq, Iowa, Iraq, Iowa?*

I ended up hugging everyone, but owing to my hug-once-a-year family I'm awkward at the best of times. This was an exercise in weird for all us, combined with a wallop of strong emotions. Just seeing me dredged up for Koch and Flattery what both called their worst day in Iraq, if not the worst day in their lives. Flattery said he had replayed it in his head like a movie every day since. He made me realize my memory loss of some of what happened at the bomb scene was a partial blessing.

They sat me down at Koch's kitchen table and filled in the blanks, even pulling up a diagram of the bomb scene on the computer (courtesy of Microsoft PowerPoint, the military's best friend).

It helped to find I'd remembered much of the scene correctly—like where I was standing before the bomb went off and where I'd lain in relation to the burning cars. Most important, they told me where the bomb had been. It helped demystify the event since all I could remember was slamming into blackness, then floating in space.

What helped the most was finding out I'd definitely been the last of both the soldiers and my team to receive hands-on first aid. Relief came in waves that day, and over the next few weeks, now that I knew for sure that no one had died because I got help first.

I hope it helped Koch and Flattery to see that one of those bloody casualties they labored over for an hour and risked their lives for that day really did walk away.

Meeting the men from the Fourth Infantry Division was a bit more fraught, simply because of the mechanics of TV. Their main interview was with CBS News anchor Katie Couric. That kind of high-level attention helped reinforce what they already knew: Their sacrifice counted.

By the time they saw me at the end of the second day of filming, their keyed-up emotions, and mine, made for an even more awkward on-camera conversation than I'd had in Iowa. So we made up for it later, meeting up at their favorite watering hole without cameras. I'm sure there's an incriminating cell phone picture or two floating around on the Internet of all of us toasting with shots of Patron Cuervo.

My toughest assignment was traveling to San Antonio to meet Jennifer Funkhouser, Capt. Alex Funkhouser's widow. She'd been wondering why no one from CBS News had reached out to her. My clumsy attempts to reach her from New Zealand through Army press officers hadn't worked. So I had to get through some apologies before we could talk about what happened that day, my last impressions of her husband, and the moments before the bomb.

The fact that she was willing to record this exchange on camera showed both her bravery and her devotion to her husband, Capt. James "Alex" Funkhauser. She told me off camera that she felt like she was only just keeping it together, but I saw a tower of strength. She was articulate, grieving but not bitter, and able to talk about all she and her two daughters were going through. She understood everything Alex had been trying to do. Most of all, she wanted Americans to understand that those daily casualty figures weren't (and aren't) just numbers.

"When they hear those numbers, I want them to think of Alex," she told me. I felt like we were ripping her heart open on film.

Off and on we have kept in touch. I told her I was writing a book, and I asked her how she'd like people to remember Alex. She swiftly wrote back:

> I've said how great he was as a father, husband, friend, and son. I've talked about his love of life and his willingness to help anyone who needed it. It gets to the point sometimes where it almost seems like I'm glorifying him in a sense, which he would hate. The truth is Alex was all of those things, but he was also simply a man doing his job.
>
> He signed up for the Army in 1991, knowing full well what he could be called to do. He moved his family to a base that he knew would send him to Iraq. This was his mission, and he was going to fulfill it. I'm proud of what he accomplished in his 35 years. And I'll never let my girls forget him.

As the months of filming *Flashpoint* flew past, I worked hard with Becca at physiotherapy—trying to bring my legs back to full strength and more after my surgery in February 2007. Just a few weeks later, now that the coral-like bone was no longer clawing at my thigh muscles, I was running, and CBS was filming.

The producers and film crew were going through it all with me, tracking my recovery. Legendary executive producer Susan Zirinsky had carved the team from her *48 Hours Mystery* crew. The rest of the year, they tracked horrific and twisted American murder stories; Z, as she is known, explained matter-of-factly that crime sells. But she said this is what it pays for: getting the chance to tell a story like this. Her team, and all those who watched *Flashpoint*, got to experience the journey of grief and ultimately recovery of all those involved that day. For me, it was the most rewarding part of returning to work.

The hardest part was overcoming people's surprising prejudices and negative expectations when it came to trauma and recovery. At work and beyond, I endured moments of sheer idiocy, born out of ignorance. There was the first-day-back comment from a work colleague I'd never met before in the middle of the newsroom in front of a crowd of people: "Oh, Kimberly, how are you feeling?"

I responded, "My legs are doing great, some swelling, but great."

The colleague said, with the large crowd hanging on every word, "Well, yes, of course, the physical side is doing well, sure. But I would imagine your greatest scars are . . . well . . . not physical." He paused. "So how *are* you?"

I was stunned into silence as I realized this man was assuming that I had posttraumatic stress disorder and that I was willing to talk about it before a large crowd. After taking a breath, I responded, "I'm fine." I paused with a grimace. "But thank you for asking."

This is how I learned one of the most important facts for surviving the aftermath of a car bomb, which has nothing to do with Iraq, bombs, surgeons, or anatomy. I found that 85 percent of the people I came across knew next to nil about trauma, surviving trauma, war zones, working in war zones, survival skills thereof, or why I did the job in the first place.

And yet 100 percent of that subset of people thinks they actually know far more than I do. They put themselves in my place and judge how they think they'd react in my shoes. If I'm not doing what they've mapped out in their heads, they decide that I'm obviously very, very sick.

It doesn't matter that I've consulted with the finest professionals in the world on the subject within weeks of the event and beyond and that those experts have deemed me a textbook example of mental strength and fortitude and have told me that I've done all the right things to process the event and get beyond it.

When you tell people, "No, no pains, no nightmares, no problems since leaving the hospital . . . two *years* ago," there's often this odd disappointment followed by hostility, as if to say, "But we were all sympathetic and spent a lot of time feeling sorry for you because you just had to be horribly screwed up. You're not? How ungrateful you are."

It's as if I lied to them somehow, and by recovering it's as if I cried wolf and obviously didn't deserve their earlier worry and sympathy.

Even close friends gently pried and probed. They listened, fascinated, as I told the story of what I remembered the day the bomb went off, and they'd interrupt me with the pro forma, "You know, you don't have to talk about this . . ." After I finished, inevitably they asked, as casually as they could muster, "So . . . um . . . having any nightmares? Any . . . um . . . flashbacks, perhaps? Are you . . . OK?" They'd let that last bit dangle, leaving the phrase "cracking up?" unspoken and yet understood. They didn't comprehend how I could lie in that hospital bed all those weeks, looking at my legs, thinking about what happened, and not go nuts.

A friend who saw *Flashpoint* was brutally honest. "It brings home all you went through, and it's just amazing to think you're mentally OK after that. I mean you *seem* OK. I wouldn't be."

As I tried to move on from the bombing, I also discovered that my bosses—like my parents had been earlier—had become accustomed to thinking of me as a victim, not as a survivor who'd put the event behind her.

It didn't help that I'd allowed the *48 Hours* team to film my very last round of surgery. Shock Trauma Hospital's Dr. Pollak chiseled out the excess bone in my leg, and his colleague, Dr. David Eisenman, created an artificial eardrum for my right ear using the tissue from my own scalp.

Images like that are powerful. I was unconscious on a gurney again. The picture didn't say, "Ready to go back to work," even though I did just a week after that surgery. People seeing it didn't think I was well. To this day I still receive get well cards and emails from strangers, so I can't blame some of my CBS colleagues for sharing that point of view.

But it was wall-punchingly frustrating.

McManus asked me to stay in Washington, D.C., for at least a year, a sort of transition time for all of us. I was ready to go back to Jerusalem, but it struck McManus as irresponsible to send a just-recovered woman back to what most Americans consider a war zone. I had only the media, including myself, to blame for that perception; we hardly ever report news from the Middle East unless something blows up.

When I saw how strongly he felt about this, I decided I'd take the temporary assignment and make it a positive. I sublet my house in Jerusalem to someone willing to take care of my cats, and I took advantage of my geography to bring some public attention to the types of injuries I'd suffered, testifying before Congress with CBS's support. Dr. Pollak had explained just before the last surgery to my right leg, minutes before I was put under, that four out of five injured troops suffer injuries to the arms and legs just like mine and they suffer all the complications I experienced.

I wrote an article for *The Washington Post* Outlook section describing what I'd been through, from the debate to save my leg to my battle against Acinetobacter to the painful surgery to remove the spiky overgrowth of bone in my femurs that's common to blast wounds. Dr. Pollak explained that doctors don't know why this heterotopic ossification grows, so they don't know how to turn it off. That means many injured troops with either blast-broken bones or amputee stumps grow this bone and then face a serious operation six to nine months after the original injury to remove it. Remove it any earlier than that and it grows back.

I pointed out that Iraqis and anyone else in war zones were also suffering blast injuries and their byproducts. This research wouldn't just help soldiers. It would save civilians' lives, as doctors had saved mine.

My activism was limited by necessity. I couldn't lobby for research money on Capitol Hill and stay impartial as a journalist. I kept having to remind some of those who reached out to me after I wrote the article that I wasn't a lobbyist, just an educator. That part was a natural extension of my job.

The hard part was my new beat: covering the war at home. It sounded great at first. But it soon became clear that with every phone call I'd make, I'd somehow end up having to relive some part of the bombing or my recovery. I didn't want to live in that moment; I wanted to move forward by returning to my career as a foreign correspondent.

Another complication: When I did a story critical of the military, I received a puzzled and hurt reaction from those I'd interviewed, as if they considered me one of their own who'd turned on them. It was hard to explain that I needed to return to what I'd always tried to be, a harsh but fair critic. Otherwise I wouldn't be true to myself or the Fourth Estate, and I wouldn't be doing anyone any good.

My CBS bosses started sending me on overseas trips, such as following Secretary of State Condoleezza Rice, a gentle transition to my old foreign beat and my old stomping grounds.

The best part of my unplanned stay in the continental United States was being there for my mom when she went in for that emergency stomach surgery while I was still filming *Flashpoint*. It kicked off a roller coaster of hospital trips and other emergency surgeries. Her painful hip and knee joints and the onset of Parkinson's became the least of our worries. She lost 50 pounds in two months and then bled out through an ulcer she'd ignored. She nearly died.

I stood over her hospital bed, looking at a woman who barely looked like my mother. She was pale with a breathing tube down her throat, just one of many pieces of medical paraphernalia that were keeping her alive. It took her three or four days to wake from the anesthesia after the worst of the operations. She looked around in fear and confusion, trying to speak before realizing something was in her throat. I understood completely. I tried to hold her eyes and explain, hoping to lessen her panic. As her pain continued and her weakness deepened, I sat by her side helpless with my dad, my brothers, and my sister.

My mom hallucinated just like I had. She was scared, especially at night, but she was too disoriented to use a call bell. So my family and I started staying with her, sleeping in the chair next to her when the doctors let us so we could respond at the faintest call for help.

She got angry at being stuck in a hospital bed. In her delirium, at one point she ordered me to call Pete and my brother Mike. "They'll protect me," she said. "They'll carry me out of here." Somewhere in her subconscious, she remembered them protecting me in Landstuhl and at Bethesda.

I coped by buying things for her room, from Mylar balloons to music for her iPod to fuzzy purple slippers—anything to help me deny my complete lack of control over the situation.

When the vigil had worn the rest of us out, from either exhaustion or because we burned through all the days we could take off work, my dad took over. He was there for her as he had been for me. He moved into her room at the rehab hospital where she had been transferred. The nurses tried to explain to him that he couldn't stay there.

"I've been with this woman for 64 years," he told them. "I intend to be with her for another 64." He wouldn't budge. They let him stay. He went for days without a shower, and he slept on a foldaway cot next to her, ready to respond to every need.

And people wondered why I recovered so fast, I thought to myself. *Just look at my parents.*

I informed Pete that my mom thought of him as her personal bodyguard, as did I.

I no longer think about the bombing every day, although the sweeping, gnarled scars and numb skin on my legs are a new constant in my life. I think about Iraq, my Iraqi colleagues I left behind, and the troops still serving in the meat grinder. I don't "cheer" for U.S. failure there, but I fear it. I hope that General David Petraeus's 2007 U.S. troop surge has produced a springboard to lasting stability. I'd seen Petraeus's counterinsurgency methods work in 2003 when he took me on tour of Mosul. But there are so many enemies waiting in the wings to fight that. Iraq was always a battlefield in gray, never in black and white. Its history guarantees a messy, bloody, ever-unfinished ending.

I often think of Paul and James. There's a picture on my office wall of the three of us at a shoot in Sadr City, all of us grinning—the way I'd like to remember them. For their memorial service in London on October 11, 2006, I wrote something for their families to be read at the service, although I imagine it was cold comfort. I was in New Zealand, still in the midst of rehab, glad for the excuse distance gave me to avoid the pain.

I still can't believe Paul and James aren't with us—in body, at least. Last I saw them they were rushing with their gear toward the soldier we were following, hurrying to get the perfect shot.

They were, as always, consummate professionals (dressed as casually as possible, of course, underneath the flak jackets). We got into the Humvees and drove off to what was to be our first and, although none of us knew it, last stop. In their last moments I saw Paul, James, and Capt. Funkhouser ahead of me, all completely focused on doing their jobs.

My thoughts are with their wives and their children. Talk to Paul and James for even five minutes and you knew they were out there doing the job for their families. The moment Paul arrived in Baghdad, every single time, he'd plaster the walls of the building with pictures of his extended clan. They were on his door . . . the door above the crew room . . . and the walls of the TV room. His family and his time with his family was his life. He loved his time with his mates, but his heart was at home.

After listening to his stories of trips he'd taken with his wife and children and grandchildren, I'd say to myself, "This guy knows how to live. The rest of us should learn from him."

James was newer to us . . . or newer to me . . . so he mostly communicated with me by teasing me that I should spend more time helping out in the kitchen, especially as he and Paul were cooking dinner for us every night.

He seemed to like to pretend around the likes of correspondents like me . . . that he was "just the soundman." But whenever I'd ask him, "Did that thing I just said make sense?" he'd launch into a carefully considered, thoughtful, and painfully intelligent explanation of why it didn't make sense and I really needed to fix it by taping it again.

His favorite story, when you could get him talking about himself, was about the time he'd gotten George Clooney to call his wife from an ABC/Diane Sawyer shoot at Clooney's Italian villa. But apparently, he says, she simply refused to believe it was Clooney. He'd tried to pull one too many jokes on her one too many times.

I miss them both, and part of me still believes that the next time I show up in some place that's just gone to hell in a hand basket they'll be there, ready to film it and/or make fun of it—preferably both.

Acknowledgments

Writing this book has sometimes been like bleeding on paper: painful, soul-wrenching, and messy. Apologies to those who found it sometimes too harsh and to those I may forget to name.

I must first thank Paul Douglas and James Brolan, whose friendship and support made Baghdad bearable, and whose example in caution and courage made me a better journalist—and I hope, a better person. They honored us all by risking their lives to tell the story of Iraq.

Pete was my anchor throughout, at my side in Landstuhl, Bethesda, and beyond.

My brother, Mike, and sister-in-law, Sherry, dropped everything to be with me—Sherry, always reminding me that faith and family are the ultimate healers. My sister, MeiLee, left her three young kids time and again, to ease me through it. (And to teach injured vets to line dance in the Bethesda waiting room—nice one, MeiLee).

Agnes Reau earned the title "Nurse Agnes," after taking care of me and several London staffers who had their own share of recent medical emergencies. (Congrats on giving up smoking, Agnes—we need you around, for as long as possible.)

Friends Beckie Ament and Denise Burgess appeared out of the blue to help.

Bob and Lee Woodruff threw me and my family a life raft, time and again, sharing the wisdom of their experience to pull me through, as they've done for so many veterans' families—turning their tragedy into a mission of education and courage.

There are literally hundreds of doctors, nurses, corpsmen, techs, and therapists to thank, who helped me recover in body, soul, and mind—too many to name, from Landstuhl to Bethesda to Kernan to the Laura Fergusson's Trust to Shock Trauma/University of Maryland Medical Center. Physiotherapist Becca Shakespeare has been there from faltering steps to running to training for a 10K, becoming a great friend in addition to her skills as trainer-tormentor.

Friends from Agnes to Kate Rydell put themselves through reading early book drafts to keep me honest, as did Chris Albert, Cami McCormick, and Robin Tobins. French foreign correspondent Laura Haim provided me moral support—and kept reminding me we do this job because we love it.

Further thanks go to Linda Mason in New York and Janet Leissner and her team in D.C. who took care of me and my family from the moment the bomb went off. They've done everything since then to make me feel welcome here, for as long as this temporary assignment lasts.

Then there's "Z" (aka Susan Zirinsky, executive producer of *Flashpoint* and *48 Hours Mystery*), who helped me put the story on TV. She patiently listened to my vision from New Zealand of telling the entire story of the war through the microcosm of one car bomb. Thanks to the entire team of *Flashpoint*—including Paul Ryan, Chris Young, Judy Tygard, Dennis Dillon, Eddie Jones, Mike McHugh (who tirelessly dug out shots for this book), and Greg McLaughlin.

Props go to Katie Couric, who took the time and energy during her frantic first year as anchor of *CBS Evening News*, to tell our story, and make it count.

Credit and thanks are also due to CBS President & CEO Les Moonves and *CBS News & Sports* President Sean McManus, who courageously backed the hour-long project at a time when viewers are increasingly tired of stories from Iraq.

Hats off to my agents who believed in me: N.S. Bienstock's Richard Leibner, who fought to get me back to the Middle East, and Trident Media Group's Paul Fedorko who fought to get my voice heard in print.

Thanks to Larry Erickson at Meredith, who took a chance on a new author, and to editor Richard Marek, who told me to go back to my first manuscript and rewrite that one, with all the raw emotion and medical detail. He guided me with a light hand, demanding more emotion than I'd have dared put in print, with his notes in the margin, "What about Pete?" or "What did you look like here? How did you feel?"

And thanks to the endlessly patient editor-at-large Alrica Goldstein, who gave me wide leeway with corrections, additions, and clarifications, understanding completely how badly I needed to get things "right."

Some who have read early editions have questioned why my personal work history comes so late in the book. I can only say that I tried to wedge it in earlier, but the stages of recovery—and everyone else's stories—seemed so much more important, that I kept shunting it to the back, which is where it stayed. I know it's a memoir, but I've never been comfortable with the fact that "it's all about me."

Finally, to my mom and dad, Dot and Ben Dozier—thank you for fighting your way to my side, and setting the example all your life that helped me get through this. I know you'll be embarrassed by seeing your lives in print, but believe me—we all need examples like yours to live by.